ANNA MAY WONG

In the series *Asian American History and Culture*, edited by Cathy Schlund-Vials, Shelley Sang-Hee Lee, and Rick Bonus. Founding editor, Sucheng Chan; editors emeriti, David Palumbo-Liu, Michael Omi, K. Scott Wong, and Linda Trinh Võ.

ALSO IN THIS SERIES:

Edward Tang, *From Confinement to Containment: Japanese/American Arts during the Early Cold War*

Patricia P. Chu, *Where I Have Never Been: Migration, Melancholia, and Memory in Asian American Narratives of Return*

Cynthia Wu, *Sticky Rice: A Politics of Intraracial Desire*

Marguerite Nguyen, *America's Vietnam: The* Longue Durée *of U.S. Literature and Empire*

Vanita Reddy, *Fashioning Diaspora: Beauty, Femininity, and South Asian American Culture*

Audrey Wu Clark, *The Asian American Avant-Garde: Universalist Aspirations in Modernist Literature and Art*

Eric Tang, *Unsettled: Cambodian Refugees in the New York City Hyperghetto*

Jeffrey Santa Ana, *Racial Feelings: Asian America in a Capitalist Culture of Emotion*

Jiemin Bao, *Creating a Buddhist Community: A Thai Temple in Silicon Valley*

Elda E. Tsou, *Unquiet Tropes: Form, Race, and Asian American Literature*

Tarry Hum, *Making a Global Immigrant Neighborhood: Brooklyn's Sunset Park*

Ruth Mayer, *Serial Fu Manchu: The Chinese Supervillain and the Spread of Yellow Peril Ideology*

Karen Kuo, *East Is West and West Is East: Gender, Culture, and Interwar Encounters between Asia and America*

Kieu-Linh Caroline Valverde, *Transnationalizing Viet Nam: Community, Culture, and Politics in the Diaspora*

Lan P. Duong, *Treacherous Subjects: Gender, Culture, and Trans-Vietnamese Feminism*

Kristi Brian, *Reframing Transracial Adoption: Adopted Koreans, White Parents, and the Politics of Kinship*

Belinda Kong, *Tiananmen Fictions outside the Square: The Chinese Literary Diaspora and the Politics of Global Culture*

Bindi V. Shah, *Laotian Daughters: Working toward Community, Belonging, and Environmental Justice*

Cherstin M. Lyon, *Prisons and Patriots: Japanese American Wartime Citizenship, Civil Disobedience, and Historical Memory*

Shelley Sang-Hee Lee, *Claiming the Oriental Gateway: Prewar Seattle and Japanese America*

Isabelle Thuy Pelaud, *This Is All I Choose to Tell: History and Hybridity in Vietnamese American Literature*

Christian Collet and Pei-te Lien, eds., *The Transnational Politics of Asian Americans*

Min Zhou, *Contemporary Chinese America: Immigration, Ethnicity, and Community Transformation*

Kathleen S. Yep, *Outside the Paint: When Basketball Ruled at the Chinese Playground*

A list of additional titles in this series appears at the back of this book.

SHIRLEY JENNIFER LIM

ANNA MAY WONG

Performing the Modern

TEMPLE UNIVERSITY PRESS
Philadelphia • Rome • Tokyo

TEMPLE UNIVERSITY PRESS
Philadelphia, Pennsylvania 19122
tupress.temple.edu

Library of Congress Cataloging-in-Publication Data

Names: Lim, Shirley Jennifer, 1968– author.
Title: Anna May Wong : performing the modern / Shirley Jennifer Lim.
Description: Philadelphia : Temple University Press, [2019] | Series: Asian
  American history and culture | Includes bibliographical references and
  index. |
Identifiers: LCCN 2018036126 (print) | LCCN 2018050041 (ebook) |
  ISBN 9781439918357 (E-book) | ISBN 9781439918333 (cloth : alk. paper)
  | ISBN 9781439918340 (paperback : alk. paper)
Subjects: LCSH: Wong, Anna May, 1905–1961. | Chinese American motion picture
  actors and actresses—Biography.
Classification: LCC PN2287.W56 (ebook) | LCC PN2287.W56 L56 2019 (print)
  | DDC 791.4302/8092 [B] —dc23
LC record available at https://lccn.loc.gov/2018036126

Printed in the United States of America

9 8 7 6 5 4 3 2 1

To Joy Adams Slingerland, Phyllis Adams,
and Soei Nio Lim

Contents

Author's Note

italicize key scenes throughout the book. By doing so, I signal to the reader that these moments represent creative historical reconstructions from Anna May Wong's point of view. On occasion I add my imaginative flare, based on archival sources, to enhance the reconstruction.

Writing about ephemeral moments such as theatrical performance presents a methodological challenge. Historians fetishize the written document as the sine qua non of all sources. Yet not all subjects and histories can be discerned through the written document or the archive. As Diana Taylor famously writes in *The Archive and the Repertoire,* "How can we think about performance in historical terms, when the archive cannot capture and store the live event?"[1] And, as Taylor persuasively argues, even if the moment is recorded, it is not the same as the actual performance. The italicized scenes mark my commitment to bringing to life the spirit of the performance. Almost all of the italicized scenes are "real." Wong's words written to Carl Van Vechten and Fania Marinoff and the scenes from "My China Film" all exist at the archive. The University of California, Los Angeles, Film and Television Archive holds the only extant copy of "My China Film." Since most readers will not have had an opportunity to screen it, I strive to make tangible the cinematic moments crucial to understanding performance and modernity.

---

1. Diana Taylor, *The Archive and the Repertoire: Performing Cultural Memory in the Americas* (Durham, NC: Duke University Press, 2003), xvi.

I maintain that the italicized scenes bring the reader closer to the multidimensional aspects of performance. Compare, for example, the sentence from Wong's visit to the Shanghai tailor shop *Like a queen extending a hand to be kissed by her subject, she holds out her arm for measurement* with a more literal "Wong held out her arm."

In a few scenes I command artistic license. Wong's theater program collection confirms that she attended Josephine Baker's performance at the Casino de Paris. Placed in italics, my rendering of what the performance looked like to the French audience combines what the theater reviews of the performance describe and what I imagine. The moment when, in my depiction, Wong causes a commotion in the audience as she appears among them is based on her impact on crowds around the world, such as the time she watched her friend Paul Robeson perform the role of Othello in London. And the moment when she is waiting on the set at Ufa Studios, ready for her close-up (readers familiar with film history will recognize the reference to the classic film *Sunset Boulevard*) is imagined, although she did work at that studio. The italicized scenes mark my desire to breathe life into the vivid and wonderful material of Wong's world.

ANNA MAY WONG

Introduction

Shanghai, 1936: Film camera held up to her right eye, the tall slender woman registers the scene around her. She stands in a busy Chinese thoroughfare, pivoting to capture on film every moment of the ceremonial procession. The camera does not disturb her perfectly coiffed bangs and long hair knotted in a bun at her nape. Her elegant, pale, patterned cheongsam flows to her ankles. Her height and activity make her, not the procession, the center of this street scene.

This scenario with Chinese American actress Anna May Wong in control of the camera is evocative. The filming of "My China Film" encapsulates one of her finest moments as a cultural worker crafting an alternative to the mainstream culture.[1] Wong created "My China Film" as her response to being rejected, in favor of Luise Rainier in yellowface, for the lead role in Metro-Goldwyn-Mayer's award-winning film about Chinese peasants, *The Good Earth* (1937). Immediately after that casting disappointment, she traveled to China for the first and only time in 1936 and had her visit there filmed. In contrast to the major Hollywood studio production *The Good Earth* (1937), "My China Film" is Wong's Chinese American artifact. *Anna May Wong: Performing the Modern* centers on a diverse array of entities, such as "My China Film," as well as encounters with other artists, such as Afri-

---

1. Since the movie does not have an official title, I call it "My China Film." Wong repeatedly refers to it as "my film" in her letters to Van Vechten and Marinoff.

can American performer Josephine Baker, in order to show Wong's cultural production and self-fashioning. Scrutinizing Wong's oeuvre outside of Hollywood A-list films opens up a whole new understanding of her career as an ingenious creative artist.

Wong stars in this book because she embodied the dominant image of Chinese and "oriental" women between 1922 and 1940.[2] Wong played groundbreaking roles in American, European, and Australian theater and cinema to become one of the major global actresses of Asian descent between the world wars.[3] Born near Los Angeles' Chinatown in 1905, Wong made more than sixty films that circulated around the world, headlined theater and vaudeville productions in locations ranging from Sydney to Paris to New York, and, in 1951, had her own television series, *The Gallery of Madame Liu-Tsong*, produced by the now defunct DuMont Television Network.[4] The sheer

---

2. Karen Leong, *China Mystique: Pearl S. Buck, Anna May Wong, Mayling Soong, and the Transformation of American Orientalism* (Berkeley: University of California Press, 2005); Shirley Jennifer Lim, *A Feeling of Belonging: Asian American Women's Public Culture* (New York: New York University Press, 2006); Judy Chu, "Anna May Wong," in *Counterpoint: Perspectives on Asian America,* ed. Emma Gee (Los Angeles: Asian American Studies Center of the University of California, 1976), 284–289; Yiman Wang, "Watching Anna May Wong in Republican China," *American and Chinese-Language Cinemas: Examining Cultural Flows,* ed. Lisa Funnell and Man-Fung Yip (New York: Routledge, 2014), 169–185; Yiman Wang, "The Art of Screen Passing: Anna May Wong's Yellow Yellowface Performance in the Art Deco Era," *Camera Obscura* 60 (2005): 159–191; Patrice Petro, "Cosmopolitan Women: Marlene Dietrich, Anna May Wong, and Leni Riefensthal," in *Border Crossings: Silent Cinema and the Politics of Space,* ed. Jennifer M. Bean, Anupama Kapse, and Laura Horak (Bloomington: Indiana University Press, 2014), 295–312; Anne Anlin Cheng, "Shine: On Race, Glamour, and the Modern," *PMLA* 126, no. 4 (2011): 1022–1041; Sean Metzger, *Chinese Looks: Fashion, Performance, Race* (Bloomington: University of Indiana Press, 2014); Sean Metzger, "Patterns of Resistance? Anna May Wong and the Fabrication of China in American Cinema of the Late 30s," *Quarterly Review of Film and Video* 23 (2006): 1–11; Celine Parreñas Shimizu, *The Hypersexuality of Race: Performing Asian/American Women on Screen and Scene* (Durham, NC: Duke University Press, 2007); Graham Russell Hodges, *Anna May Wong: From Laundryman's Daughter to Hollywood Legend* (New York: Palgrave, 2004); Philip Leibfried and Chei Mi Lane, *Anna May Wong: A Complete Guide to Her Film, Stage, Radio, and Television Work* (New York: McFarland, 2003); Anthony C. Chan, *Perpetually Cool: The Many Lives of Anna May Wong, 1905–1961* (Lanham, MD: Rowman and Littlefield, 2003).

3. Krystyn Moon, *Yellowface: Creating the Chinese in American Popular Music and Performance: 1850s–1920s* (New Brunswick, NJ: Rutgers University Press, 2005); Robert Lee, *Orientals: Asian Americans in Popular Culture* (Philadelphia: Temple University Press, 1999); Josephine Lee, *Performing Asian America: Race and Ethnicity on the Contemporary Stage* (Philadelphia: Temple University Press, 1997).

4. Shirley Jennifer Lim, "Glamorising Racial Modernity," in *Australia's Asia: From Yellow Peril to Asian Century,* ed. David Walker and Agnieszka Sobocinska (Perth: University of Western Australia Press, 2012), 145–169; Shirley Jennifer Lim, "'The Most Beautiful Chinese Girl in the World': Anna May Wong's Global Cinematic Modernity," in *Body and Na-*

number of films, theatrical productions, magazine covers, and iconic photographs rendered Wong ubiquitous. Global cultural and political interest in the "orient" propelled her fame in locales such as Germany and Mozambique. Her contemporaries noted her celebrity, for she was introduced on the 1957 American television show *Bold Journey* as the most famous Chinese [-descent] woman in the world.[5] Although she is no longer a household name, I argue that Wong remains an important twentieth-century performer because her work shaped racial modernity.

As an Asian American, there was nothing authentically "oriental" about the very American Wong, who, until 1936, had never been to China. Yet decades before the civil rights–generated category of Asian American existed, Wong grappled with how to be an Asian American actress.[6] In the early 1920s, Wong, alongside Japanese actor Sessue Hayakawa, challenged "yellowface," the film and theatrical casting norms that bypassed Asians in favor of Europeans and European Americans made up to look "oriental."[7] However, even if Wong's starring roles in early 1920s films fractured yellowface casting and marginally improved the standing of Asian Americans in Hollywood films, the racial order signaled by laws such as the 1882 Chinese Exclusion Act, Western fantasies of the oriental, and racial segregation haunted her for her entire life, denying her an opportunity to become an A-list Hollywood actress in major studio productions such as *The Good Earth*.

Despite her talent, Wong could not forge a viable Hollywood career. In the late 1920s she left the United States for Berlin, and from Africa to Australia she found appreciative audiences. Her multifaceted performances—on stage and off—had broader social significance, however, as a transnational form of interpretation that re-envisioned dominant notions of race, gender, and modernity. By contextualizing her work within the global reach of twentieth-century Western imperialism, as well as race relationally formed, this book reveals how, as a cultural worker, in her most important creative roles, she reflected the possibilities, the absurdities, and the limitations of racial and gender strictures.

---

tion: *The Global Realms of U.S. Body Politics in the Twentieth Century,* ed. Emily Rosenberg and Shanon Fitzpatrick (Durham, NC: Duke University Press, 2014), 109–124.

5. *Bold Journey,* "Native Land," ABC televised broadcast, February 14, 1957.

6. Karen Shimakawa, *National Abjection: The Asian American Body Onstage* (Durham, NC: Duke University Press, 2002); James Moy, *Marginal Sights: Staging the Chinese in America* (Iowa City: University of Iowa Press, 1993); Kandace Chuh, *Imagine Otherwise: On Asian Americanist Critique* (Durham, NC: Duke University Press, 2003); Ju Yon Kim, *The Racial Mundane: Asian American Performance and the Embodied Everyday* (New York: New York University Press, 2015).

7. Daisuke Miyao, *Sessue Hayakawa: Silent Cinema and Transnational Stardom* (Durham, NC: Duke University Press, 2007).

Methodology and Approach

The central argument of this book is that Wong's work shaped racial modernity, which made her one of the most significant actresses of the twentieth century. Rather than tracing stereotypes (oppression by power from the top down) or subversion (power from the bottom up), this book focuses on the imbrication of race and gender into modernity, paying close attention to the cultural work of self-fashioning and creation. In my first book, *A Feeling of Belonging: Asian American Women's Public Culture, 1930–1960,* I examine Wong's low-budget B-list Hollywood films as exemplars of gendered modernity and Asian American cultural citizenship.[8] That research led me to *Anna May Wong: Performing the Modern,* a serious evaluation of key moments in Wong's extraordinary career as a global symbol of the oriental. Whereas most previous scholarship has highlighted select films such as *Piccadilly* (1929), biographical details of her life, or cinematic stereotypes, this book focuses on the deliberate self-fashioning of her personas, incorporating as well as transgressing dominant ideals about womanhood, acting, and race and thereby thrusting these issues into an international public sphere. This "cultural work," as I call it, encompassed not only her film and theatrical roles but also the roles that she performed in everyday life as a celebrated actress on a world stage. This scholarly intervention draws on new research, such as the footage of "My China Film," which compels me to consider her as a cultural entrepreneur who rewrote categories of representation and produced multicultural audiences as she went along.

In this book I re-evaluate one of the major frameworks for understanding transnational racial difference, orientalism, by juxtaposing female African American and Latina performances of the "oriental" against Wong's in order to explore a more complex view of race. The normative way to study racial difference would be to focus solely on one group, in this case Asian American, and to compare that group to white European or European American culture. However, I here break out of that dualism by exploring, in conjunction with Wong, the cultural work of female performers from other racial groups. Women from various ethnic and racial backgrounds portrayed the oriental. Hence, film studios summoned Wong to portray not only Chinese women but also Southeast Asian and Pacific Islander women. Likewise, in Paris, Josephine Baker played Tonkinoise (Vietnamese), Arab North African, and Hawaiian women. In Hollywood, Dolores del Río embodied the Pacific Islander Princess Luana in *Bird of Paradise* (1932) and Lupe Vélez depicted

---

8. Lim, *A Feeling of Belonging.*

Ming Toy in *East Is West* (1930) and danced hula in *Honolulu Lu* (1941).[9] This book explores race as a relational construction by investigating how these women deployed the racial markers of the oriental.[10] It is crucial to remember that for all of the actresses, including Wong, playing oriental roles necessitated cross-cultural performance.

What is at stake? I situate this work as part of the feminist recuperation of women's experiences, and, moreover, racial minority women's responses to gender being unmarked as white. As decades of scholarship have established, this is not compensatory work but analysis that transforms how we conceptualize history.[11] Body politics still have ramifications for people's lives. What is at stake in this examination of Wong's career is the very writing of history: who can speak, who can be a subject, and how it can be done. In doing this work, I wish to validate creative and risk-taking scholarly inquiry. It is my fondest hope that this book inspires fledgling artists who have not had access to figures such as Wong to apprehend the past and, by extension, the future as a place of doing differently.

I consider Wong as a consummate artist, assembling a vital and extraordinary archive of her labor, chiefly outside of Hollywood cinema and including European film, Australian vaudeville, photography, and American television. Much of the lore around Wong centers on her never being kissed in any Hollywood film or her dying a thousand cinematic deaths in works such as

9. Karen Kuo, *East Is East and West Is East: Gender, Culture, and Interwar Encounters between Asia and America* (Philadelphia: Temple University Press, 2012); Adria Imada, *Aloha America: Hula Circuits through the U.S. Empire* (Durham, NC: Duke University Press, 2012).

10. Edward Said, *Orientalism* (New York: Random House, 1979); Lisa Lowe, *Critical Terrains: French and British Orientalisms* (Ithaca, NY: Cornell University Press, 1991). There are numerous excellent studies of race and early Hollywood cinema, including Michael Rogin, *Black Face, White Noise: Jewish Immigrants in the Hollywood Melting Pot* (Berkeley: University of California Press, 1996); Daniel Bernardi, ed., *The Birth of Whiteness: Race and the Emergence of U.S. Cinema* (New Brunswick, NJ: Rutgers University Press, 1996); Mari Yoshihara, *Embracing the East: White Women and American Orientalism* (New York: Oxford University Press, 2003); Christina Klein, *Cold War Orientalism: Asia in the Middlebrow Imagination, 1945–1961* (Berkeley: University of California Press, 2003.).

11. Wonderful examples of this kind of work include Vicki Ruiz, *From Out of the Shadows: Women in Twentieth-Century America* (New York: Oxford University Press, 1998); Valerie Matsumoto, *City Girls: The Nisei Social World in Los Angeles, 1920–1950* (New York: Oxford University Press, 2014); Judy Tzu-Chun Wu, *Dr. Mom Chung of the Fair-Haired Bastards: The Life of a Wartime Celebrity* (Berkeley: University of California Press, 2005); Valerie Smith, *Not Just Race, Not Just Gender: Black Feminist Readings* (New York: Routledge, 1998); Angela Y. Davis, *Blues Legacies and Black Feminism: Gertrude "Ma" Rainey, Bessie Smith, and Billie Holiday* (New York: Vintage, 1998); Rosa Linda Fregoso, "Lupe Vélez: Queen of the Bs," in *From Bananas to Buttocks: The Latina Body in Popular Film and Culture,* ed. Myra Mendible (Austin: University of Texas Press, 2009), 51–68.

the Fu Manchu films. If you view only widely circulated Hollywood films such as *Daughter of the Dragon* (1931) or *The Good Earth* (1937), it is easy to misinterpret Wong as an abject, almost famous film star who colluded with Hollywood in creating the worst of oriental typecasting. In contradistinction, I have written here, if you will, an anti-mainstream-Hollywood rendition of carefully curated moments in Wong's career. Rather than focusing solely on sources promoted by the dominant culture, such as those produced by Hollywood studios (which are far more abundant and easier to locate but limited in scope), I mined the historical archive to include artifacts generated by Wong and her community, both in the United States and abroad, such as self-made films, letters, personal theater program collections, newspapers, and photographs. These freshly uncovered sources compel me to re-envision Wong's opus. Housed in London, Wong's pan-European films project the breathtaking range of her talent as a starring film actress. Her letters to photographer and writer Carl Van Vechten and his wife, actress Fania Marinoff, and her self-made China film reveal her process of crafting her art. Her letters, juxtaposed against the Van Vechten portraits, hitherto unexamined except for the famed tuxedo portrait, exemplify her process of self-fashioning. Film and theater reviews throughout the world showcase Wong's sly sense of humor, filtered through the writers' oft-times admiring eyes. Through these materials, one can see Wong at the forefront of newly fabricated media forms, transitioning from silent films to the "talkies" and, finally, to television. In addition, she pioneered productions in color in both film and television: Two-Tone Technicolor in the film *The Toll of the Sea* (1922) and color in the National Broadcast Company's (NBC's) *Producer's Showcase* (1954–1957) television series.

A nontraditional imaginative archive anchors this book. It includes moments of encounter between Wong and other artists of the time such as German Jewish philosopher Walter Benjamin and Josephine Baker. Despite Wong's cultural importance, the traditional historical archive has been limited. Surviving family members have refused to grant interviews, there are no diaries, and the letters from Wong to Van Vechten and Marinoff serve as the only available extensive correspondence. Therefore, I have turned to an in-depth analysis of Wong's encounters—actual ones such as that with Benjamin as well as ones that require feats of historical imagination to actualize, such as her witnessing Baker's performance in Paris.

This book pinpoints particularly salient moments of Wong's work rather than exhaustive biographical details because I believe that her career, not romantic passion, was the driving force of her life. Historian Karen Leong

Anna May Wong, by Carl Van Vechten.

(Library of Congress, Prints & Photographs Division, Carl Van Vechten Collection [reproduction number LC-USZ62-135267].)

concurs in her excellent chapter on Wong, declaring that Wong's single status was "an expression of freedom from gender norms in both the Chinese and American communities."[12] Looking at my diverse range of sources leads me to conclude that Wong derived her emotional satisfaction from her career as well as from friendships and family. Wong declared that "work is the best Therapy

---

12. Leong, *China Mystique,* 82.

of all."[13] Her siblings were paramount—later in life she lived with her brother Richard in Santa Monica, California, traveled with him and her sister Ying to China, and persuaded her sister Lulu (Lew Ying) to accompany her to Berlin. Later, in Los Angeles, Wong reported being a "happy sister these days."[14] She never got married nor did she have children. Yet, rather than promoting the feeling that she must have been exceedingly lonely, the letters that she wrote to Van Vechten and Marinoff reveal rich networks of friends in Los Angeles and New York. Those epistles recount her meeting up with Australian actress Judith Anderson (eerily good in her Academy Award–nominated role as Mrs. Danvers in the film *Rebecca* [1940]), staying with Kitty Clements in New York City, and lunching at Paramount Pictures, even when no longer under contract. Wong's letters to Van Vechten and Marinoff become most intimate and revelatory in the 1950s, a period covered in the Epilogue of this book. Of course, although not mentioned in her letters, there exist hints of possible romance. Biographer Graham Russell Hodges links her to director Marshall Neilan in the 1920s, and in the 1930s to producer and songwriter Eric Maschwitz.[15] In Chapter 2 of this book, I hint at the tantalizing possibility of a liaison with English actor Laurence Olivier, and, in my first book, I noted that there were rumors of her involvement with German actress Marlene Dietrich. However, the letters reveal that her joys and sorrows derived first and foremost from her career, from the friendships that she built from her work, and from her family, her siblings in particular.

At its heart, this book is a work of cultural history. It owes much to performance studies and to film studies for key concepts such as "performativity" and "the modern," which undergird it. Yet those modes of analysis are not primary. The concept of "performativity" denotes the plethora of repeated acts and gestures that render gender and race socially intelligible.[16] "The modern," especially in reference to actresses, emphasizes surfaces and aesthetic modes.[17] While both frameworks denaturalize the racialized, sexualized, and gendered body, they tend to individuate, ahistoricize, and depoliticize the subject. Centering the narrative on Wong herself makes this book very different

---

13. Anna May Wong to Carl Van Vechten and Fania Marinoff, January 31, 1954, Carl Van Vechten Manuscript Collection, Beinecke Library, Yale University (hereafter, CVVMC).

14. Anna May Wong to Carl Van Vechten and Fania Marinoff, February 17, 1952, CVVMC.

15. Hodges, *Anna May Wong*, 36, 130, 178–179, 181–182, 189.

16. Judith Butler, *Gender Trouble: Feminism and the Subversion of Identity* (New York: Routledge, 1990).

17. Judith Brown, *Glamour in Six Dimensions: Modernism and the Radiance of Form* (Ithaca, NY: Cornell University Press, 2009).

from the articles by scholars such as Laura Mulvey or Anne Anlin Cheng that deploy Wong's films to prove or disprove theoretical stances, particularly psychoanalytical ones, on race, gender, politics, and film theory.[18] In contradistinction, my approach focuses on self-fashioning and cultural work as politicized cultural modes of representation and links the work of American racial minority women to a material global history of race, gender, sexuality, class, and politics. The concept of "self-fashioning," derived from literary scholar Stephen Greenblatt's *Renaissance Self-Fashioning,* describes the process of constructing one's identity and public persona according to a set of socially acceptable standards.[19] Acts of self-fashioning, originally examined in studies of the Renaissance-era upper class, have been extended by scholars to elucidate race and gender through figures such as African American writers Frederick Douglass and Nella Larsen and Latina film stars.[20] A focus on self-fashioning and cultural work situates an individual within a larger social structure and is an illuminating lens through which to view Wong's career. As a work of cultural history, this book foregrounds the broader context of politics, such as Western imperialism or the Cold War, through juxtaposing Wong against figures such as Josephine Baker.

Like a variety revue, this book presents vignettes of key moments of Wong's cultural work and analyzes their deeper meanings. It is not a traditional bildungsroman or biography. In their typical forms, both genres privilege teleological and progressive narratives, such as "coming into voice" or "going from oppression to liberation," that do not fit the ever-changing nuances of Wong's cultural work. Hodges's biographical book-length treatment, *Anna May Wong: From Laundryman's Daughter to Hollywood Legend,* does a laudable job in its attention to Chinese reactions to Wong throughout her career, but the sheer volume of detail at the expense of analysis makes me

---

18. Cheng, "Shine"; Laura Mulvey, "Love in Two British Films of the Late Silent Period: *Hindle Wakes* (Maurice Elvey, 1927) and *Piccadilly* (E.A. Dupont, 1929)," in *Europe in Love and Cinema,* ed. Luisa Passerini, Jo Labanyi, and Karen Diehl (Bristol, UK: Intellect Books, 2012), chap. 4.

19. Stephen Greenblatt, *Renaissance Self-Fashioning* (Chicago: University of Chicago Press, 1980).

20. John Stauffer, "Frederick Douglass's Self-Fashioning and the Making of a Representative American Man," in *The Cambridge Companion to the African American Slave Narrative,* ed. Audrey Fisch (Cambridge: Cambridge University Press, 2007) 201–217; Myra Mendible, "Introduction," in *From Bananas to Buttocks: The Latina Body in Popular Film and Culture* (Austin: University of Texas Press, 2007), 4; Meredith Goldsmith, "Shopping to Pass, Passing to Shop: Consumer Self-Fashioning in the Fiction of Nella Larsen," in *Middlebrow Moderns: Popular American Women Writers of the 1920s,* ed. Lisa Botshon and Meredith Goldsmith (Boston: Northeastern University Press, 2003), 263–290.

lose the forest for the trees. Instead, I here follow innovative models of race and performance historical scholarship. Hye Seung Chung characterizes her monograph on Korean American actor Philip Ahn, Wong's co-star in films such as *Daughter of Shanghai* (1937), as a "discursive critical biography" that uses Ahn as a case study in a larger examination of Asian and Asian American representation.[21] I argue that this approach, which I share, authorizes the writer to eschew the psychological and motivational analysis implicit in conventional biographical modes, instead showing such public figures as part of the structural, ideological, and cultural configurations of particular racial minority groups. Linda Hall's pathbreaking work on Mexican actress Dolores del Río interrogates the "interaction between the individual and the constructed image," an approach analogous to what I call cultural work, which enables an author to reveal both the star iconography and the steps that the actress took to achieve it.[22]

Several scholars do the vital analytical work of showcasing particular aspects of Wong's career. Leong's *China Mystique* elucidates the "gendered embodiment of orientalism."[23] Leong's chapter on Wong is complemented by chapters on Pearl S. Buck and Mayling Soong, which, as a whole, demonstrate the centrality of American cultural fascination with China. Film and theater scholar Sean Metzger interrogates "the discursive production of a wardrobe—to get readers to think differently about existing categories such as race and Asian American."[24] Metzger's chapter on Wong parses the politicized meanings of the *qipao* (cheongsam). In her important article on screen passing, film scholar Yiman Wang insists that Wong is not a performer who naturally plays Asian American roles but one who employs tactics such as screen passing or ironic ethnic masquerade in ways that can be understood as subversive of dominant racial stereotypes.[25] My analysis in this book is formed in dialogue with these works.

Instead of a simplistic story arc leading to a happy Hollywood ending or, as was common in the case of Wong, a tragic Hollywood denouement, this book makes multidimensional the challenges she faced as well as her responses to them. It seeks meaning by situating these discontinuous moments within larger historical contexts as well as analyzing them through theoretical and

---

21. Hye Seung Chung, *Hollywood Asian: Philip Ahn and the Politics of Cross-Ethnic Performance* (Philadelphia: Temple University Press, 2006), xii.

22. Linda Hall, *Dolores del Río: Beauty in Light and Shadow* (Palo Alto, CA: Stanford University Press, 2013).

23. Leong, *The China Mystique.*

24. Metzger, *Chinese Looks,* 20.

25. Wang, "The Art of Screen Passing."

conceptual frameworks. This is not a conventional biography uncovering the development of a single life. Rather, it features Wong as a historical subject cast in relation to other figures. *Anna May Wong: Performing the Modern* is structured like a globally circulating vaudeville variety show starring Wong and featuring a variety of supporting acts, locales, and stage sets. What is gained by this approach is a contingent and episodic narrative that is less conventional, but one that more accurately reflects the complicated dynamics of history.

The leading part in this story goes to Wong. Baker plays the main supporting role, with additional support by Mexican actress Lupe Vélez and a cameo appearance by Mexican actress Dolores del Río.[26] The relational formation of race and analogous work in self-fashioning instigates the other women's inclusion in this story: all of the women played oriental roles in films and/or theatrical performances. Other supporting characters include Van Vechten, Benjamin, and European American photographer Edward Steichen. Wong stars not only because she was a key figure in the United States but also because she enjoyed global fame as the ultimate "oriental" actress from Australia and China to France.

Orientalism

The gravitational force of orientalism exerts its pull on this entire book as a source of both opportunity and limitation not only for Wong but also for other groundbreaking individuals in theater and cinema, including Baker and Vélez.

---

26. Matthew Guterl, *Josephine Baker and the Rainbow Tribe* (Cambridge, MA: Harvard University Press, 2014); Bennetta Jules-Rosette, *Josephine Baker in Art and Life: The Icon and the Image* (Urbana: University of Illinois Press, 2007); Anne Anlin Cheng, *Second Skin: Josephine Baker and the Modern Surface* (New York: Oxford University Press, 2010); Jennifer Boittin, *Colonial Metropolis: The Urban Grounds of Feminism and Anti-imperialism in Interwar Paris* (Lincoln: University of Nebraska Press, 2010); Phyllis Rose, *Jazz Cleopatra: Josephine Baker in Her Time* (New York: Doubleday, 1989). Since she changed her citizenship to French and remained in Europe, Baker, unlike Wong, continued her European career into the post–World War II period. For more on Josephine Baker's 1950s politics, see Mary L. Dudziak, "Josephine Baker, Racial Protest, and the Cold War," *Journal of American History,* September 1994, 543–570. On Vélez and del Río, see Clara Rodriguez, *Heroes, Lovers, and Others: The Story of Latinos in Hollywood* (Washington, DC: Smithsonian Books, 2004); Victoria Sturtevant, "Spitfire: Lupe Vélez and the Ambivalent Pleasure of Ethnic Masquerade," *Velvet Light Trap,* no. 22 (Spring 2005): 23; Alicia Rodriquez-Estrada, "Dolores del Río and Lupe Vélez: Images on and off the Screen," in *Writing the Range: Race, Class, and Culture in the Women's West,* ed. Elizabeth Jameson and Susan Armitage (Norman: University of Oklahoma Press, 1997); Michelle Vogel, *Lupe Vélez: The Life and Career of Hollywood's "Mexican Spitfire"* (Jefferson, NC: McFarland, 2012); Hall, *Dolores del Río*; Joanne Hershfield, *The Invention of Dolores del Río* (Minneapolis: University of Minnesota Press, 2000).

As Edward Said's landmark study *Orientalism* established, European fascination with the "orient" was central to European culture, politics, and nationalism and was frequently invoked as a justification for colonialism.[27] The orient refers to geographically mutable and often unspecified places ranging from what is now Turkey and Russia to the "Middle East," the Arab world (often including Arab North Africa), and the Far East. As the foil to modernity, the orient functioned as a mirror for Europe's own desires and ambitions. Building on that European orientalism, U.S. orientalism geographically shifted focus to the eastern Pacific. U.S. orientalism combined the European version with the myth of the American frontier.[28] According to the frontier myth, American national formation was unique because class-based conflict could be solved by the promise of economic opportunity in the so-called "empty" lands in the West. As the U.S. nation-state borders reached the Pacific Ocean, historian Frederick Jackson Turner famously lamented that the United States had lost its frontier and thus its basis for class harmony. Colonizing the Pacific (the Philippines, Hawaii, Guam) through American imperialism imaginatively extended into the Pacific the function of the American West as safety valve for class conflict. Settler colonialism became naturalized and normalized as part of the American nation-state.[29] In addition, it compelled the migration of workers from Asia to the United States and its territories. In cinema as well as in journalism and the arts, American orientalism took the form of the yellow peril, namely the fear of Asian migration and the concomitant hordes of Asians taking over the United States. Both Hollywood and European versions of orientalism would affect Wong's career. As theater scholars Karen Shima-

---

27. Said, *Orientalism.*

28. Frederick Jackson Turner, "The Significance of the Frontier in American History," paper presented at the meeting of the American Historical Association in Chicago, 1893. Reprinted in Frederick Jackson Turner, *The Frontier in American History,* Project Gutenberg ebook, chap. 1, October 14, 2007, http://www.gutenberg.org/files/22994/22994-h/22994-h .htm (accessed March 19, 2018); Kerwin Klein, *Frontiers of Historical Imagination* (Berkeley: University of California Press, 1997); Harold Isaacs, *Scratches on Our Minds: American Views of China and India* (New York: Routledge, 1980); Malini Johar Schueller, *U.S. Orientalisms: Race, Nation, and Gender in Literature, 1790–1890* (Ann Arbor: University of Michigan Press, 1998); Amy Kaplan and Donald E. Pease, eds., *Cultures of United States Imperialism* (Durham, NC: Duke University Press, 1993).

29. Karen Leong and Myla Vicenti Carpio, "Carceral Subjugations: Gila River Indian Community and Incarceration of Japanese Americans on Its Lands," *Amerasia Journal* 42, no. 1 (2016): 103–120; Andrea Smith and Audra Simpson, *Theorizing Native Studies* (Durham, NC: Duke University Press, 2014); Audra Simpson, *Mohawk Interruptus: Political Life across the Borders of Settler States* (Durham, NC: Duke University Press, 2014); Glen Coulthard, *Red Skin, White Masks: Rejecting the Colonial Politics of Recognition* (Minneapolis: University of Minnesota Press, 2014).

kawa, Josephine Lee, James Moy, and Robert Lee have eloquently argued, no Asian American actor/actress steps onto a stage free of the oriental stereotypes against which he or she must struggle to be seen.[30] The transnational reach of Hollywood and European film meant that these viewpoints would circulate around the globe, including in locales such as Australia and South Africa. Wong's career contested, accommodated, and, most importantly, denaturalized various forms of orientalism.

In this book, orientalism refers to the discursive formation of otherness as well as the "orient" as an imagined amalgamation of "Eastern" cultures that loosely reference the area ranging from North Africa and Turkey to the Middle East to East Asia and the Pacific Islands. Orientalism manifested itself in films of the 1920s such as *Old San Francisco* (1927) and the Fu Manchu films, which showcased the sinister aspects of racial difference. Like the European version, American orientalism was fascinated with China in particular as evidenced by the treaty ports and Shanghai concessions, thus strengthening U.S. orientalism and Wong's cinematic career.

In the 1920s, general interest in exotic otherness through the female body meant that acting opportunities in film and theater opened up to include a few select women of color in starring oriental roles.[31] The feminized embodiment of orientalism was crucial to this casting. Patriarchal tropes combined with colonial discourse to create the female oriental in need of male Western control and mastery, creating opportunities for actresses such as Wong, Baker, Vélez, and del Río to perform "oriental" roles. American and European interest in the orient expanded to the Pacific as colonial ventures in China, Southeast Asia, and the South Pacific intensified. As cultural historian Adria Imada argues, in the context of U.S. imperialism and settler colonialism hula "helped to broker this process of incorporation and integration."[32] Through these actresses' performances, we see the paradoxes of the modern.

This book's interpretive vitality derives from the tension between the colonial/exotic/oriental roles the women were expected to play and the cultural work that they did to fashion alternatives. What is vitally important is that these alternatives render the category of the oriental unstable. I see Wong as a versatile artist, game enough to produce bad performances of the oriental that undercut any notions of authenticity while vitally engaged with self-fashioning

---

30. Shimakawa, *National Abjection*; Robert Lee, *Orientals*; Moy, *Marginal Sights*; Josephine Lee, *Performing Asian America*.

31. As historian Kathy Peiss has documented, cosmetics reflected these aesthetic changes. *Hope in a Jar: The Making of America's Beauty Culture* (1998; repr., Philadelphia: University of Pennsylvania Press, 2011).

32. Imada, *Aloha America,* 6.

and presentation of self. Women represent the ultimate modern subjects precisely because of their ability to inhabit multiple temporally complex subject positions such as those of self and other, primitive and civilized, oriental and Western. As these bodily regimes of modernity apply to everyone, it is a matter of whose body becomes visibly marked as such. Yet such an ordering of bodies is how modern Western societies organize and categorize their populations. By mapping these women's responses to the challenges that they encountered, I explore the edges and limits of modern culture.

Modernity

Changing conceptions of modernity, race, gender, and geographic mobility are central to understanding the significance of Wong's career. For *Anna May Wong: Performing the Modern,* modernity signals the changes in the Enlightenment-derived liberal subject as manifested in modern society's central organizing principles of racial and sexual difference. For those who do not bear the dominant markers of national belonging—in the case of the U.S., nonwhite and female—such narratives of belonging and citizenship are frequently renegotiated through acts of modernity. As scholar David Theo Goldberg has argued, "If premodernity lacked any conception of the differences between human beings as racial, modernity comes increasingly to be defined by and through race."[33] Modernity is a complex historical and cultural situation defined against the past, the traditional, and the "other," with shifting values attached to each category. As numerous scholars have elaborated, modernity constructs the nation as the preeminent political unit through a series of oppositions that become masked or homogenized: male and female, citizen and alien, civilized and primitive.[34] Wong's performances beautifully exemplify both the construction of as well as the contradictions at the heart of modernity.

As one of the main exemplars of the oriental, the colonial subject, and the modern American, Wong mediated the new social order. American and European nation-state modernities developed divergently, through differing imperatives of citizenship and belonging. Colonial difference was (and remains) central to the very definition of European modernity.[35] For European

---

33. D. T. Goldberg, "Modernity, Race, and Morality," *Cultural Critique,* no. 24 (Spring 1993): 202.

34. Caren Kaplan, Norma Alarcon, and Minoo Moallem, eds., *Between Woman and Nation: Nationalisms, Transnational Feminisms, and the State* (Durham, NC: Duke University Press, 1999), 1–16.

35. Arjun Appadurai, *Modernity at Large: Cultural Dimensions of Globalization* (Minneapolis: University of Minnesota Press, 1996); Dipesh Chakrabarty, *Provincializing Europe:*

colonial nations, the colonies supplied both the material and ideological underpinnings for European modernity. In addition to colonial superpowers such as Britain and France, Italy, the Netherlands, and Portugal were concurrent colonial powers. Whereas American modernity developed not only vis-à-vis imperial ventures but also in response to settler colonialism and to racial minorities within its nation-state borders, for European countries, colonial subjects chiefly resided outside.[36] Wong's American modernity, combined with her racial and, by extension, colonial difference, made her a fascinating puzzle for European and colonial audiences.

As bodies under modernity became distinguished by racial difference they also became marked by sexual difference. The twentieth century was a critical era for the changing roles of women. With the passage in 1920 of the Nineteenth Amendment to the U.S. Constitution granting the right of women to vote, women's roles in the public sphere were newly visible. These changes in the modern era were signified by the creation of the private and public spheres, the rise of industrial labor, and the shifting roles of religion and family in society. All of those currents converged in the United States at the concept of the "New Woman" and globally at the concept of the "Modern Girl," both beautifully exemplified by Wong on- and off-screen.[37] The flapper, one of the most popular incarnations of the New Woman and Modern Girl, emblemized modernity by finding new pleasures and autonomy in the public sphere away from the control of the patriarchal family. Women's reconfigured sexual, familial, and public roles, combined with their function as the main subjects of consumer culture, made the New Woman and Modern Girl significant figures of both promise and anxiety. As a career woman and a fashion icon, Wong represented the seductive dangers of the New Woman and Modern Girl even when cast as the oriental siren.

Postcolonial Thought and Historical Difference (Princeton, NJ: Princeton University Press, 2000); Fatimah Tobing Rony, *The Third Eye: Race, Cinema, and the Ethnographic Spectacle* (Durham, NC: Duke University Press, 1996); Nancy Nenno, "Femininity, the Primitive, and Modern Urban Space: Josephine Baker in Berlin," in *Women in the Metropolis: Gender and Modernity in Weimar Culture,* ed. Katharina von Ankum (Berkeley: University of California Press, 1997), 145–161; Cynthia Liu, "When Dragon Ladies Die, Do They Come Back as Butterflies? Re-Imagining Anna May Wong," in *Countervisions: Asian American Film Criticism,* ed. Darrell Hamamoto and Sandra Liu (Philadelphia: Temple University Press, 2000), 23–39.

36. Iyko Day, *Alien Capital: Asian Racialization and the Logic of Settler Colonial Capitalism* (Durham, NC: Duke University Press, 2016).

37. Modern Girl around the World Research Group, ed., *The Modern Girl around the World: Consumption, Modernity, and Globalization* (Durham, NC: Duke University Press, 2008).

Wong's career as a mass media celebrity through films, mass-circulating magazines, and consumer culture arrived at a crucial time in the 1920s. In the twentieth century, categories of difference were promoted, among other ways, through the circulation of motion pictures, images, and the commodification of the body. As eminent cultural historian Warren Susman points out, by 1922, "an exceptional and ever-growing number of Americans came to believe in a series of changes in the structure of their world, natural, technological, social, personal, and moral."[38] One way that Americans (and the rest of the world) understood this rapidly changing world was through the motion pictures. Actresses such as Wong became critical to comprehending societal transformations. As a performer, she was both symptomatic of and contributed to these changes. As Wong moved through the twentieth century, her work unfolded on new media, such as multi-language film and television. The intertextuality of film, advertisements, photography, and television displayed the shifting terrain of modernity.

In Berlin, no less an intellectual than German philosopher Walter Benjamin attempted to work through the puzzle Wong represented; his 1928 interview with her in Berlin reveals how difficult it was to fit her into dominant constructions of Chinese heritage in light of her New World modernity. Wong and Benjamin enter into a conversation with each other, and that encounter, which reverberates in his writings and in her films and letters, becomes a current in the circulation of modern culture. Yet, as I explore through Benjamin and Wong's meeting, the supposed openness of cosmopolitan culture courses up against the edges of racial mores.

The Book

The geographical scope of this book encompasses American as well as European empires that laid out the performance routes for Wong, including stops in Europe, the United States, Australia, South Africa, and China. As such, this work takes up the challenge of transnational history and U.S. history both within and outside of nation-state borders. This study focuses on a critical period when new gendered narratives of modernity, national belonging, and cosmopolitanism were in formation: from 1928, when Wong began acting in Berlin, to 1939, with the performance of her vaudeville act in Australia, and concluding in the 1950s. Although power and politics are continually

---

38. Warren Susman, *Culture as History: The Transformation of American Society in the Twentieth Century* (New York: Pantheon Books, 1984), 106.

articulated through culture, this book insists on the historical perspective, for race and its cultural meanings are not universal throughout time and location, but are mutable, contingent, and particular in time and space.

Six chapters arranged chronologically and geographically present Wong's ventures as an actress. The narrative arc of the book delineates Wong's changing relationship to power, beauty, and ingenuity. At the start of her career, Wong's youth and beauty subjected her to attention from luminaries such as Benjamin and actor Laurence Olivier and gained her starring roles in film and theater. As she aged and her beauty became less hegemonically appealing, she received fewer film roles. Yet, through the accumulation of work experience, she became skilled at finding ways to practice her craft through different media. The trajectory of this book traces Wong coming into herself as a worker and as an increasingly versatile actress. The book centers on the late 1920s, the 1930s, and, finally, the 1950s because those are the years when Wong improved her repertoire as an actress, honed her skills in finding jobs, and seized work opportunities in different countries in order to practice her craft. To me, these actions are the most interesting part of her life story.

Never daunted, Wong time and time again turned to different media and different countries: She starred in theatrical productions with Olivier in London, sang French chansons in Paris vaudeville, hired a cinematographer and made "My China Film," starred in Paramount Pictures' B-list films with Philip Ahn, and worked in television productions such as the DuMont Television Network's *The Gallery of Madame Liu-Tsong*. Her increasing repertory range yet loss of studio prestige can be seen most clearly in the *Good Earth* casting debacle. *The Good Earth* symbolized an especially cruel casting rejection because of the vast scope of MGM's production resources and because Depression-era America exhibited a strong interest in the hardships of good Chinese peasants. Wong rose to arguably her greatest power as a cultural producer when she made "My China Film" to oppose MGM's Hollywood depiction of China. Yet, because she was aging and because of the changing political climate marked by the impending Second World War, *The Good Earth* would be her last chance to star in a major Hollywood studio A-list film before the casting of the *Flower Drum Song* in 1961. Had she starred in *The Good Earth*, her name would be ubiquitous today.

Chapters 1–3 of this book focus on European and American modernities. Chapter 1, "'Speaking German Like Nobody's Business': Anna May Wong in Berlin," establishes how, in 1928, Wong journeyed to Europe to star in films that were coproduced in Germany, France, and England. Berlin was Wong's first European destination. There, she fascinated German philosopher Walter Benjamin. Benjamin's interview with her evinces the struggles of one of the most lauded European architects of modernity in puzzling through the conundrum presented by Wong's simultaneous oriental yet modern cosmopolitan body. This chapter sets the stage for the entire book by exploring the tensions between Wong's Chinese heritage, European expectations of racial difference as filtered through colonial otherness, and New World modernity. Wong rose to the challenge of being a modern American through trying to establish a career in Europe by "speaking German like nobody's business."

Although at first glance Anna May Wong's and Josephine Baker's performances displayed primitivism, exoticism, and decadence, Chapter 2, "American Moderns in Europe: Anna May Wong and Josephine Baker," probes deeper in order to explore how both women utilized dance movements, fashion, voice, and improvisation—skills gained while training in U.S. racial minority communities—to disrupt colonial culture. Wong and Baker, I argue, not only challenged the binary opposition of the primitive and the civilized underlying modernity; they also created a distinctly new form of the modern. Chapter 3, "'I Can Play Any Type of Oriental': Anna Watches Josephine at the Casino de Paris, 1932," focuses on both women's depictions of oriental roles. This chapter has two interlinked aims: first, considering France as a site of transnational performance, and second, explicating Baker's performance of the oriental, which was intertwined with Wong's. Comparing Baker and Wong demonstrates how racial modernity is a relational process. Examining the women's differing trajectories reveals that the African American body could fit into the French nation-state narratives, whereas the Chinese American one could not.

The next chapter considers the early 1930s and the creation of gendered race and ethnicity as relational categories in the United States. Chapter 4, "Glamourous American Moderns: Anna May Wong and Lupe Vélez," centers on the United States at a time when Dolores del Río and Anna May Wong emblemized ideal beauty and Lupe Vélez starred as an all-American model for 1932 Coca-Cola and 1934 Lux Soap advertisements. The chapter focuses on the central role that race plays in the development of modern aesthetics in image making and shows the overt as well as the more subtle forms of racialization that appeared through glamour photography and advertisements. One of the book's most exciting pieces of historical detective work comes to light in the final portion of this chapter. Wong's correspondence with Van Vechten provides invaluable insights into how Wong fabricated her own image.

Chapters 5 and 6 of this book feature Anna May Wong as a mature cultural worker and move geographically from the Atlantic to the Pacific. Most of the creation of Wong's Chinese persona happened in Europe and the United States, and thus it is fascinating when that persona is on display in the Pacific.

Chapter 5, "'My China Film,'" analyzes one of Wong's triumphal moments as a cultural worker forging an alternative to the mainstream culture. This chapter reveals what happened when Wong's Western-bred Chineseness encountered the actual China.

Chapter 6, "Anna May Wong in Australia," examines Chineseness, Americanness, and modernity in a settler-colonial Anglophone transnational context. Wong's portrayals of glamourous racialized modernity were the reason why she was brought to Australia in 1939 to perform on the Tivoli Theatre circuit in Sydney and Melbourne. Her visit functioned as a touchstone to examine the various meanings of Chineseness in the late 1930s both from the perspective of mainstream Australian society as well as that of Chinese Australians. In the late 1930s, Australia was considered a backwater at the edge of empire, lacking the prestige of London or Paris. In order to practice her craft, Wong was forced to go to a secondary locale because World War II preempted Western Europe as a possible worksite.

The book concludes with Wong unveiling "My China Film" for the American Broadcasting Company (ABC) television audience in 1957. American Cold War agendas regarding China not only prompted ABC to revive and promote Wong's movie; they also were made overt through the critique of Communist China and the celebration of a vanished non-Communist past that Wong had captured in her film. As a new medium, television became a way for aging Hollywood stars to revive their careers.

This book imagines otherwise in terms of Wong's cultural encounters and engagement with racial modernity.[39] Women of color in film such as Vélez and Wong have provided inspiration for me and for numerous artists. Examples include Rita Aida Gonzalez's *The Assumption of Lupe Vélez* (1999), Patty Chang's performance piece *The Product Love* (2009, based on Wong and Benjamin's encounter in Berlin), and Cheryl Dunye's *Watermelon Woman* (1996), a film whose eponymous African American actress offers Dunye's cinematic protagonist a lineage as an artistic and lesbian forebear.[40] In this current political era, when civil rights are under attack, I hope that

---

39. See Chuh, *Imagine Otherwise.*

40. See Rita Aida Gonzalez, "The Assumption of Lupe Vélez" (master's thesis, University of California, San Diego, 2014); Patty Chang, *The Product of Love* (2009), https://www .guggenheim.org/artwork/26179 (accessed August 16, 2017). On March 11, 2017, performance artist Vaginal Davis announced working on Anna May Wong, http://blog.vaginaldavis .com/2017_03_05_archive.html (accessed August 8, 2017). For more on Vaginal Davis, see Grace Dunham, "The 'Terrorist Drag' of Vaginal Davis," *New Yorker,* December 12, 2015, http://www.newyorker.com/culture/culture-desk/terrorist-drag-vaginal-davis (accessed August 8, 2017); and José Esteban Muñoz, *Disidentifications: Queers of Color and the Performance of Politics* (Minneapolis: University of Minnesota Press, 1999), chap. 4.

this book provides a reprieve through an alternative genealogy of race and gender. It is a sobering reminder that racial progress, however defined, does not move forward in a straight line. Wong's cultural creations, however, point to an earlier historical moment of possibility and creativity. It shows us how she and other women of color performed the modern despite facing extraordinary racial and gendered obstacles.

Prologue

Anna May Wong in Los Angeles

The slender large-eyed child with the glorious smile exchanges a bundle of clean clothes almost as heavy as her for a large tip. Clutching the money in her hand, instead of heading back to the laundry, she saunters off to her favorite movie palace. Mesmerized by the radiant actress walking down the staircase wearing sumptuous furs over a silk dress, she wonders, what would it be like to be her?

Anna May Wong's daily childhood experiences of grueling labor and interracial interactions punctuated by celluloid dreams prepared her for a career in the entertainment industry. Born Wong Liu Tsong (Yellow Willow Frost) on January 3, 1905, Wong was raised just outside of Los Angeles' Chinatown, the second of seven children. The family lived behind their laundry business, and, alongside her siblings, Wong performed arduous labor in the family enterprise, including delivering laundry bundles. Since she and her older sister Lulu were repeatedly racially bullied at the California Street public school, they were placed in the Presbyterian Chinese Mission School. That school represented a safe haven for them because, although the teachers were white, the other students were Chinese, and they learned both English and Cantonese there. Wong's daily life forced her to interact in English with non-Chinese people: her immediate neighbors were

Mexican and Eastern European, and the majority of her laundry customers were not Chinese.[1]

German philosopher Walter Benjamin confirms Wong's childhood interest in film, "For she [Wong] had been interested in film from very early on. She still remembers the first time she went to the cinema. School was out because of an epidemic. She bought a ticket with her pocket money. Hardly had she returned home when she tried out everything she had seen in front of a mirror."[2] Benjamin's words paint an evocative picture of Wong coming into her subjectivity through the mirror and through cinema.

Wong's upbringing in Los Angeles proved critical to her future for it gave her access to fulfilling her prodigious interest in cinema. As the film industry moved to Los Angeles, motion pictures were continually shot in her neighborhood. At age nine, Wong begged filmmakers for roles, and, by age eleven, she had developed her professional name, a combination of her Chinese last name, Wong, American first name, Anna, and her own addition of the middle name, May.[3] Wong established herself as an important ingénue in Hollywood. Cutting classes in order to frequent the back lots of Hollywood studios, Wong began her career as an extra in Alla Nazimova's classic film about China's Boxer Rebellion, *The Red Lantern* (1919). She landed her first starring role in *The Toll of the Sea* (1922) at the age of seventeen, playing a character based on Madame Butterfly.[4] Wong's well-received role in *The Toll of the Sea* led to one of national prominence—she played the Mongol slave in actor Douglas Fairbank's film *The Thief of Baghdad* (1924).

Despite that early success, Wong would leave Hollywood for Europe because typecasting, a reflection of the contemporary racial mores, discouraged her. In the 1920s, European American women dominated the main "positive" Chinese roles in Hollywood, relegating Wong to the "tragic" or "evil"

1. Karen Leong, *China Mystique: Pearl S. Buck, Anna May Wong, Mayling Soong, and the Transformation of American Orientalism* (Berkeley: University of California Press, 2005), 59–61.

2. Walter Benjamin, "Gespräch mit Anne May Wong," *Die Literarische Welt*, July 6, 1928. This article was translated by Jeff Fort specifically for this project. The entire essay appeared on the front page of the paper. Benjamin and Wong met in June of that same year. "Tried out" is translated from the verb *probte*, from *proben*, to "try" or "test." The noun *Probe* can mean "rehearsal." Benjamin, "Gespräch," 1.

3. Graham Hodges, *Anna May Wong* (New York: Palgrave, 2004), 21.

4. Cari Beauchamp, *Without Lying Down: Frances Marion and the Powerful Women of Early Hollywood* (New York: Scribner, 1997); Nick Browne, "The Undoing of the Other Woman: Madame Butterfly in the Discourse of American Orientalism," in *The Birth of Whiteness: Race and the Emergence of U.S. Cinema*, ed. Daniel Bernardi (New Brunswick, NJ: Rutgers University Press, 1996), 227–256; Josephine Lee, *The Japan of Pure Invention: Gilbert and Sullivan's "The Mikado"* (Minneapolis: University of Minnesota Press, 2010).

orientalist ones. The controlling image for Asian Americans was and still is that of the perpetual foreigner-alien, and that image originated with the Chinese.[5] Representations of China and Chinese people played key roles in the formation of American identity as white.[6] This cultural imaginary worked in conjunction with the legal limitations placed on Asians in America. The 1875 Page Law, which supposedly restricted the immigration of Chinese male and female workers and felons, in reality curtailed the immigration of only Chinese women. The 1882 Chinese Exclusion Act was the first American immigration law to bar a group by name.[7] The barring of all other immigrant groups, Asian and otherwise, resulted from that precedent. Racial segregation and anti-miscegenation laws further restricted everyday life. Everything from alien land laws and housing segregation (Asian American students at the University of California, Berkeley and Los Angeles, could not live in on-campus housing) to laws that forbade Asians from marrying whites in California circumscribed Wong's life.[8]

A prime example of how these racial mores affected Wong's film roles can be seen in the film *The Toll of the Sea* (1922), whose screenplay was written by the noted female screenwriter Frances Marion. Although only 10 percent of all silent films have an extant print, *The Toll of the Sea* survives because of its technological innovation in color through the pioneering use of Two-Tone Technicolor. Even though Wong charmed in *The Toll of the Sea,* the film reworked one of the most orientalist of all tropes, that of Madame Butterfly. Madame Butterfly, predicated on the signifiers of Eastern as female, Western as male, stands in for the dynamics of Western imperialism in Asia. Wong's

5. Lisa Lowe, *Immigrant Acts: On Asian American Cultural Politics* (Durham, NC: Duke University Press, 1996); David Palumbo-Liu, *Asian/American: Historical Crossings of a Racial Frontier* (Palo Alto, CA: Stanford University Press, 1999).

6. Jack Tchen, *New York before Chinatown: Orientalism and the Shaping of American Culture, 1776–1882* (Baltimore: Johns Hopkins University Press, 1999).

7. Erika Lee, *At America's Gates: Chinese Immigration during the Exclusion Era, 1882–1943* (Chapel Hill: University of North Carolina Press, 2003); George A. Peffer, *If They Don't Bring Their Women Here: Chinese Female Immigration before Exclusion* (Urbana: University of Illinois Press, 1999); Sucheng Chan, "The Exclusion of Chinese Women, 1870–1943," in *Entry Denied: Exclusion and the Chinese Community in America,* ed. Sucheng Chan (Philadelphia: Temple University Press, 1991), 94–146; Lucie Cheng Hirata, "Free, Indentured, Enslaved: Chinese Prostitutes in Nineteenth-Century America," *Signs: Journal of Women in Culture and Society* 5, no. 1 (Autumn 1979): 3–29; Andrew Gyory, *Closing the Gate: Race, Politics, and the Chinese Exclusion Act* (Chapel Hill: University of North Carolina Press, 1998).

8. Judy Yung, *Unbound Feet: A Social History of Chinese Women in San Francisco* (Berkeley: University of California Press, 1995); Peggy Pascoe, *What Comes Naturally: Miscegenation Law and the Making of Race in America* (New York: Oxford University Press, 2009).

character, Lotus Flower, has a baby with an American ship's captain (Allen) under the illusion that they are married and he will bring her to America. However, Allen becomes engaged to a white European American woman, he takes Wong's (and his) baby away to America, and, at the end of the film, she, still in China, commits suicide. The colonial metaphors and tropes—substitute baby for laboring bodies or raw goods that the colonizers ship to the metropole and elsewhere—are rife.

Wong's clothing in *The Toll of the Sea* situated her as nonmodern and (both her and China) as a colonial subject. Throughout the movie Wong wears silk Chinese garments. However, when Captain Allen announces his return to the United States, Wong's character strives to prove that she is ready to live in America through her knowledge of appropriate fashion. Copying from her grandmother's fashion guide, Wong's character emerges in full nineteenth-century long skirts, mistakenly believing that her ensemble represents contemporary chic. The 1922 audience would have howled with laughter, knowing her character appeared at least fifty years out of date. To underscore that point, when Allen returns to China a second time, his European American wife, Elsie, wears modern short skirts made from softer, lighter materials. Wong's clothing displays her as unfit for modernity: she does not know what is modern; therefore, she cannot raise a modern child, and thus

Anna May Wong in *The Toll of the Sea* (1922).
(Film still, *The Toll of the Sea*.)

her son is better off with the modern white couple, to be raised in America. One could extend the metaphor to colonial relations. Colonial subjects do not understand modernity; therefore, they cannot rule themselves or their own people. Screenwriter Marion's key plot device is that Wong confides in Elsie that the child is Allen's and does so because of the sisterly mutual understanding of women around the world. This sentiment rings hollow as it provides the justification for Allen and Elsie to take the child away from Wong. Under colonial regimes, white women like Elsie gained status at the expense of the colonialized women.[9]

Modernity factored into orientalism and was heightened by the need to manage the yellow peril and Asian menace, which manifested itself in films. Through a strong Americanization movement, World War I set the tone for the ensuing decades' xenophobia. *Old San Francisco* (1927), in which Wong played a nameless Chinese girl, secured the American West for European Americans and excised the Mexican American and Asian American contributions by situating them as nonmodern.[10] Genre movies, which highlighted sinister orientals as being decadent, savage, and nonmodern, worked in tandem with legal cases such as *Takao Ozawa v. United States* (1922) and *United States v. Bhagat Singh Thind* (1923). Both of the U.S. Supreme Court decisions invoked a "common" understanding of race to rule that Asians were nonwhite. That common understanding of race had derived in part from the movies.[11]

Within that 1920s racial framework, Wong's options as an actress were limited. Hollywood orientalism and yellowface in particular could simultaneously conjure up and ameliorate racial anxieties most effectively if actual Asian American bodies were banned. As theater scholar Karen Shimakawa has influentially argued, the category of Asian American operates as abject in relation to America, which means that the Asian American figure works as a state and a process of being made present and discarded.[12] In other words, American culture requires a constitutive figure such as the oriental who would ultimately be cast off in order to consolidate and affirm who could be American and who could not. These cultural dynamics were codified in Hollywood cinema production codes and anti-miscegenation laws that prohibited the depiction of interracial romance between actors of European

9. Mari Yoshihara, *Embracing the East: White Women and American Orientalism* (New York: Oxford University Press, 2003).

10. Moy, *Marginal Sights*, 89.

11. Rogin, *Blackface, White Noise*; Lee, *Orientals*.

12. Karen Shimakawa, *National Abjection: The Asian American Body Onstage* (Durham, NC: Duke University Press, 2002), 3.

descent and those of Asian descent, making it almost impossible to have female Asian characters on screen embodied by Asian Americans.[13] Therefore, in the United States, Wong struggled to be cast in roles as a Chinese woman against European American actresses in yellowface such as Myrna Loy, Colleen Moore, and Luise Rainer.[14] Wong was ready for starring roles outside of the United States.

Imagine, if you will, that you are Anna May Wong. After starring in the films The Toll of the Sea, The Thief of Bagdad, *and* Peter Pan, *you have not received any appealing roles. When Hollywood sends out invitations, your mailbox clangs shut—hollow, empty. Then, a starring role offer from Berlin! With trepidation, you traverse the American continent and sail across the Atlantic. Your fellow thespians crowd to see you at Ufa Studios. Suddenly, you are invited to the Berlin Press Ball. Famed intellectual Walter Benjamin clamors to meet with you. Why are you, a twenty-three-year-old American, born just outside of Los Angeles' Chinatown, the toast of Berlin's intellectual and cultural life?*

13. Nancy Courtney, *Hollywood Fantasies of Miscegenation: Spectacular Narratives of Gender and Race, 1903–1967* (Princeton, NJ: Princeton University Press, 2005).

14. Gina Marchetti, *Romance and the "Yellow Peril": Race, Sex, and Discursive Strategies in Hollywood Fiction* (Berkeley: University of California Press, 1993); Karla Rae Fuller, *Hollywood Goes Oriental: CaucAsian Performance in American Film* (Detroit, MI: Wayne State University Press, 2010).

1

"Speaking German Like Nobody's Business"

Anna May Wong in Berlin

Neubabelsberg, Germany, 1928: To get here, Wong travels with her sister Mary across the United States and the Atlantic Ocean for the first time in her life. The melee at the Berlin Hauptbahnhof overwhelms the young American actress. Stately yet lively, Berlin's wide, tree-lined avenues bustle with streetcars and fashionable people. She waits onstage at the famed Ufa Studios in Neubabelsberg just outside of the city. The lights dim; the cameras are poised to roll. She is ready for her close-up.

The central story of Anna May Wong's self-fashioning and cultural work commences in Berlin in 1928 with her first film role outside of the United States. The acts of leaving her family, Los Angeles, and Hollywood denoted a bid for greater authority. This Berlin sojourn marked Wong's emergence as a truly cosmopolitan and global actress, which would prove crucial throughout the rest of her career. Being an international celebrity gave her leverage, publicity, and access to a whole host of influential cultural figures. Her time in Berlin served as important tutelage in her understanding of her own appeal as a global star. This initial foray to Europe shaped how she, for the rest of her life, handled the limitations placed on her as an Asian American woman.

The starring role in the film *Song/Show Life/Schmutziges Geld* (1928) enticed Wong across the United States and the Atlantic Ocean to Berlin.[1] German director Richard Eichberg cast Wong in films such as this and *Hai-Tang/Flame of Love/Le Chemin du Déshounneur/The Road to Dishonour* (1930), which were co-produced in Germany, France, and England and subtitled or shot in multiple languages so that they could screen throughout Europe and, most crucially, the colonial world. Hence the multiple titles for the films. Those films played not only in France and Germany but also in locations such as Mozambique and South Africa.[2] Wong became a transnational symbol of racialized femininity, and her star persona helped to create a new pan-European cinema, construed more broadly as global cinema. Doubtless Wong found these starring roles appealing in comparison to Hollywood's exploitative orientalist roles and her reception in Europe welcome compared to the host of race-based laws that circumscribed her life in California.

Courtesy of her starring role in the first of these pan-European films, *Song/Show Life,* in the summer of 1928 in Berlin, Wong and German Jewish philosopher Walter Benjamin (1892–1940) shared an unlikely encounter that set in relief European and American conceptions of modernity. On July 6, 1928, Benjamin published the results as "Gespräch mit Anne May Wong: Un Chinoiserie auf dem Westens" (Speaking with Anna May Wong: A Chinoiserie from the Old West) on the front page of a leading German literary review.[3] The resulting article reveals the complexities of Wong's Asian American cosmopolitan modernity. Benjamin justified his choice to interview a nonliterary figure to his audience by explaining, "As everyone knows, May Wong has a central part in the great film now being directed by Eichberg."[4] Benjamin's essay, juxtaposed against a cache of Wong's writings, neither of which has yet to receive serious scholarly attention, is significant not just for what Benjamin says about Wong, or what Wong reveals, but for how it intervenes in constructions of racial and gendered difference. It is precisely the complex blend of Wong's American cosmopolitanism, Chinese heritage,

---

1. *Song/Show Life/Schmutziges Geld* (1928) was directed by Richard Eichberg and co-produced in France, England, and Germany by Ufa Studios, headquartered in Neubabelsberg, Germany.

2. Reviews and stories appeared in *O Brado Africano* and *South Africa Film and Screen.*

3. Walter Benjamin was a regular contributor to *Die Literarische Welt,* edited by Wally Haas in Berlin. According to Susan Buck-Morss, it published his works almost weekly. Susan Buck-Morss, *The Dialectics of Seeing: Walter Benjamin and the Arcades Project* (Cambridge, MA: MIT Press, 1991), 34; Catherine Russell, *Archiveology: Walter Benjamin and Archival Film Practice* (Durham, NC: Duke University Press, 2018).

4. Walter Benjamin, "Gespräch mit Anne May Wong," *Die Literarische Welt,* July 6, 1928, 2. The article was translated by Jeff Fort specifically for this project. The entire essay appeared on the front page of the paper, and Benjamin and Wong met in June of that same year.

and fashionable European sensibility, the seemingly contradictory aspects of which Benjamin stumbles over during the meeting, that were critical for Wong's cinematic success.

Europe in general and Benjamin in particular were interested in Wong as a film star because her body and her career symbolized key aspects of modernity. As the premier film actress of Asian descent, Wong represented multiple facets of racial and gendered difference central to modernity, most importantly the oriental. In the late 1920s Germany used its fantasies of the orient—Turkey, Russia, the Middle East, and East Asia—to work through national and imperial ambitions. Being an oriental and a film star accentuated Wong's importance. As Frankfurt School intellectuals such as Theodor W. Adorno and Siegfried Kracauer theorized, mass media, film, and consumer culture, all made legible through Wong's body, were key sites of modernity. Another critical characteristic of modernity is mobility, the geographic movement of bodies prompted by forces such as slavery, imperialism, and global capitalism. That mobility led to the mingling of bodies and cultures, which are the prerequisites of cosmopolitanism. As a Chinese American film actress in Berlin, Wong was uniquely situated to represent all of those racialized, gendered, orientalized, imperial, New World settler-colonial, mass media, and geographic mobility components of modernity.

Unhappily we do not have many of Wong's own writings from this heady Berlin period; therefore, her conversation with Benjamin becomes an important means to understanding her allure. Examining this interaction as well as other markers of Wong's fame in Germany such as *Song/Show Life* and Wong's meetings with actress and film director Leni Riefenstahl and actress Marlene Dietrich permits me to open up questions about the relationship between Asian America, modernity, race, and gender. Even though these events take place in Berlin, most significantly they link notions of cosmopolitanism to a discourse of race in the transnational American context.[5] Wong's time in Berlin tells us about Europe, but more importantly it helps us rethink the U.S. configuration of transnational racial modernity. This initial trip to Eu-

---

5. I use the concept of "transnational American racial modernity" to refer to the ways in which empire and American domestic racial hierarchies are intermeshed. Works useful to this concept are too many to list but include Amy Kaplan and Donald E. Pease, eds., *Cultures of United States Imperialism* (Durham, NC: Duke University Press, 1993); Shelly Streeby, *American Sensations: Class, Empire, and the Production of Popular Culture* (Berkeley: University of California Press, 2002); Daphne Brooks, *Bodies in Dissent: Spectacular Performances of Race and Freedom, 1850–1910* (Durham, NC: Duke University Press, 2006); D. T. Goldberg, "Modernity, Race, and Morality," *Cultural Critique,* no. 24 (Spring 1993): 193–227. I argue that modernity itself is a process.

rope set the stage for Wong's subsequent cultural work and self-fashioning. It showed Wong both the limits and the possibilities of being a global Asian American star.

Anna May Wong in Berlin (Seducing Berlin)

Vollmoeller wrote it [the film screenplay] specifically for her. And for that reason, it will have a great deal of passion and misfortune, for she loves to play scenes of sorrow. Her weeping is famous among her colleagues. They come all the way out to Neubabelsberg to see it.

—WALTER BENJAMIN, "Gespräch mit Anne May Wong"

For Anna May Wong, the global film industry in Berlin provided a critical opportunity for her to become an international star, an opportunity that would not have been available had she remained in the United States. Benjamin's essay shows how Wong came to Europe through cosmopolitan Hollywood. Wong had met author Karl Vollmoeller in Hollywood, and he persuaded Eichberg to cast Wong in *Song,* which was based on Vollmoeller's novel.[6] The Ufa film studios were in the Berlin suburb of Neubabelsberg, and the film was released in the summer of 1928.

Because Wong played the title role, the film focused on her. Numerous close-ups of her face ensured that film audiences around the globe could witness her ability to play "passion and misfortune." In one particularly moving scene, Wong's face fills the screen, her eyes filling with tears that slowly roll down her face. The black-and-white cinematography and the squalor of her surroundings all accentuate Wong's pathos. Her expressive facial gestures and eloquent eyes as well as her reported ability to cry on demand proved irresistible for fans of silent film, including Benjamin. As he reported, such artistry commanded her fellow thespians to attend the film shoots at the Ufa Studios in Neubabelsberg in order to admire and learn from Wong.

One of the most compelling reasons to situate Wong as a significant figure in the production of an interwar cosmopolitan culture is by recognizing that film industry practitioners construed film to be a universal, globally circulating medium. Each of Wong's early European films, shot in multiple languages, became a building block of "Film Europe" and circulated around

---

6. Karen J. Leong, "Anna May Wong and the British Film Industry," *Quarterly Review of Film and Video* 21 (2006): 14.

Anna May Wong crying.
(Film still, *Song/Show Life.*)

the globe.[7] As the central part of a dream to make film an international language, Film Europe used producers, directors, and actors from multiple nation-states.[8] Intended as an alternative to Hollywood, much of the production centered on Neubabelsberg as well as Elstree Studios in Britain and Gaumont in France. Ufa's aesthetics, developed in part through Wong's work, became central to the creation of this European cinema. Not costumed in oriental robes (unlike in her Hollywood productions), Wong's angular body accentuates the drama of the black-and-white scenes. Her jazz-era dances, derived from African American performance such as the Charleston and the Shimmy, provide modern atmosphere. As film scholar Yiman Wang has argued, part of Wong's appeal was how her physical form fit beautifully into

7. Tim Bergfelder, "Negotiating Exoticism: Hollywood, Film Europe and the Cultural Reception of Anna May Wong," in *"Film Europe" and "Film America": Cinema, Commerce and Cultural Exchange, 1920–1939,* ed. Andrew Higson and Richard Maltby (Exeter, UK: University of Exeter Press, 1999), 302–384.

8. Sabine Hake, *German National Cinema* (New York: Routledge, 2007) 50.

Art Deco aesthetics.[9] Co-produced by British International Pictures, *Song, Pavement Butterfly,* and *Hai-Tang* were set in ambiguous urban settings well suited to Wong's mysterious glamour.

Wong's star persona aided and abetted the technological innovations of cinematic modernity: her European films bridged the silent and the talking-picture eras through a new form known as the multiple-language version (MLV) film. Although *Song/Show Life/Schmutziges Geld* was a silent film released in different countries with the appropriate language title and dialogue cards, other films, such as *Hai-Tang/Flame of Love/Le Chemin du Déshounneur/ The Road to Dishonour* and *Pavement Butterfly* (1929), were multiple-language films. Developed as a means to address the new problem of the monolingual sound film in a multilingual world with studio heads intent on building global cinematic distribution, German and French studios pioneered the MLV in 1929, and Hollywood studios such as MGM and Paramount followed suit. Generally, MLVs reshot an entire film in several different languages, using the same director, costumes, props, and plot but with different actors fluent in the appropriate language. Casts were typically different for each language variation, but stars such as Marlene Dietrich (in Josef von Sternberg's *The Blue Angel* [1930]) and legendary comedians Laurel and Hardy starred in all versions of their respective multiple-language productions, as did the irreplaceable Wong.[10]

Anxiety over racialized and gendered otherness had historical and geographical resonances for European audiences when played out through the guise of the female oriental. It is not surprising that Wong performed "oriental" roles: the construction of orientalism is intertwined with constructions of gender and sexuality.[11] In the German imaginary, Russia, Turkey, the Middle East, and East Asia all represented the "oriental" other. As the converse to modernity and to the West, the idea of the orient was malleable and rife with substitution and, most important of all, had very little to do with the actual geographic and cultural regions themselves. Wong's pan-European films reflected this: she played a nationally ambiguous title character in *Song,*

9. Yiman Wang, "The Art of Screen Passing: Anna May Wong's Yellow Yellowface Performance in the Art Deco Era," *Camera Obscura* 60 (2005): 159–191.

10. Gemma King, "The Multiple-Language Film: A Curious Moment in Cinema History," June 17, 2015, http://www.brentonfilm.com/articles/the-multiple-language-version-film-a-curious-moment-in-cinema-history (accessed July 26, 2017). See also Tessa Dwyer, "Universally Speaking: Lost in Translation and Polyglot Cinema," *Linguistica Antverpiensia* 4 (2005): 295–310.

11. Lisa Lowe, *Critical Terrains: French and British Orientalisms* (Ithaca, NY: Cornell University Press, 1991), 136.

a film located in a nonspecific Middle Eastern port, and portrayed an oriental temptress in imperial Russia in the film *Hai-Tang*. The construction of the oriental as female conjoined with that of the racialized other, hence Wong's resonance in 1920s and 1930s Europe. Orientalism was a vexed cultural construct for Wong. It channeled the types of roles she could play and set limits on their parameters. But it also gave her the opportunity to practice her craft and to mediate yellowface performance.

Although small in terms of the numbers of actual inhabitants of Asian descent living in Germany, the orient figured large in the German psyche.[12] From 1884 to 1919, Germany had formal colonies in China, the South Pacific, and Africa, and the German imperial imaginary extended far beyond the actual possession of those colonies. As Jennifer Jenkins argues, "the Orient was the site upon which and through which German national and imperial visions were articulated and acted upon."[13] Germany's overseas empire was dismantled following its defeat in World War I. With the concluding Treaty of Versailles, German colonies were divided between Belgium, the United Kingdom, certain British dominions, France, and Japan with the determination that none of them would be returned to Germany. Afterward, Germany's territorial attention focused East, chiefly on Central and Eastern Europe, but also the Middle East and East Asia. In addition, the orient stood as the antithesis to Germany's own modernity. In Weimar Germany, colonial loss echoed the German defeat in World War I, and films such as *Song/Show Life* could ameliorate the ensuing malaise through Wong's oriental body.

Wong loved her role as Song. In "Gespräch mit Anne May Wong," Benjamin wrote, "We do not learn very much about this film, of course. 'But the role,' she says, 'is perfect. It is a role that belongs to me like no other before.'" This revelation from Wong is poignant, for it conveys how she felt that her previous Hollywood roles had not "belonged" to her. In other words, she had to leave the United States and come to Europe in order to find an acting role

---

12. The Chinese in Germany, who comprised a small but visible population, were "mostly men, ranging from peddlers, laborers, seamen at one end of the social ladder, to diplomats and students at the other." Maggi W. H. Leung, "Notions of Home among Diaspora Chinese in Germany," in *The Chinese Diaspora: Space, Place, Mobility and Identity,* ed. Laurence J. C. Ma and Carolyn Cartier (Lanham, MD: Rowman and Littlefield, 2003), 242. Before Wong's arrival there were "747 Chinese were living in the Weimar republic. Berlin alone had 312 Chinese residents, including 30 women." Erich Gutinger, "A Sketch of the Chinese Community in Germany: Past and Present," in *The Chinese in Europe,* ed. Gregor Benton and Frank Pieke (New York: St. Martin's Press, 1998), 201.

13. Jennifer Jenkins, "German Orientalism: Introduction," *Comparative Studies of South Asia, Africa and the Middle East* 24, no. 2 (2004): 98; Uta Poinger, "Imperialism and Empire in Twentieth-Century Germany," *History and Memory* 17, nos. 1–2 (2005): 117–143.

that suited her. The language of belonging is very much tied up with nation-state citizenship. For Wong, these pan-European films were different from the Hollywood films that distressed her and caused her to leave the United States because she starred in these films and utilized her formidable screen presence to transform the roles.

What is remarkable is that at no point during the film is Wong's character Song's provenance or race identified. In *Song,* the film's text frame reveals that "the ancient beauty of the mosques and palaces is reflected in the quiet waters of this Eastern harbour." Accompanying those words is a camera shot of Istanbul. The title card tells us, "Song is just one of Fate's castaways ". . . Anna May Wong." *Song* tells the story of Wong as a shipwrecked young lady who becomes a performing star. This overall ambiguity through lack of national specificity was part of a larger strategy of making Wong's star image exportable to numerous countries with differing racial codes and meanings.[14] Wong's gestures and movements, born out of the Chinese American community in Los Angeles, tutored in Hollywood, and refined in Europe, became exported to the world as the signifiers of the oriental. The fact that films such as *Song* and *Hai-Tang* screened in locations such as Mozambique, Australia, and South Africa reflects the appeal of Wong as a global figure of exotic otherness. Through *Song/Show Life* Wong becomes the ultimate cosmopolitan star.

Examining the film *Song/Show Life* reveals an entirely new aspect of Wong's cultural work. The film has not received much critical attention, which I attribute to the obstacle of there being only three extant copies (of which I am aware) housed in film archives in Berlin, London, and Canberra. In contrast, the film *Piccadilly* (1929), one computer click away through Amazon, has been scrutinized in academic articles by luminaries such as psychoanalytical film scholar Laura Mulvey, literary scholar Anne Anlin Cheng, and East Asian film studies scholar Yiman Wang.[15] German literary and film studies professor emerita Cynthia Walk is the only other scholar who has written about *Song/Show Life.* In the three pages devoted specifically to the film, Walk does not see anything ironic or subversive in Wong's performance and, placing the film in the context of Germany's orientalism and imperial ambitions, argues that Wong "embraced and promoted orientalism as the strategic key to

---

14. Bergfelder, "Negotiating Exoticism," 317.

15. Anne Anlin Cheng, "Shine: On Race, Glamour, and the Modern," *PMLA* 126, no. 4 (2011): 1022–1041; Laura Mulvey, "Love in Two British Films of the Late Silent Period: *Hindle Wakes* (Maurice Elvey, 1927) and *Piccadilly* (E.A. Dupont, 1929)," in *Europe in Love and Cinema,* ed. Luisa Passerini, Jo Labanyi, and Karen Diehl (Bristol, UK: Intellect Books, 2012), chap. 4; Wang, "The Art of Screen Passing."

her success."[16] While Wong's earnest self-orientalizing is part of her cultural work, it is not the entire story. Walk conflates Wong's oriental body with the naturalness of her performance, missing out on her skilled performance as an active heroine.[17]

What about the film caused Wong to declare to Benjamin that the role was perfect and belonged to her?[18] *Song/Show Life,* I argue, captures Wong's exuberance, glee, and an encompassing joy in her work. In the opening scene of the film, Wong exhibits her feistiness in gathering food and fighting off her attackers. The camera first reveals Wong spearing crustaceans and eating them raw with her bare hands, staving off starvation. Her zest for life and for the food manifests in her seizing of the sea creatures, and in her eyes and facial expression. Then, when two strangers start to attack her and her co-star and future love interest Heinrich George, she triumphs in two-against-two fisticuffs. Walk writes that George rescues Wong, but I disagree and assert to the contrary that Wong's actions in the fight scene save George. When he loses his knife, her slippered foot recovers it. When he is about to get hit by one of the assailants, Wong intervenes and foils the attack with her own counterattack. With these moves Wong is an active heroine, not one awaiting rescue. Her eyes flash while she restrains herself from chortling with glee as she trumps her attackers. Her words that the role "belongs to me like no other before" exhibits her enjoyment playing it. It is possible that her nonwhiteness allows her to fight.

Wong's clothing throughout the film and her dance performance finale offers a modern or even postmodern pastiche of the oriental. Her grand finale is strikingly difficult to attribute to any one nation-state. She wears a head-dress, and beads hanging from her arms, which references an unspecified Eastern culture, but her skirt displays a Western cut and pattern. She dances a modern dance, moving from side to side as she holds the edge of her skirt. Her costume barely hints of the Middle East in its beads as well as its veil, but does not contain any references to East Asia. This is especially noteworthy because other well-known films such as *Piccadilly* or *Shanghai Express* (1932) are replete with markers that label Wong as Chinese. In the film's dramatic

---

16. Cynthia Walk, "Anna May Wong and Weimar Cinema: Orientalism in Postcolonial Germany," in *Beyond Alterity: German Encounters with Modern East Asia,* ed. Qinna Shen and Martin Rosenstock (New York: Berghahn Books, 2014), 137–167, 152.

17. Yiman Wang and I agree on this position, which she skillfully puts forth in "The Art of Screen Passing."

18. Centering the narrative on Wong herself makes this book very different from the articles by scholars who are chiefly interested in using Wong's films to prove or disprove theoretical stances, particularly psychoanalytical ones, on race, gender, politics, and film theory.

Anna May Wong spearing seafood.
(Film still, *Song/Show Life.*)

Anna May Wong fight scene.
(Film still, *Song/Show Life.*)

Anna May Wong dance finale.

(Film still, *Song/Show Life.*)

conclusion, Wong glimpses George while she is dancing and accidentally falls on her sword. That mishap kills her, but mercifully the blade does not exsanguinate her heart onto the glittering stage.

In one of the most poignant scenes in the film, Wong's character Song impersonates the white female dancer Gloria (Mary Kid). Passing for white is unprecedented in Wong's career as well as for other Asian American actors and actresses.[19] This scene is a revolutionary remaking of the racial masquerade. Throughout cinematic history, white women have continually been cast as Asian/oriental women, whereas the racial logic of white supremacy dictates that women of Asian descent, like Wong, do not portray white women. Her racial impersonation tricks George into believing that she is Gloria. How does the film make this ruse work? Midway through the film George becomes blind when he tries to rob a train to get money to buy jewelry for Gloria and thus win her affection over her wealthy sponsor. Wong bravely asks Glo-

19. For more on passing in Asian American theater, see Josephine Lee, *Performing Asian America: Race and Ethnicity on the Contemporary Stage* (Philadelphia: Temple University Press, 1997), chap. 7.

Anna May Wong in Gloria's clothing.
(Film still, *Song/Show Life.*)

ria for money for an operation to restore George's eyesight. Gloria refuses Wong, instead instructing her maid to give her old clothes to her. While the maid bundles Gloria's castoffs, Wong stealthily steals money from Gloria for George's operation. Back at home, enrobed in Gloria's perfume-infused fur-collared coat, Wong slips George the money. George's blindness makes the racial deception work. He smells her and touches her face. His fingertips cannot detect the difference between the two women. The close-up shot reveals Wong's anguish in pretending to be someone she is not in order to bring relief to the man she loves. The soft-focus lens and light-colored fur collar soften Wong's features while beautifully accentuating her star aura. Wong's acting prowess was noted by contemporary German film critic Hans Stahl, who enthused that it was not just Wong's exotic appeal that garnered attention but her "mesmerizing, fascinating aura similar to the first films of [Lillian] Gish."[20] What this meant for Wong was that it opened up avenues for her career as a cultural worker. It signaled the momentary possibility of detaching her racialized oriental body from Chinese or oriental scripts.

What is remarkable about *Song/Show Life* is that it is the first film to medi-

---

20. Hans Stahl, "GrossStadtschmetterling," *Der Montag Morgen,* no. 15, April 15, 1929. Cited in Walk, "Anna May Wong and Weimar Cinema," 149.

tate on Wong's stardom and, moreover, reveals how she embraced the human. My findings are very different from those revealed in Anne Anlin Cheng's article "Shine," which is based solely on the film *Piccadilly*. Although Cheng boldly claims that "*Piccadilly* is the only film in Wong's extensive catalog that meditates on the making of her celebrity," I argue that *Song/Show Life* divulges the birth of her screen character's stardom and that it not only does so before *Piccadilly* but also sets the script for that film.[21] "Shine," a Freudian-derived concept that drives Cheng's argument, is not the only way to understand the power of Wong's cinematic presence. One can use Cheng's metric of epidermal schema to reach a different conclusion. In *Song/Show Life* Wong exudes a hazy, feminized, vulnerable surface akin to Lillian Gish's. Cheng makes much of the cellophane plastic shine, based on Judith Brown's work on glamour, which she finds in Wong's costuming in *Piccadilly* and interprets to signify Wong's refusal of the human.[22] However, though in Wong's final dance number in *Song/Show Life* she is suffused with glinting light, throughout most of the film and, most importantly at her death at the end of the film, cinematographer Heinrich Gärtner filmed Wong in soft focus. I argue that it is Wong's embrace of the human through her tears that brought the German and international acting community all the way to Neubabelsberg to see her. Those tears reveal that Wong, far from refusing the human, embodied the human.

"Gespräch mit Anne May Wong"

May Wong—the name resonates with color around the edges, it is sharp and light like the tiny specks[23] that open into scentless full-moon blossoms in a bowl of tea.[24] My questions were the tepid bath in which the destinies concealed in this name could divulge a little something of themselves. In this friendly house in Berlin, we formed a little community that had gathered around the low table to watch this process unfold. But as is said in Yu-Kia-Li: "Useless prattle about the affairs of people prevents important discussion."[25]

---

21. Cheng, "Shine," 1026.

22. Ibid., 1031. See Judith Brown, *Glamour in Six Dimensions: Modernism and the Radiance of Form* (Ithaca, NY: Cornell University Press, 2009).

23. Translator's note: "*Stäbchen* (diminutive of *Stab,* stick or rod)—it also means chopsticks. . . . Hard to say if this is supposed to be some kind of pun."

24. Translator's note: The image as a whole seems to be a vague reference to Proust, who compares the sudden expansion of his memory (through the madeleine and the tea) to small Japanese pieces of paper that unfold into particular objects when placed in water.

25. Benjamin, "Gespräch," 1.

Benjamin's essay on Wong stands out within the body of his work both in its subject matter and its style. Three years after the rejection of his Habilitation dissertation (the passing of which was necessary to become a full professor in the German academic system), 1928 is the point in Benjamin's career when he was becoming a public intellectual whose writings forged the intellectual parameters of twentieth-century modernity. He had recently traveled to Paris to interview writer André Gide, had begun the renowned arcades project, and had just published his Proust translation.[26] "Gespräch mit Anne May Wong" is striking for the ways in which he seeks to understand avant-garde European culture through the paradox of a Chinese American star in a leading German-made film with pan-European and global ambitions.

Benjamin conceived of the encounter with Wong that resulted in "Gespräch mit Anne May Wong" as a free-flowing conversation in which she could muse as she pleased. It does not read like a typical news account of an interview with a film star for we do not hear Benjamin's questions. Instead, it was a meeting that unfolded over the course of an afternoon. As Benjamin wrote in the ensuing essay, "At first nothing much came of it, and we all had time to form a picture of one another."[27] Meeting with Wong gives Benjamin the opportunity to ponder a wide range of topics related to film and to worldliness. A small drawing of Wong in profile, but no photograph, accompanied the front-page essay. Benjamin explains right away who was present: "There was the *romancier* [novelist], whom May Wong later asked whether she practices her roles before a mirror; there was the artist, whom May Wong indicated on her left, and the female American journalist, whom she indicated on her right, and there was Anna's sister, who was accompanying her."[28] However, although the other participants did ask questions, their interlocutions disappear as the meeting progresses. Throughout the encounter, Wong and her film career as filtered through Benjamin were the main topic of conversation. This quotation appears at the beginning of the article, and it is the only time, aside from the title, that Benjamin uses the name Anna—which he uses not to refer directly to her but in reference to her sister. Instead, throughout the discussion he calls Wong by her middle name, May. In all subsequent press reportage, Wong reveals that May is a name she chose for herself, believing that Anna Wong did not have the same harmonious flow as Anna May Wong, which made the latter a better name for an actress. Yet Benjamin's continued insis-

---

26. David S. Ferris, ed., *The Cambridge Companion to Walter Benjamin* (Cambridge: Cambridge University Press, 2004).

27. Benjamin, "Gespräch," 1.

28. Ibid.

tence on using May Wong as her name instead of Anna or Anna May raises an issue. Could it be that he found Anna too Western a name, too Northern European, and instead preferred to use the less-jarring-to-his-ears as well as more "oriental" name of May? From the beginning Benjamin signals that at least one of the lenses through which he views her is an "oriental" one.

Benjamin did not typically interact with film stars. If you compare "Gespräch mit Anne May Wong" with one of his other writings on a film star, "Chaplin in Retrospect," published in the same periodical, "Chaplin" focuses on the film rather than on the actor, for Benjamin did not actually interview Charlie Chaplin. By contrast, in the discussion-based "Gespräch mit Anne May Wong," Benjamin (who had not yet seen Wong's films) reads Wong's staging of self as a manifestation of cosmopolitanism. Stylistically, "Gespräch" is not as journalistic in tone as Benjamin's other *Die Literarische Welt* pieces, such as "Toys and Play" (June 1928) and "Conversation with André Gide" (February 1928), nor his other writings of the time, but reads much more like poetic musings on a subject he cannot master or contain. Although "Gespräch" marks the only words we have from Benjamin on Wong, Benjamin's other writings, such as *On Hashish,* indicate his indirect stake in orientalism.

Cosmopolitanism

Benjamin's "Gespräch mit Anne May Wong" reveals how cosmopolitanism flows through Wong. Benjamin introduces her to his audience as a global traveler. As he states in the essay, "there was the inhabitant of this room, an influential and worldly woman, who wanted to offer us the gift of her last hours before her departure."[29] Benjamin's choice of terms such as "worldly" and "departure" denote Wong as being the opposite of provincial. Wong's imminent travel signals her cosmopolitanism, in this case her departure for Paris and then London, where she would make films such as *Piccadilly* (1929) and star in the play *The Circle of Chalk.*

As Benjamin's invocation of the word "worldly" signals, Wong gracefully performs the cosmopolitan persona in its Eurocentric framework of the time. Then, as now, Europe holds a privileged place for claims to cosmopolitanism. It was critical that Wong mastered speaking European languages such as German and French. As cosmopolitan culture attained its reach and supposed universality through the imperialist project, had Wong instead been "speaking Swahili," she would not have attained the same cachet. Although her actions fit in with Eurocentric definitions of cosmopolitanism and those quali-

---

29. Ibid.

ties attracted Benjamin to Wong, they also caused him to stumble when he tried to reconcile them with her Chinese face and American colloquialisms.

Cosmopolitanism is one of the means through which modernity interfaces with colonialism as well as American racial constructions. Scholars have used the term in a variety of ways, but it usually refers to the ideology that all human beings belong to a single cosmos, a single universe based on a shared morality. This is extracted from its Greek etymology of "citizen of the world." Frequently cosmopolitanism has been cast as the opposite of nationalism. The concept's academic salience has increased because of its ability to characterize global flows of people and cultures beyond nation-state paradigms. Yet its analytical strength is also its challenge; its fluid, situated, and historical meanings do not yield a static definition, nor do most proponents account for discrepant geopolitical power relations. Attributed to Diogenes, modified by Immanuel Kant, and promulgated by critic Martha Nussbaum, one strand of cosmopolitanism refers to the worldwide community of human beings.[30] As other works have argued, however, rather than being "some known entity" with the aforementioned genealogy, there are multiple forms of cosmopolitanism "awaiting realization" that "sometimes work with nationalism" rather than being its opposite or are "local and embodied" rather than universal.[31]

The term "cosmopolitanism" holds relevance for this discussion because both Wong and Benjamin used it to refer to the global reach of Wong's cinematic stardom. Later on Wong employed the term "cosmopolitan" to distinguish between those in China who knew her as a global film star and those who did not. According to Wong, her fame spread to cities such as Shanghai, "where there are more cosmopolitan [people]," whereas those who lived in the Chinese countryside typically did not.[32] For Wong, cosmopolitanism encompassed knowledge of Western films and culture, and the occupation of Western spaces—Shanghai as a colonial treaty port city replete with Western sectors—where such encounters are possible. At this particular moment between the world wars, it was the global production and reach of her cinematic persona that render Wong cosmopolitan. Through this formulation, Wong signaled the process of people from Shanghai becoming cosmopolitan through movie attendance. Given the colonial Western presence in Shanghai

30. Martha Nussbaum, "Kant and Stoic Cosmopolitanism," *Journal of Political Philosophy* 5, no. 1 (1997): 1–25.

31. Pheng Cheah and Bruce Robbins, eds., *Cosmopolitics: Thinking and Feeling beyond the Nation* (Minneapolis: University of Minnesota Press, 1998); Carol A. Breckinridge et al., eds., *Cosmopolitanism* (Durham, NC: Duke University Press, 2002), 2.

32. Wong, quoted in *Bold Journey,* "Native Land," which was filmed in 1936 and screened on ABC on February 14, 1957, at 9:30 P.M.

during the interwar period, Wong's remarks attest how film itself can act as a medium of cultural imperialism.

Benjamin and Wong's conversation can be understood within the historical context of the intellectual debates of the 1930s. For example, influential thinkers such as Kracauer and Adorno focused on the relationship between capitalism, technology, and mass consumption.[33] As members of the "Frankfurt School," these philosophers thought through the problems of extent capitalist, fascist, and communist systems. Though drawing from Karl Marx, these theorists, including Herbert Marcuse and Max Horkheimer, used ideas from thinkers such as Immanuel Kant, Sigmund Freud, and Georg Wihelm Friedrich Hegel. Benjamin was associated with these theorists and with the Frankfurt School. What makes Benjamin and Wong's encounter particularly noteworthy is that it was both a theoretically enriching one as well as an exploratory one. The encounter with Wong enabled Benjamin to think through cosmopolitanism and modernity. For Wong, the meeting with Benjamin allowed her to not only claim cosmopolitanism but also obtain further tutelage in how to strategically stage orientalism.[34]

Yet, as Benjamin displays throughout the conversation, as a Chinese American, Wong presents a conundrum for the possibilities of cosmopolitanism. When confronting the paradox of Wong's Chineseness and Americanness, Benjamin becomes baffled and reverts to the national to invoke the racial. For example, he describes her clothing at the meeting as follows, "Her outfit would not be at all unsuitable for such garden games; a dark blue suit, a light blue blouse, a yellow tie over that—one would like to know a Chinese verse to describe this. She has always dressed this way, for she was in fact not born in China but in Chinatown in Los Angeles."[35] It is striking that the conjunction of Wong's modern Western clothing yet racialized Chinese body causes him to struggle for words. It is clear that he admires her clothing, figure, and femininity. Benjamin's desire to at first cast about for a "Chinese verse to describe this" then acknowledging her Los Angeles birth would indicate that he at first wants to use a potentially orientalizing phrase to capture her but then admits that that kind of phrase does not quite suit her. An eloquent man of letters, Benjamin is stymied by the paradox of Wong's cosmopolitan Western modernity and racialized Chinese body. Although he does invoke the national to describe the racial, he clearly recognizes and wants to be able

---

33. Founded in 1973, the journal *New German Critique* was devoted to this issue.

34. Julia Phillips Cohen, "Oriental by Design: Ottoman Jews, Imperial Style, and the Performance of Heritage," *American Historical Review* (April 2014): 364–398.

35. Benjamin, "Gespräch," 1.

to bring both Chinese and Western together. In fact, the subtitle of this essay, "A Chinoiserie from the Old West," indicates his fascination with her complicated and contradictory star image. It is significant that he uses the term "chinoiserie" rather than the German noun for Chinese. Chinoiserie indicates Western items stylized as Chinese rather than authentic Chinese objects. By using the term, Benjamin acknowledges that Wong has a Chinese-appearing surface with a Western interior.

Wong's American citizenship combined with her Chinese diasporic origins presents us with a different spatiality of the dynamics of modernity than that of the typical European center-colony model in that it forces (at minimum) a triangulation of spaces and cultures. Imperialism and the subsequent flows of culture between colonies and European centers gave cosmopolitanism its claims to universality.[36] Race and difference were imbricated into the supposedly universal construct of European cosmopolitanism.[37] Scholars interested in racial difference and cosmopolitanism have analyzed the flows of culture between the European metropole and the colony. However, they do not take into account the triangulation of flows of culture that includes the United States as a critical node in the creation of a cosmopolitical culture.

As an American, Wong presents additional complications to that dynamic of cosmopolitanism because her culture is not "native culture" and her relationship to Europe is more complex than that of colonial subject to the metropole. The United States' deeply racialized history begins pre-nation-state as a slave-holding colony of Spain, France, and Britain, on which are grafted the U.S. nation-state's colonial ventures in Asia, the Pacific, and the Caribbean, the continued genocide of indigenous peoples, and reterritorialization of Mexico. In the twentieth century, the United States is the preeminent modern nation-state precisely because of those global flows of people and cultures. Wong's Chinese heritage in particular subjects her to the slipperiness of American racial categories vis-à-vis national citizenship and affiliation. Wong's career in Europe helps us rethink the process of the creation of Asian American racial categories. If "denationalization," to use Sau-ling Wong's critical phrase, "entails a relaxation of between what is Asian American and what is Asian," by thinking through Wong's framework within a European context, then the Asian American diasporic perspective is one not only between Asia and America but also between Asian America and Europe.[38]

---

36. Pheng Cheah, "Given Culture," in *Cosmopolitics: Thinking and Feeling beyond the Nation*, ed. Pheng Cheah and Bruce Robbins (Minneapolis: University of Minnesota Press, 1998), 293.
37. Ibid.
38. Sau-ling Wong, "Denationalization Reconsidered: Asian American Cultural Criticism at a Theoretical Crossroads," in *Postcolonial Theory and the United States: Race, Ethnic-*

As a subject of an American nation-state that is settler colonial, postcolonial, and colonizer, Wong has a life history that adds complexity to the Eurocentric imperial models of racial spatiality. Because she was a Chinese American, her citizenship was made tenuous by laws such as the Cable Act (1922), which would have stripped her of her citizenship if she married an "alien ineligible for citizenship," such as a Chinese immigrant. Her ability to travel and be at home in the world was circumscribed by race-based migration laws such as the 1882 Chinese Exclusion Act. Wong brings all of that historical baggage with her to Europe. Temporality is the other way Wong's case makes us rethink cosmopolitanism. The term "orientalism" tends toward nostalgia or the past and the nonmodern, whereas "cosmopolitanism" makes gestures toward the modern and contemporary. Of course, there are slippages, contradictions, and overlap between the terms. In fact, as a modern cosmopolitan Chinese American "flapper," Wong's persona exposed those slippages and contradictions.

There is a simultaneous incommensurability yet hypercompatibility of the terms "Asian American" and "cosmopolitanism." On the one hand, the concepts are incommensurable because Asian American is an ethnic-specific category, while cosmopolitanism is conceived in opposition to ethnic particularity. On the other hand, the terms "Asian American" and "cosmopolitanism" are hypercompatible because of the particular position of Asians in the Americas. The American citizen has been defined historically against the Asian immigrant. Asian immigrants are simultaneously bodies to be integrated into the national political sphere and foreign objects always subjected to their alien origins. In material terms, this subjection to alien origins translated into American racial codes such as Asian immigrants being legally barred from becoming American citizens, alien land laws that forbade noncitizens from owning land, anti-miscegenation laws that forbade "Mongolians" from marrying whites, and a whole host of official and unofficial segregation practices that regulated everything from swimming pools and movie theaters to jobs and residential housing. The production of the United States as a nation-state as well as its Asian American subjects is predicated on drawing the lines of belonging and exclusion. Yet that continual expulsion to alien origins places Asian Americans in an ambiguous nation-state subjectivity, hence opening up the possibility of extranational affiliation, including cosmopolitanism. Paradoxically, it is that "foreigner-within" conception of the Asian American that allows for cosmopolitanism.

Whereas European cosmopolitanism was made universal through im-

---

ity, Literature, ed. Amritjit Singh and Peter Schmidt (Jackson, MS: University of Mississippi Press, 2000), 129.

perialism, the United States was made cosmopolitan through not only colonialism and conquest but also transnational European migration. As American intellectual Randolph Bourne observed in "Trans-National America" (1916), "What we have achieved has been rather a cosmopolitan federation of national colonies, of foreign cultures, from which the sting of devastating competition has been removed."[39] Yet, under Bourne's formulation, America as a cosmopolitan nation is still a Eurocentric one. In this article Bourne discusses how the migrations of the Jews, Greeks, Scandinavians, and Germans allowed what was formerly colonialism to grow into cosmopolitanism. What we see in Bourne's articulation of cosmopolitan America is the consolidation of whiteness at the expense of the marginalization of the other. The place of Asian Americans as well as Latinos, Native Americans, and African Americans is effaced. Dangerously, U.S. settler colonialism becomes naturalized and normalized. If Europe achieved cosmopolitanism through the imperialist project, then the United States achieved Eurocentrism through expulsion of the racial minority other and ignoring its indigenous populations. What is important is that the United States, not just Europe, is a locus of cosmopolitanism. Hence, using Bourne's formulation, it could be argued that as an American, Wong was cosmopolitan before she went to Europe.

Given the complex dynamics of modernity, primitivism, and exoticism, it is not surprising that Benjamin misreads Wong, for she emerged out of a specific racialized performance tradition that invoked an alternate American modernity. Growing up in Los Angeles just outside of Chinatown and Hollywood, Wong, and many other Chinese Americans, capitalized on early cinema's fascination with race and otherness.[40] As movies about Asia were filmed around Los Angeles, numerous members of the Southern California community became part of Chinese American Hollywood, forming a branch of the Chinese Screen Actors Extras Guild and developing community networks for finding jobs in Hollywood.

---

39. Randolph Bourne, "Trans-National America," in *The History of a Literary Radical and Other Papers* (New York: S. A. Russell, 1956), originally published in *The Atlantic,* July 1916, 276; Marilyn Fischer, "A Pragmatist Cosmopolitan Moment: Reconfiguring Nussbaum's Cosmopolitan Concentric Circles," *Journal of Speculative Philosophy* 21, no. 3 (2007): 151–165.

40. Gina Marchetti, *Romance and the "Yellow Peril": Race, Sex, and Discursive Strategies in Hollywood Fiction* (Berkeley: University of California Press, 1993), 1; Henry Yu, *Thinking Orientals: Migration, Contact, and Exoticism in Modern America* (Oxford: Oxford University Press, 2001).

Wong herself was very much part of this dynamic of becoming an "authentic" Chinese subject through the movies. Benjamin's words reveal this aspect of Wong donning clothing in order to feel and become oriental, "But when her roles call for it, she is glad to wear traditional clothing. Her imagination has a freer rein [works more freely] in them. Her favorite dress was cut from her father's wedding coat, and she also wears it at home from time to time."[41] What is particularly interesting about this quotation is that the dress cut from her father's wedding coat is actually not a traditional garment per se but one that is refashioned and repurposed. Given Wong's history of self-fashioning as oriental it is possible that this is another fabricated story meant to underscore her supposed authentic orientalness, acting as a counterargument to yellow-face casting.[42] Yet Benjamin places her dress in the realm of the authentic. As authenticity is fundamental to modernity's discourse on orientalism, Chinese Americans having to learn how to play "authentic" Hollywood-style Chinese people ruptures that seamless construction of the modern. Wong would find that, despite her lack of Chinese authenticity, she would nonetheless be expected to represent that culture. Most importantly, through self-fashioning courtesy of the training within her community, she could try out differing strategies for performing the female racial minority body. Wong learned how performance could contain subversive elements and how one could inhabit multiple temporalities simultaneously.[43] Instead of Benjamin looking at Wong in only orientalist terms, he is compelled by her racial and cinematically mediated modernity to dialogue with her cosmopolitanism.

Yet, with Wong as the subject, cosmopolitanism could dangerously veer into a version of orientalism through poetic national containment. Benjamin resorts to metaphor when prose is not sufficient to describe her. Although Wong was a second- or third-generation American-born actress who had not been to China, the encounter is striking in Benjamin's continual insistence

---

41. Benjamin, "Gespräch," 1.

42. MGM replicates this story in one of its publicity stills for Wong. Anna May Wong, MGM Stills Collection, Margaret Herrick Library, Academy of Motion Pictures, Arts and Sciences, Los Angeles (hereafter, AMPAS). In another example of self-orientalizing as self-fashioning, Wong's Chinese autograph did not match her supposed Chinese name. I thank one of my anonymous readers for highlighting this link.

43. Apparently Hollywood directors asked various extras to say something in Chinese to make the scenes more authentic. Unconfirmed rumors (Chinese Screen Extras Guild) declare that those extras would either make something up in gibberish or would say insults in Chinese. Whether or not these disruptive speech acts occurred or not, the fact that there are rumors about them is in itself extremely significant for they show a desire for contestatory subjects.

in linking her with Chinese sayings.[44] The opening article line reads: "May Wong—the name resonates with color around the edges, it is sharp and light like the tiny specks that open into scentless full-moon blossoms in a bowl of tea." Words like "specks," a possible reference to chopsticks, as well as "bowl of tea" and "full-moon blossoms" all immediately situate Wong's "orientalness" for not only the literary weekly's audience but also Benjamin himself. The words Benjamin invokes are very feminine ones in Western discourse—blossoms, moon, and tiny specks. With these words, Benjamin is still working through his language, invoking the poetic in his attempts to describe her. It is striking that regular prose cannot define the paradox that her Chinese American cosmopolitanism presents. Wong's racialized body calls into question the notion that cosmopolitanism can indeed belong to anyone but certifies that it is privileged along the lines of gender, race, and class.

Despite all the possibilities of understanding and presumed equality embedded in liberal formulations of cosmopolitanism, such equivalence was not always possible to achieve. Several years before Benjamin met Wong, he developed his ideas on translation and history in his oft-cited article "The Task of the Translator." In that piece, which lends us insights into how to understand "Gespräch mit Anne May Wong," he states, "In the same way a translation, instead of resembling the meaning of the original, must lovingly and in detail incorporate the original's mode of signification, thus making both the original and translation recognizable as fragments of a greater language, just as fragments are part of a vessel. . . . [The] work reflects the great longing for linguistic complementation [and] ". . . a literal rendering of the syntax ". . . proves words rather than sentences to be the primary element of the translator."[45] In order to "incorporate the original [Wong's] mode of signification," Benjamin peppers in Chinese phrases, sincerely believing that he is being faithful to her meaning as a Chinese subject. This statement on translation gives Benjamin license to interpret Wong, which, though intended to add clarity and truth, opens up the conversation to the danger that it is about Benjamin and his abilities to project, rather than being about Wong.

What is particularly interesting about this theory of translation is that contemporary critics have used this Benjamin piece to generate a reading

---

44. Like many other Chinese Americans of her generation, due to Chinese immigration exclusion, differing official migration histories exist in the official records. Chinese migrants routinely claimed "paper son" status in order to be allowed into the United States. They could be actual sons/daughters/wives, or fictitious ones. So, depending on which sets of paper one wishes to believe, Wong was either second- or third-generation Chinese American.

45. Walter Benjamin, "The Task of the Translator," in *Illuminations* (New York: Schocken, 1969), 79.

methodology that claims to avoid "othering" through an elision of orientalism or other such tropes. According to Chinese film scholar Rey Chow, Benjamin's essay on translation outlines a useful method for her as a critic to further elucidate Chinese film to Western academic audiences (though she does not examine Wong's films), characterizing this approach as a mutual and reciprocal "liberation."[46] In this mode of thinking, using a phrase like "dragons romping in water" would be an attempt at liberation between Wong as subject and Benjamin as interviewer. Chow argues that, according to Benjamin, "translation is a process in which the 'native' should let the foreign affect, or infect itself and vice-versa."[47] Even if Benjamin is trying to have the foreign (Wong) not sound like the native (him, Europe, Germany) in order not to reduce her to Western terms, as she is an American, this theory does not allow for the multiple axes of translation necessitated by her American modernity. The Chinese becomes infected with orientalism. Chow, on the other hand, lauds this theoretical move by Benjamin as one that does not perpetuate the reduction of the other, of the translated, into terms solely dictated by the translator.[48] Yet I argue that Benjamin's model runs into difficulties when it is forced to deal with greater complexities than merely the dichotomy between primitive and civilized or oriental and Western. Understanding Wong's historical and cultural significance requires reading and translation practices on multiple valences, not just a dichotomous one. "Gespräch mit Anne May Wong" reveals what happens if the translator is confused as to what constitutes the other. I contend that, despite his use of a translation methodology intended to safeguard against orientalism, when Benjamin is asked to perform a translation between "Chinese American" (and all the translation between those terms to begin with), "China," and "Europe," what results in the essay is that the sheer complexity of Wong's Chinese American modernity in Europe does not yield to easy explication. This moment offers a cautionary tale as well as a justification for considering racial, national, and temporal complexity beyond the binary.

Benjamin's description of Wong's physical movements during the meeting reveals her as a resistant interview subject, possibly uncomfortable with his "translation." He writes, "May Wong turns question and answer into a kind of swinging: she leans back and rises up, sinks down, rises up, and I fancy that from time to time I am giving her a push. She laughs, that is all."[49] This quo-

---

46. Rey Chow, *Primitive Passions: Visuality, Sexuality, Ethnography and Contemporary Chinese Cinema* (New York: Columbia University Press, 1995), 188.

47. Ibid., 189.

48. Chow, *Primitive Passions,* 189.

49. Benjamin, "Gespräch," 1.

tation suggests that Wong refuses to articulate what he wants and expects to hear. The phrase "giving her a push" could be construed as a helpful gesture, especially in the context of swinging, but could also be interpreted as invasive. Could it be that she is refusing to answer the question and instead swings up and down, back and forth? He hints as much when he says "she laughs, that is all." It is possible that she laughs instead of answering his questions because she knows her answer is not what he wants to hear. Or maybe he is unable to hear or to understand if she were to answer. Perhaps she cannot answer the question, which is quite interesting given that her interviews tend toward the revelatory rather than the secretive. The expression "that is all" could mean "that is all" in the sense that it empowers her to evade any further response, or that she does not retort or reply critically but leaves it as a laugh. Perhaps what is revealed is not so much resistance as the static that occurs when such incomplete translations of culture happen.

Germans View Wong

Walter Benjamin's understanding of Anna May Wong is reflected in the broader German print culture of the time. German film critic Erick Jaeger, like Benjamin, used nature metaphors, especially floral ones, to describe Wong. According to him she honed her craft in the "erotic gardens of California" and demonstrated "the plum blossom dance of her country of origin."[50] Given that the plum blossom dance alludes to a dance from China, not the United States, with those words Jaeger implies that Wong's country of origin is China. Benjamin, to his credit, does acknowledge Wong's American birth. Other German film critics, though using orientalist language analogous to Benjamin's, were unable to reconcile her Chinese face with her American birth. As the *New York Times* reported, "Berlin critics, who were unanimous in praise of both the star and the production, neglect to mention that Anna May is of American birth. They stress only her Chinese origin. She is acclaimed as not only an actress of transcendent talent but also a great beauty. Such phrases as 'this exquisite Oriental maiden,' 'porcelain loveliness' and 'exotic pulchritude' are common in all the reviews."[51] With words like "Oriental," "porcelain," and "exotic," these Berlin critics echoed the sentiments revealed by Benjamin.

---

50. Graham Hodges, *Anna May Wong* (New York: Palgrave, 2004), 84–85.

51. "Berlin Praises Miss Wong: Her First Film Produced in Germany Acclaimed at Premerie," *New York Times,* August 22, 1928, http: //www.nytimes.com/movie/review?res=9C02 E7D6103AE03ABC4A51DFBE668383639EDE (accessed January 25, 2018).

Oriental cosmopolitanism manifested itself in early twentieth-century German culture as refracted through the body of the Asian, in this case, Wong. Oriental cosmopolitanism was a way for Westerners to feel like citizens of the world through selective adoption of "oriental" traits courtesy of consumer culture. This could range from the rage for coolie hats to the "bob" haircut with bangs exemplified by European American actress Louise Brooks as well as Wong's hair ensemble with bangs to "oriental" fonts and other features of art deco and art nouveau. German historian Uta Poinger has found that, before World War I, advertisements repeatedly featured "diminutive non-white figures, including Chinese, as servants with childlike proportions."[52] Those images disappeared by the second half of the 1920s, replaced by visions of "universal modernity" that featured "ethnically ambiguous, 'cosmopolitan' types."[53] Poinger's prime example was an illustrated perfume advertisement that featured a modern woman with short hair dressed in a "bathing-suit-like gown" and whose "most outstanding feature was her East Asian eyes."[54] Created in 1929, this advertisement looks remarkably like a previously published newspaper photograph of Wong.[55] Even if it was not a literal representation of Wong, it is striking that it employed the figure of an ethnically ambiguous but nonetheless Asian woman. These advertisements promoted the female figure as modern rather than antiquated.

European American actress Louise Brooks's career provides an analog to Wong's. Brooks, like Wong, left Hollywood to work in the Berlin film industry and made two silent motion pictures there with G. W. Pabst, *Pandora's Box* (1929) and *Diary of a Lost Girl* (1929). In addition, Brooks made a French film, *Prix de Beauté* (1930), under the direction of Augusto Genina. It is highly significant that a white American actress associated with "dangerous" sexuality (lesbianism) worked in Europe at the same time as Wong. In fact, contemporary film writer Cedric Belfarge grouped Brooks and Wong together as two of the people "really born European—though they didn't know it at the time."[56] Such a remark speaks to how he as a European film critic did not consider Brooks and Wong as Hollywood products but as European cosmopolitans. As Brooks's director Pabst reportedly said to Belfarge, "'She [Brooks] belongs

52. Uta Poinger, "Imperialism and Empire in Twentieth-Century Germany," *History and Memory* 17, nos. 1–2 (2005): 131.

53. Ibid., 32.

54. Ibid., 132.

55. *Sunday Pictorial,* January 23, 1927, 12. I thank Celia Marshik for bringing my attention to this photograph.

56. Cedric Belfarge, *Motion Picture Magazine,* February 1930. Cited in Barry Paris, *Louise Brooks* (1990; repr., London: Mandarin Paperbacks, 1991), 317.

in Europe and to Europeans. She has been a sensational hit in her German pictures. I do not have her play silly little cuties. She plays real women, and plays them marvelously.'"[57] By extension, these remarks could apply to Wong. Brooks's film work in Germany and France helps explain Wong's success in those film industries.

Wong's reception in Germany can also be gauged through the famous 1928 Alfred Eisenstaedt photographs of Wong with actress Marlene Dietrich and filmmaker Leni Riefenstahl. These mementos record the process of Wong becoming a world-renowned film star.[58] Even though her character dies at the end of *Song/Show Life,* the film brought to life Wong's celebrity. Creating a record of her fame through these photographs, Wong gazes smilingly at the audience through the camera. She is clad in a completely Western sleeveless flapper dress in dark material with a sheer overlay, accented by a knotted long single-strand pearl necklace. Like Wong, Dietrich sports a flapper-style dress accessorized by a multistrand beaded necklace. Film scholar Patrice Petro argues that Wong centers the photograph because she is the best known of the three women; Dietrich and Riefenstahl flank Wong in order to absorb some of her glamour.[59] People have speculated about the three women's sexuality and possible sexual relations with each other. Regardless of what actually may have happened, Petro reads their relationship as "indicative of an emergent form of cosmopolitanism, especially for women, newly enfranchised and eager to think, dress, and perform beyond national borders and traditional identities."[60]

Wong's association with Riefenstahl is important because the German dancer, actress, and director became known in the 1930s for her direction of Nazi propaganda films. Her film *Triumph of the Will* (1934) is still acknowledged as a landmark work in documentary film. In *Olympia* (1936) she

---

57. Ibid.

58. I did not include this photograph in the book because Getty Images would have charged a prohibitively expensive licensing fee, despite this book's being published by a nonprofit academic press. The image can easily be found by Googling "Anna May Wong, Marlene Dietrich, Leni Riefenstahl." For more on Getty Images' licensing practices, see the very interesting article by Michael Hiltzik, "Getty Images Will Bill You Thousands to Use a Photo That Belongs to the Public. Is That Legal?," *Los Angeles Times,* August 2, 2016, http://www.latimes.com/business/hiltzik/la-fi-hiltzik-getty-photos-20160801-snap-story.html (accessed April 27, 2018).

59. Patrice Petro, "Cosmopolitan Women: Marlene Dietrich, Anna May Wong, and Leni Riefensthal," in *Border Crossings: Silent Cinema and the Politics of Space,* ed. Jennifer M. Bean, Anupama Kapse, and Laura Horak (Bloomington: Indiana University Press, 2014), 295–312; Patrice Petro, *Idols of Modernity* (New Brunswick, NJ: Rutgers University Press, 2010).

60. Petro, "Cosmopolitan Women," 300.

developed techniques such as the tracking shot (film footage with the camera mounted on rails). Both films received awards at the time and are still considered masterpieces. Through these propaganda films Riefenstahl became the foremost Nazi film director, and after the war she was unable to shake her association with Nazi filmmaking. Wong's circle in Berlin included both left-wing notables such as Benjamin and fascist artists such as Riefenstahl.

Speaking German Like Nobody's Business

What, then, do Anna May Wong's own words reveal about her time in Berlin? Witness her letter to her new acquaintances, photographer and writer Carl Van Vechten and his spouse, the actress Fania Marinoff, written more than a year after her conversation with Benjamin, in which she comments on her film career in Germany: "So all I've accomplished since I saw you is speaking German like nobody's business as I have to speak both German and English in the new film. It's been most interesting to master what formerly seemed like an impossibility but we sometimes even surprise ourselves at what we can do."[61] Wong's presentation of self as an American comes out in her formulation of mastering an impossibility with a "can-do" attitude. The phrase "like nobody's business" demonstrates her fluidity with American colloquial language, not surprising given her birth, upbringing, and adult life spent chiefly in Los Angeles. Her terminology "all I've accomplished" can be considered a statement both of pride and false modesty. "Speaking German like nobody's business" can be interpreted as saying to her friends that hey, nobody thought a Chinese girl from Los Angeles could "speak German" at all and look at me, here I am doing it extremely well. "Speaking German," of course, refers to not only the actual acquisition of German language skills but also the successful adoption of European cosmopolitan behaviors. For Wong, acting in German-produced films was clearly a challenge, but one that she relished, for it tutored her to become an international film star.

Even the beginning stages of Wong's correspondence with Van Vechten and Marinoff, which continued until her death in 1961, revealed an appealingly playful facility with language. Proud of her ability to "speak German," on August 12, 1929, she composed a short telegram to them entirely in German: "Glueckliche Reise Auf Wiedersehen [Good luck until we meet again] Anna May Wong." Demonstrating more of her engaging sense of humor, she signed the "speaking German" letter in colloquial American idiom: "Ginger

---

61. Anna May Wong to Carl Van Vechten and Fania Marinoff, September 26, 1929, Carl Van Vechten Manuscript Collection, Beinecke Library, Yale University.

snaps to you." That sense of fun carried through the rest of the letter. Wong enthused: "I was most frightfully sorry you weren't able to get over this way and give the Berliners a treat. A great many friends have been here and hello and goodbye was a continuous performance by me, but it[']s been much fun and I was having a holiday on salary so I've been having a glorious time."[62] Through her language Wong pens an enchanting narration of her life.

In a 1934 *Los Angeles Times* interview (published after more favorable American attitudes toward China had emerged), Wong explained how her sojourn in Europe paradoxically made her more "Chinese," especially now that it was culturally safer to claim the term in the United States. The term "Chinese" does not mean the same thing at all times to all people but indexes a range of temporal and racial positions. Deploying "Chinese" in that cosmopolitan sense permits us to explore the contradictions posed by Wong's restaged persona. According to her own formulation, she left the United States a young female American flapper and came back a cosmopolitan Chinese woman of the world. She stated for the *Los Angeles Times* in 1934, "My next milepost was in Berlin. The first picture in which I appeared made a hit. Crowds waited in the lobby for me to come out. Weaving my way through that pack of admiring fans, I seemed suddenly to be standing at one side watching myself with complete detachment. It was my Chinese soul coming back to claim me. Up to that time I had been more of an American flapper than Chinese."[63] Wong reported later in the interview that the more she studied French, German, and music, the more Chinese she became. This is not entirely surprising, for in London, Paris, and Berlin, European valorization of the oriental worked not only to control the oriental but also to give status and admiration to an exceptional few performers, such as Wong. While in Europe, Wong realized that playing the oriental could be of great use to her as an actress. Plus, in the 1930s, the image of the Chinese in the United States shifted to a much more positive one, allowing her to claim her Chinese heritage in more public ways. Although Benjamin's admiration of her "oriental" beauty was not the only factor that prompted Wong to realize that she could capitalize on her Chinese heritage in order to advance her career, it was nonetheless influential. Wong's reclamation of the Chinese aspects of her persona took place in Europe, outside of the United States and China.

Wong's claiming of the sign "Chinese" returns us to the conundrum of Asian American cosmopolitanism. In some ways, her invocation of the term

---

62. Ibid.

63. Harry Carr, "'I Am Growing More Chinese—Each Passing Year!' Says Anna May Wong to Harry Carr," *Los Angeles Times,* September 9, 1934, H3.

"Chinese" is a sign of her inability to comfortably claim Eurocentric cosmopolitanism. One can also make the case that it is a move to shift the semantics of cosmopolitanism away from its Eurocentrism. Perhaps it is an indication that she is trapped within the delimiting conceptual vocabulary produced by high-culture theorists like Benjamin; in other words, it is difficult for her to claim anything other than the ethnic and nation-state signifier of China to represent herself as a worldly American. A wholesale uncritical adoption of the limitless possibilities of transnational and diasporic perspectives breaks down in the face of material reality. All of these struggles display the complex and vexed possibilities of Asian American cosmopolitanism.

Wong's career in Europe invokes the limits and the possibilities of Asian American cosmopolitanism. The dynamic of American citizenship in which people of Asian descent are perpetually expunged paradoxically offers Wong the possibility of cosmopolitanism because of the impossibility of full national affiliation. However, Wong is in a very different subject position than that of a privileged Protestant white male subject voluntarily "choosing" to be cosmopolitan, who has the luxury of choice according to the liberal model of the citizen-subject. As an assimilated German Jew who identified as a cultural Zionist, Benjamin himself was acutely aware of his distance from Protestant culture. For that white male, who represents the typical and unmarked subject, cosmopolitanism has the sense of being at home everywhere in the world. I here caution us against celebrating the limitless possibilities of denationalization, including cosmopolitanism, for we do not live in a classless or borderless world. Class and nation-states regulate the body and draw racialized lines that continually cordon off whiteness. For an Asian American woman such as Wong, her case is diametrically different from that of an elite white man. She travels because she is working, not because she is a member of the leisured class on a grand tour. Instead of being at home everywhere, she is at home nowhere, even and especially in her hometown of Los Angeles, where she was subject to racial segregation, migration restrictions, and anti-miscegenation laws. That sense of displacement and expulsion within her supposed home country gave her a certain longing to find home and explore other geographic possibilities, while ultimately feeling a sense of difference. Wong's yearning for China and desire to claim belonging there speaks to the lack of home in the United States or Europe. In some ways Wong was not making a liberal choice; she was forced into cosmopolitanism by virtue of her delimited "choice" at the same time that she was excluded from cosmopolitanism's freedoms.

Wong's racialized body reveals the limits of cosmopolitanism and the fact that not just anyone can claim it. Likewise, Benjamin's struggle to fully characterize Wong points to the difficulties of intersecting racialized American modern femininity with a Eurocentric cosmopolitanism. These are the configurations of a particular historical moment. The end of the Weimar republic and the rise of National Socialism spelled the end of the possibility of Wong making films in Berlin. Although cosmopolitanism appears to be a neutral and open category, under the weight of racialized categories, it splits open and cannot be realized.

The issues raised in this chapter resonate throughout this book. The issue of cosmopolitanism and the knowledge of European languages, and, by extension, European manners and customs, is revisited in Chapter 2 as well as in Chapter 6, which discusses Australia. European languages were central to creating a "White Australia." White Australia was created through a dictation test, typically given in English, with exceptions for European languages but not for Asian ones. Just as the U.S. Gentleman's Agreement did not specify Japan by name but targeted Japanese Americans, Australia's dictation test masked the race-specific Chinese target of the immigration exclusion policy. Not just a question of language, "speaking German" in the Australian context refers to not only manners, cosmopolitanism, and other markers of modernity but also the very core of being Australian.

Chapter 2, "American Moderns in Europe," focuses on the challenges, comedic and otherwise, that arose from the disjuncture between European audiences who expected colonial, primitive, and oriental performances and the Americans who performed. Wong's story is enhanced by that of African American performer Josephine Baker. By examining the experiences of both women, we can see how colonial, national, racial, and gender dynamics interplay, a fruitful juxtaposition I have hinted at in this chapter. Through their performances, both women disrupted concepts central to the modern and modernity: primitive and civilized, other and Western, male and female, colonial subject and metropole.

American Moderns in Europe

Anna May Wong and Josephine Baker

Elstree Calling (1930): A heap of tires, chairs, and tables rain down the stairs. In this comic scene, Katherine first appears at the top of the stairs shouting in Cantonese. Her expressive eyes flash anger. With devastating accuracy she hurls cream pies at her husband. Pies spatter as they hit the other men in the scene, including her father, the footmen in the main hall, and the character representing William Shakespeare. This sketch reveals Katherine in control of the space and the men around her.

The film *Elstree Calling,* named after the Elstree (film) Studios in London, England, is a series of Shakespeare-based sketches starring chiefly British actors and actresses. In the scene described above, Chinese American actress Anna May Wong plays Katherine, the cantankerous wife from *The Taming of the Shrew.* Alfred Hitchcock directed some of the scenes, although not the one with Wong. Given the British cinematic prohibition on interracial relationships, Wong's Chinese heritage heightens the incommensurability and therefore the comedy of Katherine and Petrucchio's fraught marital relationship. Since Donald Calthrop, who plays Petrucchio, is white, this is a marriage that cannot be. Shouting in Cantonese makes the communication gap and thus the impossibility of the marriage even more pronounced. Yet the fact that Wong played such a prominent role within a cast of notable British thespians proclaims her success in London.

This brief but noteworthy appearance in *Elstree Calling* was just one of the many markers of Wong's celebrity in London. After her time in Berlin being interviewed by German philosopher Walter Benjamin and making the film *Song/Show Life* (1928), Wong worked in London. She portrayed the dancer Shosho, who is the toast of London, in the film *Piccadilly* (1929) directed by E. A. Dupont. She starred in the play *The Circle of Chalk* and received top billing over famed British actor Laurence Olivier. Olivier graciously remained friends with Wong: on her subsequent visit to London, he suggestively scrawled his home address on her theater program, presumably so she could visit.[1] She graced the covers of the society magazines *Tatler* and *The Sketch*. Living the life of an upper-class socialite, she met the Prince of Wales, learning to curtsy to royalty in the process. Her elegance and beauty stopped Parliament when she sauntered into the visitor's gallery.[2] Wong stated, "I had a very marvelous time socially in London. Many of the finest people became my friends and were wonderful to me."[3] Wong's fame and adulation in Europe were very different from her stereotyped roles and lukewarm reception in the United States.

Wong's ability to become a superstar in Berlin and London was part of a larger trend of racial minority American performers finding success in Europe. This chapter and Chapter 3 look at Wong in conjunction with African American performer Josephine Baker. The life stories of Wong and Baker overlap in several ways. Neither woman achieved stardom in the United States and both found better work opportunities in Europe. As American moderns in Europe, being American was both a source of power and of vexation. As Americans training in the United States, they had learned how to be the ultimate modern performers, yet the American racial climate had been characterized by Asian immigration exclusion, institutionalized racial segregation, and wage-labor stratification. Both women trained in Europe to further their craft and there became stars. Their performance reviews and films circulated not only throughout Europe and the United States but in Africa and Asia as well. Although the two women never worked together, Wong witnessed Baker perform at the Casino de Paris in 1932.

Examining the lives of both women highlights three issues. First, the comparison encapsulates the importance of American modernity and American performing traditions. One cannot comprehend Wong's and Baker's stories

---

1. Program, *The Circle of Chalk*, 1929, Anna May Wong Gift Collection, Billy Rose Theatre Collection, New York Public Library, Performing Arts Branch.

2. Audrey Rivers, "Anna May Sorry She Cannot Be Kissed," *Movie Classics,* November 1929, Anna May Wong Clipping File, Margaret Herrick Library, Academy of Motion Pictures, Arts and Sciences, Los Angeles (hereafter, AMPAS).

3. Anthony C. Chan, *Perpetually Cool: The Many Lives of Anna May Wong, 1905–1961* (Lanham, MD: Rowman and Littlefield, 2003), 64.

without understanding race in the United States. They were born into a complex settler-colonial nation-state, which affected everything from their initial training to how they handled their lives in Europe. Second, examining both women reveals the dynamics of European fascination with racial difference, sexuality, and colonial otherness. Looking at both a Chinese American and an African American performer substantiates a broader spectrum of racial and colonial difference than scrutinizing just one of them. Through this comparison, the convergences and divergences of orientalism, primitivism, and colonialism become apparent. Third, and most importantly, both women were involved in self-fashioning. They took advantage of fascination with racial otherness. But experts such as dance choreographers, accent coaches, and clothing designers trained them. Their performances on and off stage became deliberate and multifaceted strategies. Baker redefined Africanness and Wong redefined Chineseness by appropriating them as performances from which they could step in and out. Although frequently their performances were understood as "natural," they were crafted entities, sometimes improvised, with roots in American performance.

American Beginnings

Anna May Wong and Josephine Baker brought their American racial identities and performance traditions to Europe. Their ability to be successful performers in Europe had everything to do with their experiences as racialized subjects and performers in the United States. Race is the constitutive element of the American nation-state, and performance as a means to signify race is deeply imbued within American history.[4] Racial minorities have had to respond to the contradictions racial hierarchy posed to the U.S. democratic ideal.[5] Those contradictions between racial hierarchy and liberal humanist democracy are deeply embedded within American culture; racial minorities have responded by pointing out them out through performance.

For African Americans, performance was a formative means of transition

---

4. Michael Rogin, *Black Face, White Noise: Jewish Immigrants in the Hollywood Melting Pot* (Berkeley: University of California Press, 1996); Daniel Bernardi, ed., *The Birth of Whiteness: Race and the Emergence of U.S. Cinema* (New Brunswick, NJ: Rutgers University Press, 1996).

5. Eric Lott, *Love and Theft: Blackface Minstrelsy and the American Working Class* (New York: Oxford University Press, 1993); Thomas Cripps, *Slow Fade to Black: The Negro in American Film, 1900–1942* (New York: Oxford University Press, 1993). As film scholar Gina Marchetti's study's opening line states, "Hollywood has long been fascinated by Asia, Asians, and Asian themes." Gina Marchetti, *Romance and the "Yellow Peril": Race, Sex, and Discursive Strategies in Hollywood Fiction* (Berkeley: University of California Press, 1993), 1.

to the Americas. During the Middle Passage between Africa and the New World, enslaved Africans were brought up from the ship's hold and forced to dance, both for entertainment and for health.[6] A healthy slave would command a higher price than a sickly one. In the United States, dance and song became both a coerced mode—by the slave master—as well as a means of not only retaining African culture but also creating an African American culture.[7] Thus oppression laid the groundwork for contestation.

Likewise, performance identified Chinese women from the beginning of their entry to the United States. After the end of the African slave trade, Chinese and South Asian laborers were brought to the Americas. Beginning in 1835, a steady number of Chinese contract laborers were brought to Hawaii, and customs officials recorded that approximately 370,000 Chinese arrived in Hawaii and California between the late 1840s and early 1880s.[8] This caused such turmoil in American political culture that one of the first American laws to restrict immigration, the Page Law (1875), targeted Chinese women.[9] Although the law was originally written to exclude the entire Chinese working class, anxiety around prostitution ensured that the law was enforced exclusively against Chinese female migration. Hence, sexually disreputable, working-class, single Chinese women became the specter against whose body the boundaries of the U.S. nation-state were drawn.

Through performance, Chinese migrant women covertly challenged U.S. immigration laws. They responded to the exclusion laws through their enactment of class-inflected respectability during the immigration review process at the Angel Island detention center in San Francisco Bay. For example, working-class Chinese women who aimed to migrate to the United States deliberately dressed in fine clothing and displayed an upper-class manner in order to convince U.S. immigration officials that they should be admitted.[10]

6. Jacqui Malone, *Steppin' on the Blues: The Visible Rhythms of African American Dance* (Chicago: University of Illinois Press, 1996); Brenda Dixon Gottschild, *Digging the Africanist Presence in American Performance Dance and Other Contexts* (Westport, CT: Greenwood Press, 1996); Lynne Fauley Emery, *Black Dance: From 1619 to Today* (Princeton, NJ: Princeton Book, 1988).

7. Paul Gilroy, *Black Atlantic: Modernity and Double-Consciousness* (Cambridge, MA: Harvard University Press, 1995); April Masten, "Challenge Dancing in Antebellum America: Sporting Men, Vulgar Women, and Blacked-Up Boys," *Journal of Social History* 48, no. 3 (Spring 2015): 605–634; Michael Gomez, *Exchanging Our Country Marks: The Transformation of African Identities in the Colonial and Antebellum South* (Chapel Hill: University of North Carolina Press, 1998).

8. Sucheng Chan, *Asian Americans: An Interpretive History* (Boston: Twayne, 1991), 3.

9. The Alien Act of 1798 allowed the United States to deport noncitizens.

10. Erika Lee, *At America's Gates: Chinese Immigration during the Exclusion Era, 1882–1943* (Chapel Hill: University of North Carolina Press, 2003); Him Mark Lai, Genny Lim,

Baker and Wong emerged from a historical backdrop when American imperialism and white supremacy dominated and, in turn, shaped cultural production. Racial segregation, authorized by the U.S. Supreme Court decision *Plessy v. Ferguson* (1896), combined with U.S. imperial ambitions in the Pacific, including the Philippines, Hawaii, and the Shanghai concessions.[11] Minstrel shows that featured white performers in blackface or yellowface were one of the most popular forms of nineteenth-century entertainment and consolidated white privilege for the American working class.[12] This creation of white privilege through mockery of blacks continued in films such as *Birth of a Nation* (1915).[13] In 1881 Chinese were put into P. T. Barnum circus "freak" shows, and Filipino "savages" were displayed in the 1904 St. Louis World's Fair.[14] In the United States, such ethnographic displays were some of the most important venues for enacting and understanding racial difference. As such, racial hierarchy was created and maintained through performance.

African American entertainer Josephine Baker's story is well known. Born Freda Josephine McDonald in St. Louis, Missouri, in 1906, Baker took her last name from her husband from a short-lived marriage. She was best known for her variety vaudeville performances. She began her career as a dancer, then expanded her repertoire to include singing and the motion pictures. Baker emerged from the African American vaudeville circuit. She learned her craft while traveling as blues singer Clara Smith's dresser, assisting her with her costuming for the revue *The Dixie Steppers.* Both being a dresser and witnessing the show were significant spaces for learning the importance of self-fashioning. She then worked her way from being a dresser for Noble Sissle and Eubie Blake's landmark musical *Shuffle Along* to touring in the chorus with the production.[15] Baker was well known for her scene-stealing eye-rolling and comic performances. What seemed like "natural" improvisa-

and Judy Yung, *Island: Poetry and History of Chinese Immigration on Angel Island, 1910–1940* (Seattle: University of Washington Press, 1999).

11. Amy Kaplan and Donald E. Pease, eds., *Cultures of United States Imperialism* (Durham, NC: Duke University Press, 1993).

12. David R. Roediger, *The Wages of Whiteness: Race and the Making of the American Working Class* (New York: Verso, 1991); Matthew Frye Jacobson, *Whiteness of a Different Color: European Immigrants and the Alchemy of Race* (Cambridge, MA: Harvard University Press, 1998).

13. Cripps, *Slow Fade to Black.*

14. Robert Rydell, *All the World's a Fair: Visions of Empire at American International Expositions, 1876–1916* (Chicago: University of Chicago Press, 1984); Adria Imada, *Aloha America: Hula Circuits through the U.S. Empire* (Durham, NC: Duke University Press, 2012).

15. Phyllis Rose, *Jazz Cleopatra: Josephine Baker in Her Time* (New York: Doubleday, 1989), 46–64; Karen C. C. Dalton and Henry Louis Gates Jr., "Josephine Baker and Paul Colin: African American Dance Seen through Parisian Eyes," *Critical Inquiry* 24, no. 4 (1998): 903–934.

tion was really the result of decades of hard work, training, and observation. Underlying her supposedly spontaneous performances were steps such as the "Mess Around" and "Tack Annie," and she even practiced her eye rolling.[16]

Because African Americans in the United States chiefly played in front of black audiences, if Baker wanted to earn more money and become famous, she would have to perform in front of white audiences and thus racialize herself in order to fit in with their expectations. According to biographer Phyllis Rose, an African American performer could either try to achieve artistic excellence and thus lose white audiences who expected to see racial stereotypes, or could play those stereotypes, which compromised artistic excellence.[17] In her last act before leaving for Paris, Baker played a pickaninny in blackface in *Chocolate Dandies.* Although money was doubtlessly an inducement, receiving the starring role in Caroline Dudley's *Revue Nègre* compelled Baker to journey across the ocean for work.

Unhappy with their roles in the United States, Baker and Wong departed for Europe, Baker in 1925 to France, Wong, as shown in Chapter 1, in 1928 to Germany. What both women found in Europe was a different but nonetheless strongly racialized social order. Undoubtedly appealing was 1920s Europe's reputation of allowing racial minorities to stay in public accommodations, eat in restaurants, have interracial relationships, and perform for multiracial audiences, all of which were forbidden or highly contested in the United States.[18] Although there was no formal racial segregation in Europe, as there was in the United States, there existed longstanding ideas about the colonial "other." This racial and primitive other was the foil against which imperial Europe not only proved its civilization but also justified colonialism.[19] For European audiences, Wong and Baker presented a complicated image of exoticized Americanness and colonial otherness—ethnically other and sexually primitive. These are enduring tropes of European fascination with the "new" and colonial worlds, ones that both Baker and Wong played on and exploited, and to which Europe continues to respond.[20]

---

16. Rose, *Jazz Cleopatra,* 47; Ramsay Burt, "'Savage' Dancer: Tout Paris Goes to See Josephine Baker," in *Alien Bodies: Representations of Modernity, "Race" and Nation in Early Modern Dance* (London: Routledge, 1998), 57–83.

17. Rose, *Jazz Cleopatra,* 61.

18. Tyler Stovall, *Paris Noir: African Americans in the City of Light* (New York: Mariner Books, 1996).

19. Robert Young, *Colonial Desire: Hybridity in Theory, Culture, and Race* (London: Routledge, 1995); Kathleen Wilson, *Island Race: Englishmen, Empire, and Gender in the Eighteenth Century* (New York: Routledge, 2002).

20. Daphne Brooks, *Bodies in Dissent: Spectacular Performances of Race and Freedom, 1850–1910* (Durham, NC: Duke University Press, 2006); Tracy Denean Shapley-Whiting,

The two women arrived in a Europe primed for them by interests in jazz and chinoiserie. Although for centuries Europeans had exhibited performers of color, in the aftermath of World War I, modernity's obsession with "primitive" cultures encouraged striking numbers of African and Asian diaspora musicians, writers, and artists to create visible cultures.[21] Pablo Picasso and Paul Gauguin were just two of the European painters borrowing from African and Asian aesthetics to fabricate modern art.[22] During and after World War I, African American male musicians, writers, and other artists flocked to Paris. World War I segregated armed forces bands such as the 369th Regiment (Hellfighters) directed by James Reese Europe popularized jazz in France. In addition, World War I increased the numbers of African and Asian diasporic peoples in Europe through migration and settlement.[23] Colonial African and Asian soldiers were key to their colonial rulers' victory.[24] A horrific event that signified the evils of modern civilization, World War I led many white Europeans to seek redemption in the supposedly primitive and exotic. The

Black Venus: Sexualized Savages, Primal Fears, and Primitive Narratives in French (Durham, NC: Duke University Press, 1999); Fatimah Tobing Rony, _The Third Eye: Race, Cinema, and the Ethnographic Spectacle_ (Durham, NC: Duke University Press, 1996); Bunny McBride, _Molly Spotted Elk: A Penobscot in Paris_ (Norman: University of Oklahoma Press, 1995); Jayna Brown, _Babylon Girls: Black Women Performers and the Shaping of the Modern_ (Durham, NC: Duke University Press, 2008); Joy S. Kasson, _Buffalo Bill's Wild West: Celebrity, Memory, and Popular History_ (New York: Hill and Wang, 2000). Postwar Germans impersonated Native Americans in order to cope with the guilt of the Holocaust. See Katrin Sieg, _Ethnic Drag: Performing Race, Nation, Sexuality in West Germany_ (Ann Arbor: University of Michigan Press, 2002), 73–150.

21. During and after World War I, African American male musicians, writers, and other artists flocked to Paris. Stovall, _Paris Noir_; Andre Levinson, "The Negro Dance under European Eyes," _Theater Arts,_ April 1927, 282–293; Tricia Danielle Keaton, T. Denean Sharpley-Whiting, and Tyler Stovall, eds., _Black France/France Noire: The History and Politics of Blackness_ (Durham, NC: Duke University Press, 2012).

22. Simon Gikandi, "Picasso, Africa, and the Schemata of Difference," _Modernism/Modernity_ 10, no. 3 (2003): 455–480. Jean Cocteau devised Josephine Baker's infamous banana skirt. See Mariana Torgovnik, _Gone Primitive: Savage Intellects, Modern Lives_ (Chicago: University of Chicago Press, 1990); Anne Anlin Cheng, _Second Skin: Josephine Baker and the Modern Surface_ (New York: Oxford University Press, 2010); Sieglinde Lemke, _Primitivist Modernism: Black Culture and the Origins of Transatlantic Modernism_ (New York: Oxford University Press, 1998).

23. Sue Peabody and Tyler Stovall, eds., _The Color of Liberty: Histories of Race in France_ (Durham, NC: Duke University Press, 2003). For more on black internationalism, see Brent Hayes Edwards, _The Practice of Diaspora: Literature, Translation, and the Rise of Black Internationalism_ (Cambridge, MA: Harvard University Press, 2003); Heike Raphael-Hernandez, _Blackening Europe: The African American Presence_ (New York: Routledge, 2003).

24. Gregory Mann, _Native Sons: West African Veterans and France in the 20th Century_ (Durham, NC: Duke University Press, 2006); Myron Echenberg, _Colonial Conscripts: The Tirailleurs Sénégalais in French West Africa, 1857–1960_ (Portsmouth, NH: Heinemann, 1991).

primitive could be a positive aspect of the modern because it signaled a way out of the technological mass destruction of World War I. It also represented the negative effects of 1920s European colonialism in Africa and Asia.

If Europe was a seductive site for performers of color such as Anna May Wong or Josephine Baker, performers of color in turn seduced European audiences, albeit through layers of racial exoticism and orientalism. The importance of both Wong's and Baker's presence in Berlin in 1928 was duly noted on the May 28 cover of *Simplicissimus,* as drawn by artist Thomas Theodor Heine. Now defunct, *Simplicissimus* (1896–1967) was a weekly satirical magazine published out of Munich and Stuttgart.[25] Although Wong and Baker never performed together in actuality, they did so in the mind of the German press; above the *Simplicissimus* cover image the heading announces "Josephine Baker und Anna May Wong." The presence of Wong alongside Baker underscores how European interest in oriental and black cultures was mediated through American racialized bodies. There is no story about Baker or Wong inside the issue, leaving the cover as the site of their meeting. A short white man stands between them, partially blocked by Wong, representing possibly either the publisher Albert Langen or Heine. Baker is on the left. She looks male, androgynous, portrayed quite differently from the hyperfeminized and sexualized bare bosomed banana skirt look that even today persists in cultural representations of her. She is fully clothed in a white shirt, black unitard, white socks, and black shoes. She stands, with her hands on her hips and with her knee and elbow protruding outside the frame of the red background. Like a minstrel sketch, her face bears exaggerated features and colors: her face is black, lips and nostrils red, and eyes grey-rimmed. She has no visible hair on her head. Looking like a yellow Greek statue that sports her iconographic hairstyle of bangs and hair pulled back, Wong is seated on the right. Her skin and dress are unmistakably yellow, the same shade making them blend into each other. Her pink-rimmed eyes are closed, and her lips red. Her feet are bare and one leg is up and bent. The Grecian gown bares her left (her right, our left) breast and is open almost to the top of her hip. The German man is fully clothed, standing slightly behind Wong. He wears a long dark jacket, there is red in his tie and striped pants, and he is balding and wears eyeglasses. He appears shorter than Baker, at the same head level as Wong, who is seated. Caricature, parody, and exaggeration are all part of this ensemble. It is a curious portrait.

---

25. Peter J. Hugill, "German Great-Power Relations in the Pages of 'Simplicissimus,' 1896–1914," *Geographical Review* 98, no. 1 (2008): 1–23.

Anna May Wong and Josephine Baker on *Simplicissimus* cover.

This cover opens up the possibility of the orient representing a mode of modernity and temporality alternate to the one outlined by Edward Said or the film *Toll of the Sea*. The composition of the *Simplicissimus* cover and its brief caption place Baker and Wong in dichotomy to each other. The cover caption reads: "A part of the black continent and a handful of Light from the east. Kids, it gives a daring cultural twilight." The metaphor of black and light makes it seem as if Baker and Wong are opposing forces. Geographically, they are presented as from the East versus the African continent. The unspecified orient is cast as "East" as opposed to an unspecified location within a specific continent. Together the light and the dark form a "daring cultural twilight," which probably refers to the juxtaposition of the two forms of racial difference or the demise of white civilization. Racial and geographic polarization is augmented by gender binaries. Although their femininity is not part of the caption's text, in the actual image, Wong appears feminized and Baker masculinized, fitting in with how racial tropes of Africanness and Asianness were and still are gendered. What is interesting is that the images did not derive from colonial stereotypes of the savage or the primitive or the antiquated oriental. Instead, Baker harkens to an androgynous dancer, perhaps a French mime, and Wong to ancient Greece. Their American heritage is only implicitly noted by their sharing the cover.

American Moderns in Europe

Even though Baker and Wong seduced audiences in Europe with their supposed exoticism, their performances off- and onstage represented key moments in creating modern culture. Despite being born American, their race meant that they were continually read as exotics or primitives or colonial subjects. Training in American ethnic communities empowered both women to intervene in the construction of the modern predicated on the binary between primitive and civilized in colonizing Europe. Both women would portray European colonial subjects. During those performances, Wong's and Baker's ridiculous, comic, and "bad" improvisations disrupted seamless fictions of colonial otherness and civilized self, thus calling into question the underpinnings of modernity and imperialism. As both women asserted their American modernity, they insisted on being temporally located in the modern. There are three key moments that illustrate this: Baker dancing the Charleston in the streets of the Netherlands, Wong's *The Circle of Chalk* performance in London, and the cosmopolitan deployment of fashion, especially Baker's sophisticated clothes that took her image beyond the banana skirt.

Perhaps the dance that best illustrates how performance affected the construction of American race and modernity is one that Baker popularized in Europe, namely the Charleston. Within dance history itself, the Charleston is a multiply mediated entity, both jazz-influenced, with African antecedents, and as an innovation within modern dance. As jazz composition plays with improvisation, rhythm, and the melding of multiple musical influences, many consider it the ultimate engagement with modernity. The history of the Charleston reveals multiple traversals of the performative Black Atlantic.[26] A quintessential African American creation, the Charleston's Congolese antecedents have been documented by Robert Farris-Thompson and Brenda Dixon Gottschild.[27] Baker's rendition originates with African dance transposed to the American context, and transformed into American jazz dance, which was then brought back across the Atlantic to northern and Western Europe.

Baker's performance of the Charleston utilized parody to challenge Western preconceptions of black performance. There is a long tradition of African Americans imitating European Americans with exaggerated gestures in order to expose historical inequities. The cakewalk, a precursor to the Charleston, was developed under slavery and segregation.[28] The dance received its name because, for the masters' amusement, African Americans would be compelled to dance in competition for the prize of a cake. The dancers performing the cakewalk would parody the masters' dances such as the minuet and perform them back to the masters as "authentic" black dances. Minstrel shows also depended on an analogous back-and-forth dynamic.[29] Baker's trademark Charleston had its roots in historically subversive parody. As literary scholar Henry Louis Gates argues, parody in particular is subversive because of how African Americans under slavery used it for survival and understood its reference to the trickster figure.[30] Understanding this dynamic is critical to comprehending the meaning of Baker's Charleston.

By moving the body in a multiplicity of directions with dense rhythms, the Charleston transformed modern dance by shattering the unity of the Western body.[31] Though there are quintessential Charleston movements,

---

26. Gilroy, *The Black Atlantic*.

27. Robert Farris Thompson, *African Art in Motion: Icon and Art in the Collection of Katherine Coryton White* (Berkeley: University of California Press, 1974).

28. Marshall Stearns and Jean Stearns, *Jazz Dance: The Story of American Vernacular Dance* (New York: Macmillan, 1968). The cakewalk allegedly has Seminole Indian and African Kaffir influences.

29. Lott, *Love and Theft*.

30. Henry Louis Gates Jr., *Signifying Monkey: A Theory of African American Literary Criticism* (New York: Oxford University Press, 1988).

31. Mura Dehn, *The Spirit Moves*, USA, 1952, video recording. Available at the New York Public Library, Performing Arts Branch.

improvisation was key to its origins in jazz dance and critical to its innovation from modern dance. Modern dance itself was a conscious break from ballet, especially from dancing on point, on the tips of the toes. Frequently the Charleston body was poised parallel to the floor, which counterpoised ballet's upright body. The Charleston both ensured jazz dance's break from modern dance and further differentiated that genre from ballet. Baker's variation performed in the Netherlands continued its evolution and centered the black body at the heart of the modern.

One of the most incredible sequences of multiple cultural transpositions in Baker's early European career occurred in the Netherlands. In a 1926 Fox Movietone News clip, Baker is first shown souvenir shopping dressed in the height of contemporary fashion. She wears a pleated skirt, knit sweater and jacket, silk scarf and hat.[32] This type of narrative clip, shown in movie theaters before feature films, supposedly captured "real" news about stars, though, of course, it was staged. As a tourist, Baker was both the spectator and the spectacle, and thus we follow Baker's gaze around the souvenir shop. She spins the spokes of a toy miniature windmill and is entranced by a little Dutch girl. In the next scene she emerges out of a souvenir shop dressed in a "traditional" Dutch outfit. A tricorn lace hat on her head, she is now wearing a full-skirted mid-calf-length dress with wooden clogs on her feet. Baker shed her contemporary outfit for one that marked her as rural and timeless. She holds hands with the little Dutch girl, attired in a matching outfit. Baker's costuming is a lesson in colonial pedagogy that reveals the comic in the colonizing project. Essentially, Baker wears Dutch drag. The intended humor of the scene stems from the juxtaposition of Baker's black skin with the assumed whiteness of Dutch culture and national identity. Yet it is an uneasy joke because of Dutch colonial possessions in Suriname, the Caribbean, and Indonesia.[33] I speculate that it is Baker's Americanness that entitles her to slip in and out of black Dutch character in ways that might be too threatening for an actual black Dutch colonial to perform. That black Dutch colonial would have to remain primitive.

Baker then breaks into a "spontaneous" Charleston performance and disrupts the fiction of her colonial subjectivity. As she dances the Charleston in

---

32. "Josephine Baker Visits Volendam," Fox News Story C8059, August 24, 1928, https://mirc.sc.edu/islandora/object/usc%3A1750 (accessed October 15, 2018).

33. Allison Blakely, *Blacks in the Dutch World: The Evolution of Racial Imagery in a Modern Society* (Bloomington: Indiana University Press, 1993); Julia Ann Clancy-Smith and Frances Gouda, *Domesticating the Empire: Race, Gender, and Family Life in French and Dutch Colonialism* (Charlottesville: University of Virginia Press, 1998).

the streets, her wooden shoes fly off her feet. Baker stumbles, collapses to her knees, hands to chest, clearly laughing. Baker's laughter acknowledges the absurdity of the moment. The shoes weigh her down, fall off her feet, and prevent her from properly dancing the Charleston. Baker was fully aware of the incongruity of dancing the Charleston in a traditional Dutch outfit. She revealed in her autobiography: "I was dressed in Dutch clothing, with a white hair-covering, a long dress so large I was lost in it, and yellow wooden shoes. You see: the Charleston in yellow wooden shoes."[34]

Although this particular dance may have been staged for the Fox Movietone News camera, Baker's performances were never perfectly scripted. Her response to dancing the Charleston in Western drag demonstrates the improvisation at the heart of American jazz.[35] Since the shoes do not permit her to dance her usual steps, she modifies the steps to fit the situation. After falling, she gamely continues. Rather than feet flying out in front and in back, which would have dislodged the shoes, she dances energetically, swaying from side to side with feet firmly planted on the floor. Her quick thinking enables her to continue her performance in front of the Dutch audience. In this performance, grounded by her yellow wooden shoes, Baker exemplifies dancing with modern planted feet.[36] The ability to improvise was a key skill for African Americans living under racialized regimes of power such as slavery and segregation.[37] Indeed, noted African American writer and critic Ralph Ellison has argued that black American artistic performance under slavery and segregation was improvisatory, subversive, and life sustaining.[38] With Baker's improvisation she asserts control of the scene by rooting her feet, which undermines the colonial gaze.

34. Marcel Sauvage and Josephine Baker, *Les Mémoires de Josephine Baker* (Paris: KRA, 1927), 18. Translation mine.

35. Krin Gabbard, ed., *Representing Jazz* (Durham, NC: Duke University Press, 1995); Krin Gabbard, ed., *Jazz among the Discourses* (Durham, NC: Duke University Press, 1995); Michael Borshuk, "An Intelligence of the Body: Disruptive Parody through Dance in the Early Performances of Josephine Baker," in *Embodying Liberation: The Black Body in American Dance,* ed. Dorothea Fischer-Hornung and Allison Goeller (Piscataway, NJ: Transaction, 2001), 41–58.

36. Burt, "'Savage Dancer.'"

37. Wynton Marsalis, quoted in "Gumbo," Ken Burns, producer, *Jazz* (documentary) (PBS, 2000). For example, if you were caught in a location without a pass, you could improvise and act as if you did have permission to be there, and avert punishment.

38. Ralph Ellison, "Change the Joke and Slip the Yoke," in *Shadow and Act* (New York: Random House, 1953).

London, 1928–1929

In London, Anna May Wong struggled to retain her body as temporally, spatially, and aurally in the modern. At first, British culture cast Wong as an "oriental" subject but that soon changed into hybrid modernity. Like the French and Dutch obsession with Baker, British fascination with Wong was so great that, soon after she arrived in Europe, she graced the covers of the society magazines *Tatler* and *The Sketch,* dressed in oriental regalia.[39] Britain's Shanghai concessions, Chinese treaty ports, and the colonies of Hong Kong and Singapore gave it strong national and imperial interests in knowing about and imagining the "orient." In the twentieth century, European interest in the orient shifted from the Middle East to East Asia.[40] Wong's oriental costumes on the covers of both magazines showed her exotic appeal, which was quickly interrupted by her American modernity.[41] As she became established in her career in the 1930s, she became legendary for wearing sophisticated designer gowns that contradicted (or perhaps even further adorned) her sexualized and "primitive" performances.[42]

Wong's Americanness, typically a metaphor for temporal modernity, was at first largely ignored in the British press. Instead, Wong's Chineseness came to the forefront, frequently in inaccurate ways. In *The Sketch* on August 22, 1928, the cover reads "Miss Anna May Wong, in National Dress: By N. Michailow." The caption accompanying the illustration states: "Miss Anna May Wong, the famous Chinese screen star who is visiting England and will shortly make her British screen debut in 'Piccadilly,' usually wears European dress; but when she sat to Professor Nic Michailow, the well-known artist, she chose to be painted in a superb Chinese coat, and with her hair arranged in national style." Hence Wong's American national identity is obfuscated in favor of a high-class Chinese appearance; Chineseness is collapsed into a "national style" associated with China's elite. Note that the piece presents the Chinese dress as Wong's choice and stated that Wong usually wore modern or "European" dress. *Tatler* placed her on the cover on March 20, 1929, also in Chinese dress. These two magazine covers display how Wong's Chineseness in London is an anachronistic, antiquated one, albeit one with high-class standing. In this

---

39. *Tatler,* March 20, 1929, cover; *The Sketch,* August 22, 1928, cover.

40. Lisa Lowe, *Critical Terrains: French and British Orientalisms* (Ithaca, NY: Cornell University Press, 1991).

41. These early covers contrast with later magazine and newspaper depictions, where she is much more Western and cosmopolitan.

42. Shirley Jennifer Lim, *A Feeling of Belonging: Asian American Women's Public Culture* (New York: New York University Press, 2006), chap. 2.

London press coverage, not only does Wong's Chinese heritage get collapsed into nation-state historical signifiers; China and the Chinese also become subsumed in temporal noncoevalness.[43]

By insisting on temporal contemporaneity, Wong and Baker disrupted how European colonialism depended on placing its subjects under noncontemporaneous (noncoeval) time in order to craft this new type of modern. As Johannes Fabian documents in *Time and the Other,* placing the other in noncoeval time is central to European domination of the other.[44] Fabian calls it the "denial of coevalness," which he defines as a "persistent and systematic tendency to place the referent (s) of anthropology in a Time other than the present of the producer of anthropological discourse."[45] Primitive societies were defined by anthropology and colonial discourse as being trapped in the ethnographic past. Baker's and Wong's work offers concrete evidence of Fabian's point that the temporal component to modernity is critical. In an age that measured civilization's progress through a linear timeline that posited the modern West as the most evolved stage, the colonized were constructed as primitive (Polynesia, Africa) or decadent (China, Middle East), which meant less evolved and emphatically not modern. Although white Europeans forayed into the primitive and the decadent to ameliorate as well as revitalize the modern, because they were racially unmarked as white, they kept their higher civilized status. Witnessing Baker's or Wong's performances was one way that they did this. Wong and Baker, on the other hand, created their modernity through the racially marked body that contested white privilege's sole claim to modernity.

This collapsing of Chinese heritage into Chinese nation-state belonging was not confined to Wong. Numerous writers confused race and national origins for other actresses of Chinese descent. For example, on March 20, 1929, referring to Wong's star turn in *The Circle of Chalk, The Sketch* reported that "This celebrated screen star of Chinese birth has been featured in many successful pictures, including the much discussed 'Piccadilly,' but has never before been seen on stage."[46] The article went on to state that "The part of the jealous wife is played by another Chinese actress, Miss Rose Quong." As historian Angela Woollacott has researched, Rose Quong was actually a Chinese Australian from Melbourne who settled in London and capitalized on

---

43. Johannes Fabian, *Time and the Other: How Anthropology Makes Its Object* (New York: Columbia University Press, 1983).

44. Ibid.

45. Ibid., 31.

46. *The Sketch,* March 20, 1929, 557.

her Chineseness.[47] So, in referring to Wong's "Chinese birth" and Quong as "another Chinese actress," both the American and Australian actresses were cast as Chinese.

Despite efforts to orientalize her, Wong articulated and re-historicized the modern through her theater performances in London. In the modern aesthetic, national affinity is marked through gestures such as vocal intonation, and Wong's American accent called into question the colonial fantasies surrounding her. One of the most striking aspects of the press coverage of Wong's performance is the theater critics' amazement at the disjuncture between what they assumed was an authentic oriental appearance and the reality of Wong's American voice.

Perhaps the ultimate testament to the Chinese mode of Wong's appeal came in a theater review of *The Circle of Chalk*. Referring to her role, critic Hubert Griffith wrote, "I have rarely seen anything more completely beautiful. Rhythm, gesture, the expressiveness of motion—she is mistress of them all. One could sit back and watch the lithe little figure moving across the stage and see how in all the complicated movements of the dance never as much as a finger-tip departed from patterns of the highest grace of felicity."[48] Indeed, as he continued, "The dance was a miracle, a masterpiece. And once again, at the end of the evening, when she at first refused to make a speech at the curtain fall, the actress did so in a gesture that was again arresting in its expressiveness and beauty." Griffith's enchantment with Wong as a physical object was complete.

The critic Griffith, however, preferred Wong mute. He continued in his review: "It is at first a shock to hear that the accent that falls from Celestial lips is a highly Americanised one, and then, when one gets over this as unimportant, to find that it is further an undistinguished one, clipping words leaving many of them almost inaudible. She got no variety into the long speeches, and generally, if I may say so without unpardonable rudeness, was at her most effective when silent. I return in memory to the dance, which I thank her for as a real experience." Sadly for the critics, the shock of her American voice ruined the illusion of Wong's perfect "Celestial" dance. In addition to Wong's lack of proper theatrical intonations, Griffith observed that almost the entire cast lacked elocution skills. Although Griffith backed away from his initial distress at Wong's American accent, nonetheless he

---

47. Angela Woollacott, "Rose Quong Becomes Chinese: An Australian in London and New York," *Australian Historical Studies* 129 (2007): 16–31.

48. Hubert Griffith, "Anna May Wong on the Stage: Her Dance the One Perfect Moment in a Play," *Daily Telegraph*, March 15, 1929.

completely elided the history of migration of the Chinese to the United States as a response to British and Western imperialism in China during the middle of the nineteenth century. Such colonial disruptions were effaced through the journalists' categorization of the Chinese as belonging to China, not the United States or Australia.

Although the theater critics for *The Circle of Chalk* expressed shock at Wong's accent, some press reports underscored her American birth. Perhaps because of its greater familiarity with Hollywood, the British periodical *Film Weekly* reported that "Anna May Wong ". . . though Oriental from her almond-shaped eyes to her long finger nails, was actually born and brought up in Los Angeles, California."[49] With her image on the February 11, 1929, cover, the text explained, "She became known to the public by playing the role of a Chinese slave girl in 'The Thief of Bagdad.' Since then, her name has grown famous in such productions as 'Show Life,' 'A Trip to Chinatown,' 'The Chinese Parrot,' and lastly, 'Piccadilly.'" The text continued, "Anna May Wong, in English, means Frosted Yellow Willow, a beautiful name for a talented actress."

Not all of the critics identified Wong as oriental; some of the British critics pinpointed Wong's American regional specificity, calling her voice "Californian." As another critic lamented, Wong was "Vurra Chinese.—The surprise in 'The Circle of Chalk' at the New was Anna May Wong, whom we expected to be so Chinese, but who turned out to be so American. In appearance her heroine is faultless. In accent it is hopeless."[50] Wong's American accent prevented the theater critics from continuing to construct the world as modern (Britain) and premodern (Chinese). Instead, her voice signaled the reality of contemporary migration patterns, which forced them to confront the dislocations caused by European imperialism, colonialism, warfare, and disruption of local economies. In other words, the British audiences could consider why a Chinese person spoke with perfect American twang. This break between voice and appearance interrupted colonial expectations. Wong's American voice and contemporary intonation woke British audiences out of their colonial imaginary and took her out of decaying Chinese empire time. Indeed, British press coverage of Wong's career sought to reconcile her voice with her appearance by discussing her American heritage.[51]

---

49. *Film Weekly*, February 11, 1929, cover.

50. Review glued inside *The Circle of Chalk* program, Theater Museum, London.

51. A further analysis of Wong's voice and language can be found in Yiman Wang, "Star Talk: Anna May Wong's Scriptural Orientalism and Poly-phonic (Dis-)play," in *The Multilingual Screen: New Reflections on Cinema and Linguistic Difference,* ed. Tijana Mamula and Lisa Patti (New York: Bloomsbury, 2016), 297–316.

As Wong explained in her own defense, her American accent jarred the audiences more than an English one would have. She stated in an interview: "The critics liked me, but said my American accent seemed out of place. Later, at a press luncheon, I pointed out to them that since the play was Chinese, even an English accent would have been out of place. But I explained I was sorry I had offended their ears and would try not to do it again. My next move was to get an accent coach."[52] Wong's dry sense of humor comes out when she apologizes for having "offended their ears" and recognizes that the expected English accent would be out of place. Which raises the question—would the critics have balked had she had an English accent? Were they expecting a Chinese one?

After the theater critics decried her American twang, Wong invested in elocution lessons in order to master an upper-class British accent. Note that she did not hire an accent coach to perfect a Chinese accent. Wong countered the criticism of her voice with all-American aplomb and paid a tutor to rid her of the American vulgarisms and to transform her voice into that of an upper-class British socialite. For private acting lessons, Wong sought out theater legends such as Kate Rork and Mabel Terry Lewis.[53] So these elocution lessons would presumably allow British audiences to accept her speaking voice as authentic when portraying Chinese roles. Later, to lend distinction to her work, she invoked traces of that same accent in her American movie parts. Such a move to hire theater voice coaching was a significant step in Wong's self-fashioning. That step enabled Wong to win starring film and theater roles and authorized her to claim the persona of a cosmopolitan woman of the world—important cultural capital for a person of color in the interwar period. This was especially valuable as it enabled Wong to successfully transition into the talking picture era, corroborating her ability as an ingenious cultural worker to adapt to technological changes under modernity.

By insisting on temporal contemporaneity through actions such as elocution lessons, Wong disrupted how European colonialism depended on placing its subjects under noncoeval time. While in London, Paris, and Berlin, Wong acquired the credentials that would permit her to become coeval and enter into modernity. In addition to her English-language accent training, she learned French and German, utilizing her German in films such as *Pavement Butterfly* (1929) and to sing in the Viennese opera *Springtime*.[54] As befits a

---

52. Harrison Carroll, "Oriental Girl Crashes Gates Via Footlights," *Herald Express,* no. 6 (June 5, 1931), Anna May Wong Clipping File, AMPAS.

53. Anna May Wong Clipping File, October 26, 1932, AMPAS.

54. *Wiener Zietung,* August 17, 1930, and September 10, 1930.

modern movie star, Wong learned how to handle the press and the numerous photo shoots. She gained the social skills and acting polish that, upon her return to the United States, would win her a broader repertoire of starring theater and film roles. All of those acquired upper-class English mannerisms, including voice, ensured that Wong's charms would translate on a global scale.

Wong's American modernity placed her in a complex situation with regard to her Chinese heritage. Being a person of Chinese descent, racialized meanings of her body became enmeshed in multiple and overlapping meanings of Chinese, ranging from national, antiquated, racial to transnational Chineseness. The term "Chinese" as applied to Wong can change from a racial signifier to a nation-state signifier to a temporality signifier. One key distinction was between modern transnational Chinese and antiquated national Chinese. Modern transnational Chinese could encompass Wong's Americanness as well as modernity. Antiquated national Chinese posited her as noncoeval and as a silent museum curiosity, to be admired but not a threat. Wong's self-fashioning was her attempt to be a modern transnational.

On these points, it is instructive to contrast Wong with Japanese-born actor Sessue Hayakawa, which brings out the gendered and orientalist dimensions at play in this time and space. In addition, it demonstrates the efficacy of Wong's self-fashioning. Often compared to silent movie legend Rudolph Valentino, Hayakawa's expressive facial gestures and smoldering sexuality ensured the success of silent movies such as Cecil B. DeMille's *The Cheat* (1919).[55] Hayakawa biographer Daisuke Miyao argues that given the persistence of the Madame Butterfly trope, Hayakawa as a male actor had more flexibility to forge his star image than did female Asian actresses such as Tsuruko Aoki or Wong.[56] Although this was certainly true in Hollywood during the silent era, Wong's film work in Europe gave her greater clout upon entering Hollywood's subsequent talking-picture era.

In 1931, the fan magazine *Motion Picture* highlighted how Wong's and Hayakawa's cultural differences were popularly understood: "Sessue Hayakawa smokes Japanese cigarettes, has Japanese people around him, talks with a completely bewildering Japanese accent, looks oriental, and above all thinks with the oriental attitude. 'Never make plan,' says Sessue with his difficult accent. 'Never plan ahead.' Anna May, with Western verbosity, is more explicit in expressing her philosophy." As the passage testifies, the two stars of

---

55. Sumiko Higashi, "DeMille's *The Cheat*," in *Unspeakable Images: Ethnicity and the American Cinema,* ed. Lester Friedman (Urbana: University of Illinois Press, 1991), 112–139.

56. Daisuke Miyao, *Sessue Hayakawa: Silent Cinema and Transnational Stardom* (Durham, NC: Duke University Press, 2007), 143.

Asian descent had divergent cultural careers in the 1930s. Even though both worked in Europe, Wong's mastery of British English proved essential to her success in sound motion picture productions. The comparison in *Motion Picture* confirms the popular belief that Wong was far more cosmopolitan, modern, and Westernized than Hayakawa. The article further racially differentiated them:

> She is glad to be back.
> She went away a Chinese flapper—and now many tell her that she no longer even looks Oriental.
>
> He [Sessue Hayakawa] has remained completely Oriental.[57]

Hayakawa's foreign appeal served him well in the late 1910s and early 1920s, but not in the 1930s. In a political climate hostile to immigrants exemplified by the 1924 Immigration Act, it is not surprising that the article promoted American-born Wong in a far more positive light than immigrant Hayakawa. This passage displays how the inscrutable, unintelligible male "oriental" was not as palatable as the hybrid, cosmopolitan, Westernized female.

Demonstrating the importance of accent and national origin in claiming modernity, the contrast in their speaking voices was starkly apparent in a 1931 Hollywood movie that starred both Wong and Hayakawa, *Daughter of the Dragon*. In *Daughter*, Wong's clear lilting diction made all of her lines intelligible, whereas Hayakawa's thick accent made him difficult to comprehend. Like many other silent movie actors in the talking era, Hayakawa's unacceptable voice overshadowed the memorable facial gestures that served him so well in the silent era.[58] *Daughter of the Dragon* became one of Hayakawa's last major Hollywood roles until the 1957 feature *Bridge on the River Kwai*.[59]

Wong's fame in English film circles can be witnessed through *Elstree Calling*. In it, Wong has a short scene-stealing role as Katherine from Wil-

---

57. *Motion Picture Magazine,* October 1931.

58. Miyao, *Sessue Hayakawa.* For an insightful analysis of Sessue Hayakawa's creation and use of stereotypes in his silent movie roles, see Donald Kirihara, "The Accepted Idea Displaced: Stereotype and Sessue Hayakawa," in *The Birth of Whiteness: Race and the Emergence of U.S. Cinema,* ed. Daniel Bernardi (New Brunswick, NJ: Rutgers University Press, 1996), 81–99.

59. In *Bridge,* like the foreign-born actresses Umeki, Nuyen, and Kwan, Hayakawa found an opportunity to display his acting talents and non-American-accented English voice and was rewarded with an Academy Award nomination for best supporting actor.

liam Shakespeare's *The Taming of the Shrew*.[60] The equivalent of an all-star Hollywood revue, *Elstree Calling* consists of nineteen interlinked vignettes with the common thread of a thwarted aspiring Shakespearean actor. The film is renowned for Hitchcock's appearance in one of the vignettes as well as his direction of some of them and for its exceedingly early reference to television as represented by a nonworking television set. The humor in the film derives from British actor Donald Calthrop's satirically thwarted attempts to play Shakespearean roles. For example, in one clip, the multiple stage curtains keep closing in front of him as he tries to perform, hiding him time after time. Another episode features a magic show with tricks that go wrong as he discusses Shakespeare. The host who introduces *The Taming of the Shrew* announces that Calthrop will do a "marvelous impersonation" of Douglas Fairbanks and he has the "good taste" to have chosen Wong as his leading lady. The host refers to *Thief of Baghdad* (1924) in which the dashing Douglas Fairbanks Jr. stars and Wong plays the lovely albeit scantily clad maiden. Calthrop's Petrucchio "woos" Wong to no avail. As he heads up the stairs to find her, tires, chairs, and tables tumble down. Wong as Katherine, who has thrown the furniture, appears at the top of the stairs, hurling insults in Cantonese. This is another example of playing Shakespeare going awry, for instead of being wooed, an enraged Katherine throws cream pies. Wong wears a costume similar to the one she sported for the Siamese dance in *Piccadilly*. This is a marvelous moment when one likes to imagine that Wong's anger on-screen stands in for the multitude of issues that probably made her furious: not being cast in critically respected Shakespearean roles but being typecast instead in oriental ones, the white male establishment, and portraying a colonial female subject wearing a revealing costume. As befits such an enraged female heroine, the scene ends with Wong throwing the pie squarely in Shakespeare's face. In this particular instance, the shrew does not get tamed.

Fashion: Beyond the Banana Skirt

Wong and Baker generated a new type of modern through glamour and fashion. In the 1920s and 1930s, glamourous racial modernity had an uneasy relationship to orientalism and primitivism, which explains the women's appeal. As literary scholar Judith Brown argues: "Glamour derives from a paradoxical indulgence in an aestheticizing distancing of the primitive through formal

---

60. *Elstree Calling* (1930), "Anna May Wong Throws a Cream Pie at Shakespeare," Minute 7:43: Donald Calthrop.

control and brings into relation orientalist and Africanist primitivism."[61] German film star Marlene Dietrich is a prime example of this dynamic. She underscored her star persona through embodying the primitive or the other, which highlighted her whiteness and glamour.[62] Wong would have been one of Dietrich's early exemplars of race and glamour when they met in Berlin in 1928. Later, as Wong's costar, Dietrich played Shanghai Lily, foil to Wong's Hu-Fei, in the Josef von Sternberg film *Shanghai Express* (1932). Both Wong and Dietrich acted as sexually threatening women shot through with the exotic, but glamour operated in different ways for each woman. As a nonwhite woman, Wong embodied the threat of the oriental and the primitive; therefore, her elegance was necessary to mitigate the threat. In other words, just as Dietrich needed characters such as Shanghai Lily or the gorilla costume in *Blond Venus* (1932) to offset her whiteness and heighten her glamour, Wong utilized elegance to counteract the threat of her racialized body. Wong's ability to play with both the modern and the primitive, in her case the oriental, gave her glamour and powered her stardom.

Wong and Baker challenged colonial culture not only onstage and onscreen but also offstage, through their attire. Wong and Baker deployed gendered modernity and performed upper-class mores through fashions that contravened their typecasting as premodern. Although in their stage and film performances they represented the "oriental," the "African," and the "other," their alterity was mediated by, contradicted by, and, in fact, predicated on their adoption of offstage elite Westernized fashion and manners. In response to primitivism, of which someone like Sarah Bartmann, also known as the Hottentot Venus, was symbolic, with her combined Asian and African features, both Wong and Baker transcended their working-class American backgrounds by not only learning how to dress like upper-class European white women but also trumping them.[63] Initially both Wong and Baker wore clothes in noncontemporary ways—Wong in the Chinese robes on the covers of *The Sketch* and *Tatler,* Baker topless in a banana skirt—while offstage they quickly established their visual modernity. While America's *Time* magazine called Baker a "Negro wench" and "buck-toothed," in France, conversely, the

61. Judith Brown, *Glamour in Six Dimensions: Modernism and the Radiance of Form* (Ithaca, NY: Cornell University Press, 2009), 189n13.

62. Mary Ann Doane, "Dark Continent: Epistemologies of Racial and Sexual Difference in Psychoanalysis and the Cinema," in *Femmes Fatales: Feminism, Film Theory, and Psychoanalysis* (London: Routledge, 1991), 215; E. Ann Kaplan, *Looking for the Other: Feminism, Film, and the Imperial Gaze* (New York: Routledge, 1997), 73.

63. Sander Gilman, *Difference and Pathology: Stereotypes of Sexuality, Race, and Madness* (Ithaca, NY: Cornell University Press, 1985).

press dwelled on Baker's beauty and talent. Baker became the wealthiest and best-dressed woman of African descent in Europe, complete with a chateau, designer clothing, and a pet leopard. The Mayfair Mannequin Society of New York acknowledged Wong's efforts by crowning her the "Best Dressed Woman of the Year." In their public lives, both Wong and Baker contervened their typecasting.[64]

As fashion icons, Wong and Baker shaped the modern. Although they dressed like white European and American women, frequently they utilized "exotic" touches in ways that created a distinctly new modern. Wong transformed the coolie hat from a symbol of Chinese peasantry into a high-fashion item. She would model the hat with a suit that had fashionable Western tailoring. At times that suit would be hybrid, made with Asian silk or a frog fastening detail, but as cutting-edge concoctions rather than primitive or traditional ones.[65] Instead, it was European American women who would wear Asian fashions as exotic and antiquated. Wong's fashion iconography embedded the exotic within the modern, breaking down the artificial temporal and spatial distance between traditional and modern, East and West, and in doing so furthered the changing aesthetics of modernity. Unlike Picasso and Gauguin, who created modern art by not only depicting African and Pacific Islander cultures but also borrowing from those aesthetics, the women themselves were supposed to "naturally" embody primitive and non-Western cultures. As their bodies reflected the primitive, applying contemporary touches fashioned an even more complex version of modernity. Baker dressed in upper-class high fashion to complicate any notion of primitivism or exoticism. Both women insisted on temporal contemporaneity. This was different from the white female "star" image and lifestyle because of the highly charged issues of sexuality and respectability as well as because of the commodification of exoticism.

Then and now, Wong became lauded for wearing the latest fashion with panache. Take, for example, her famous culottes outfit. It was a riff on menswear, yet the bows on her shoes and her cloche hat mark her as female and as a flapper. So while the jacket, tie, and shirt were menswear, the culottes themselves were a skirtlike version of trousers. Wong was pictured wearing culottes in Chicago as well as London. In a nod to contemporary relevance, *New York* magazine's fashion spread on culottes through history featured the image of Wong representing culottes in the 1920s.[66]

64. "Josephine Baker Is a St. Louis Washerwoman's Daughter," *Time*, February 10, 1936; Alma Whitaker, "Which Star Really Deserves the Best Dressed Woman Title?," *Los Angeles Times*, October 28, 1943, 2.

65. Anna May Wong, photograph, Paramount Pictures files, AMPAS.

66. *New York* magazine, June 15–28, 2015, 58.

In France, Baker shifted her image from that of a savage dancer to a modern superstar. In the United States today, it is Baker bare chested in a banana skirt that continues to be the enduring image. However, in France starting in the late 1920s, she deliberately changed that image. In variety shows at the Casino de Paris such as *Paris qui Remue* and *La Joie de Paris,* Baker evolved a glamourous modern persona intermixed with her performances of the colonial and racial other. From the beginning, there were displays of the modern. Baker's first performance in France merged American modernism with the colonial primitive. In one critical scene in the 1925 *La Revue Nègre,* Baker, engulfed by a stage set comprising urban American skyscrapers, leaves civilization to become an African jungle woman.[67] You can see the emergence of an American-influenced modern star in Baker's January 1928 *Les Adieum de Josephine à Paris* song titles: "Chants et Danses Américaines," "The Man I Love," "Muddy Water," and "Charleston Chante et Danse par Josephine Baker."[68] Gustave Beer designed her costumes, which were quite modern. It was precisely because she was the modern black star that she could play the colonial subject over and over again.

Baker's portrayals of oriental roles such as "L'Hawaïenne" and "La Petite Tonkinoise," the subject of the next chapter, occurred as she transformed her image.[69] Her particular brand of the modern as well as her visual importance to French culture is evident in the magazine coverage of her fashions and of her film roles. For those without access to the variety show performances, periodicals would more broadly distribute striking images of her. For example, Baker graced the cover of *Ciné-Mirroir* on January 6, 1928. She presents the ultimate portrait of the glamourous film star who, like an actual star, radiates light all around her. Her smile accentuates her luminescence, as do her eyes and teeth that gleam, capturing the light that is further refracted in her round sparkling necklace and earrings. The white background further illuminates Baker as a star, for the darkness of her skin tone and hair pop out against that paleness. Baker personified the racial minority colonial woman as a civilized radiant star. French fashion magazines echoed the cinema magazines' portrayal of Baker as a modern woman by depicting her in ensembles designed by fashion luminaries such as Vionnet, Poiret, and Schiaparelli.

---

67. Jacques Patin, *Le Figaro,* October 7, 1925.

68. Program, *Les Adieum de Josephine à Paris,* 1928, Josephine Baker Clipping File, Bibliothèque Nationale de France Richelieu.

69. For more on the concept of performance, see Karen Shimakawa, *National Abjection: The Asian American Body Onstage* (Durham, NC: Duke University Press, 2002); Brooks, *Bodies in Dissent.*

Josephine Baker, by Stanislaus Julian Walery.

(National Portrait Gallery, Smithsonian Institution.)

Josephine Baker as a New Woman, by Carl Van Vechten.

(Library of Congress, Prints & Photographs Division, Carl Van Vechten Collection [reproduction number LOT 12735, no. 76].)

The French press depicted Baker in a variety of outfits emblematic of the "New Woman." The New Woman of that era typically worked for a living, enjoyed adventures, and operated in the public sphere.[70] The French newspaper *Figaro* reported on "Josephine Baker Aviatrice," complete with photographs.[71] Newspapers also printed photographs of Baker as a newsboy, wearing a newsboy cap and holding a copy of *L'instransige* in her hands.[72] Baker's play with androgyny and male clothing received publicity. In fact, wearing male clothing was a sign of Baker's comfort with her femininity, and worked to accentuate that femininity. This resonates with Baker's cover image for the aforementioned *Simplicissimus*.

Mixing high and low cultures, Baker paraded her avant-garde panache. In one newspaper photograph, Baker is en pointe (on the tips of her toes), wearing ballet slippers. She wears a dress with a white collar, possibly a sailor suit. Her fingers are on top of her head, pointing down and touching, pinky and thumb extended 180 degrees. Her feet are crossed, legs bent, knees splayed out, almost like a Charleston en pointe with her upper body reminiscent of the photographs of Baker with her eyes crossed.[73] Baker mixes the high culture of formal ballet with the popular culture of a comic dance outfit all combined into her Charleston-like pose.

Traveling Modernity

As part of the civilizing and colonizing project, the European (and American) film industry exported their products to their colonial territories. Through the mass media, Wong's, and to a lesser extent Baker's, American modernity was put on display in colonial Africa. The images and portrayals of modernity they represented did not always mean the same thing that they did in Europe or the United States.

Press coverage divulged how Wong's performances affected those confronting colonialism directly. For example, Wong's role in her first talking picture, the *Flame of Love* (1930), merited front-page discussion in Mozambique's bourgeois black African and *mestiço* (mixed-race) newspaper, *O Brado*

70. Modern Girl around the World Research Group, ed., *The Modern Girl around the World: Consumption, Modernity, and Globalization* (Durham, NC: Duke University Press, 2008).

71. "Josephine Baker Aviatrice," *Figaro,* November 5, 1935, Bibliothèque Nationale de France Richelieu, Arts et Spectacles, 4-ICO PER 1326.

72. Ibid.

73. Folies Bergère interview/story about Baker, *Le Matin,* April 24, 1934, 7, Bibliothèque Nationale de France Richelieu, Arts et Spectacles, 4-ICO PER 1326.

Africano. This newspaper was the mouthpiece of the small bourgeois group of Africans and *mestiços* in Lorenço Marques (Maputo). Until the 1930s, when Portuguese prime minister Antonio de Oliviera Salazar instituted strict censorship, the paper was fairly critical of the Portuguese, although it could never have been considered more than liberal. An article called "Do Estrañero" appeared on the front page of the paper on June 20, 1931. The writer praised Wong's singing voice, deeming it "as splendid as the oriental flutes."[74] The writer raved about the "oriental ballads" in the film. The Mozambicans may not have had access to all of the other media forms in which Wong's American modernity played out. As a *Variety* review stated, in *Flame of Love,* "Miss Wong talks flat American."[75] Given that Mozambique was a Portuguese colony, audiences were not native English speakers, making the distinction between American English and British English moot. Wong's lack of power to speak to the press in these colonies demonstrates how her American modernity could be subsumed to colonial projects.

On April 25, 1928, Wong and Baker appeared on facing pages in *South African Pictorial: Stage and Screen,* a magazine chiefly aimed at South Africa's white, well-to-do, English-speaking settlers.[76] On page 8, a story about Baker appeared, on page 9, a photograph of Wong, and directly below the picture of Wong, an advertisement for Shem el Nessim, an exotic fragrance of Araby. Looking pensive with eyes modestly cast sideways and down, Wong is dressed in elaborate Chinese robes. She is seated with her legs crossed on cushions, leaning against a silk backdrop. There is no text, just a caption with her name, Wong. Wong's American modernity is subsumed in an orientalized portrait. Yet the perfume advertisement directly below her touts the "subtle alluring perfume of a modern women's dainty charm. It comes from the East and weaves a spell with the haunting, thrilling night scents of a slumbering English garden." Although Wong is not promoting the perfume, the advertisement's placement implies it. Yet that same page 9 indicates ambivalence about race and performance, specifically jazz. Immediately to the left of the picture of Wong and the Shem el Nessim advertisement is a brief story about Muriel George and Ernest Butcher. The two, who typically sang folk songs, had found a welcoming reception despite the introduction of jazz to London by other artists. As an American and African American perform-

74. "Do Estrañero," *O Brado Africano,* June 20, 1931, front page. I thank Lloys Frates for calling my attention to this article.

75. *Variety,* November 5, 1930.

76. *South African Pictorial: Stage and Screen,* April 25, 1928, 8–9.

ing art, jazz had taken London by storm, which potentially marginalized white South African performers such as George and Butcher.

On the opposite page, Pamela Tavers's weekly *South African Pictorial* column featured Baker. According to Tavers, actresses habitually pull publicity stunts ranging from faking jewelry losses to promenading with monkeys. As she states: "Josephine Baker has outshone them all."[77] Tavers referred to Baker driving an ostrich-drawn dogcart through the streets of Vienna as an apology to Johann Strauss, with whom she had quarreled. Tavers ends her column by suggesting that, given all of the ostriches in the country, South Africans should emulate Baker's example. Given South Africa's white colonial rule, the suggestion that Baker could be a role model startles. Perhaps the distance between Vienna and South Africa allowed that suggestion, or perhaps Tavers believed that star power offset racial difference. Possibly the suggestion is sarcastic. It is worth noting that there was no picture of Baker, nor any reference to her blackness. Instead, Tavers discussed Baker in a matter-of-fact manner, as if the audience should know her.

Baker became a touchstone for black Antillean communities in Paris in the early 1930s. Baker was a racialized colonial symbol not just for white French audiences but for the actual colonial populations. As historian Jennifer Boittin has found, the Antillean Paris newspaper *La Dépêche Africaine* (the African dispatch) in 1930 responded to right-wing journalism in other publications by publishing defenses of Baker.[78] In addition, Baker was used by black Parisian groups such as the Union des Travailleurs Nègres to attract audiences to their events. As Boittin writes, "The ease with which anti-imperialist men latched onto Baker as the perfect vehicle for their undertaking—both as a representative of colonialism and as a celebrity bound to attract an audience—shows how reverse exoticism permitted them to manipulate existing representations of otherness to their own political ends."[79] Parisian blacks did not approve of Baker's support of Mussolini and fascism nor her lack of support for black artists in the Folies Bergère in 1936. Yet disapproval of Baker was significant, for as Boittin argues, "members of the subversive racial counterculture of anti-imperialists supported Baker's position as a cultural symbol by developing their rhetoric around her actions, imagined or real, and stances."[80] Beloved or not, Baker was an important symbol for black Parisians.

---

77. Ibid., 8.

78. Jennifer Boittin, *Colonial Metropolis: The Urban Grounds of Feminism and Anti-imperialism in Interwar Paris* (Lincoln: University of Nebraska Press, 2010), 28–29.

79. Ibid., 116.

80. Ibid., 33.

Conclusion

Through dance, cinematic, and stage performances, Wong and Baker utilized their training in American racial minority communities to reinvent the modern in Europe. Performing in Europe at the height of French and British colonialism, they were called on to depict colonial, primitive, and sexually "other" women. As women have been made the bearers of culture, modernity and tradition fall disproportionately on them. Through onstage and offstage performative gestures such as voice, clothing, and dance improvisation, both Wong and Baker broke down the binaries at the heart of modernity, creating a new type of modern.

Chapter 3, "'I Can Play Any Type of Oriental,'" continues the examination of both Baker and Wong. As an imperial center, France was a primary site of transnational performance. Comparing Baker's and Wong's oriental performances attests to divergences and convergences of the racialized body and how racial modernity is a relational process. Examining the women's differing trajectories reveals that the black colonial body could fit into French nation-state narratives, whereas the oriental one could not and was subject to diasporic belonging.

"I Can Play Any Type of Oriental"

Anna Watches Josephine
at the Casino de Paris, 1932

Paris, 1932: Amid stares and murmurs, Chinese American actress Anna May Wong takes her seat in a mezzanine box at the Casino de Paris. The curtains open onto a tropical island set with palm trees, a waterfall, and canoes shooting the rapids. At center stage American entertainer Josephine Baker chants, gesticulating with her trademark energy in order to personify "L'Hawaïenne" (The Female Hawaiian). At the dramatic apex the entire cast appears on stage with Baker. The audience roars with approval, from time to time gazing at Wong to gauge her reaction. Wong applauds enthusiastically with the crowd.

This moment opens up questions about the dynamics of race in the heart of imperial France. Why is Anna May Wong, the leading "oriental" actress in the world, watching one of the greatest African American comedic singers and dancers of all time perform a Hawaiian role in Paris? Why were both American women playing Southeast Asian and Pacific Islander roles? How were these performances manifestations of race and American modernity? Through moments like Wong looking at Josephine Baker perform "L'Hawaïenne," this chapter diagrams a complicated nexus of colonialism and orientalism, nation-state and diasporic belonging, temporality, and gender and sexuality.

Baker, in turn, registered Wong as someone who served as the iconographic referent for all things "oriental." In addition to exploring Baker's oriental roles, this chapter reveals Wong's stardom in France. There, she made films, performed vaudeville, granted press interviews, vacationed, and published a piece on interracial romance. Not only did Wong's films circulate throughout France, Europe, and the colonial world; her image also graced the covers of magazines, making her one of the most ubiquitous of "oriental" women. By the time she witnessed Baker's performance of "L'Hawaïenne," Wong had adorned the covers of the French magazines *Cinémonde* and *Ciné-Mirroir*, and her films *Song/Show Life* (1928), *Piccadilly* (1929), and *Hai-Tang/Flame of Love/Le Chemin du Déshounneur/The Road to Dishonour* (1930) had screened in France. Traces of Wong's impact can be detected in Baker's performances. Baker's oriental roles were created later than Wong's, yet Baker's "oriental" costuming was very similar, particularly in the 1930 production of "La Petite Tonkinoise," where her headdress and dance costume bore a striking resemblance to Wong's from the 1929 film *Piccadilly* as well as in the film *Hai-Tang*.[1] The two women mutually informed each other's enactments of racial difference. Most scholarship about Baker or Wong examines them as creators as well as creations of their white audiences. Rather than situating them vis-à-vis their white audiences, I consider what it means for these women to be influenced by each other.

This chapter remedies the tunnel vision prompted by looking at Baker as the dominant, often sole, racial minority performer in France by analyzing Wong's performances. Examining both women's portrayals of the oriental highlights how racial modernity forms as a relational process. At the height of colonialism, Baker was the touchstone of racial difference in France. Most scholars have focused on Baker's portrayals of Africanness and blackness, including her Arab North African roles. What scholars who examine Baker's oeuvre neglect to do is to scrutinize her colonial roles, such as "L'Hawaïenne" and "La Petite Tonkinoise," within the broader context of oriental performances.

Race in general and orientalism in particular were mutually constitutive poles of otherness. The relationship between performing oriental roles and temporality was a quixotic one, with different valences for each woman. One of the most important points I make throughout this book is that when Wong played "oriental roles," she engaged in cross-cultural and cross-racial performance. Yet confused audiences frequently misinterpreted as authentic Wong's typically antiquated and noncontemporary oriental roles. My second finding in this chapter is that each woman had different relationships to na-

---

1. *Film Weekly*, February 11, 1929, cover; "The Flame of Love" publicity materials, James Anderson Collection, Box 20, British Film Institute Special Collections; *La Rampe*, December 1930, Josephine Baker Dossier, Opèra Paris, Bibliothèque Nationale de France.

tion-state belonging. When I examine the women's trajectories I demonstrate that the black colonial body could fit into French nation-state narratives, whereas the oriental one could not. It is through depicting oriental roles that Baker as an African American became incorporated into the French nation-state, whereas Wong as an Asian American became diasporic.

American Racial Modernity Meets Paris, the Capital of Modernity

It is not entirely surprising that Anna May Wong witnessed Josephine Baker's performance at the Casino de Paris; Paris was predisposed to embrace American racial modernity. As the "capital of modernity," to use David Harvey's evocative phrase, Paris had enjoyed decades of welcoming expatriates as well as avant-garde artists.[2] Paris represented the epitome of public modern culture, a "City of Light" with vivid nightlife, restaurants, and cafés and a great global center for the fine arts, music, film, and theater. Walter Benjamin, the protagonist of Chapter 1, immortalized Paris as the preeminent modern city with his arcades project and his writings about the flâneur. Noted modern writers such as Americans Gertrude Stein, Ernest Hemingway, and Ezra Pound called the city home, as did a plethora of visual artists such as Spanish expatriate Pablo Picasso. The ban on alcohol in the United States during the Prohibition era and the relatively inexpensive cost of living in Paris made the French capital especially alluring. There was no formal legal racial segregation in France as there was in the United States, so African American artists and writers made Paris home, which made it an expatriate site of the Harlem Renaissance.[3]

In the 1920s and 1930s, European colonialism in general and French colonialism in particular collapsed and elided varying modalities of racial difference into a more generalized colonial otherness that met at the oriental. As the opening moment of Baker playing a Hawaiian woman reveals, she could portray a variety of races in a homogenization of racialized histories. In Paris, Baker depicted Vietnamese, Pacific Islander, North African, and Arab women. Given French interests in the South Pacific, the appeal of watching Baker play a Pacific Islander/Hawaiian role fit orientalist tropes. Hawaii's mixed-race population and geographically hybrid location at the edge of both

---

2. David Harvey, *Paris, Capital of Modernity* (New York: Routledge, 2003).

3. Tyler Stovall, *Paris Noir: African Americans in the City of Light* (New York: Mariner Books, 1996); Sue Peabody and Tyler Stovall, eds., *The Color of Liberty: Histories of Race in France* (Durham, NC: Duke University Press, 2003); Heike Raphael-Hernandez, *Blackening Europe: The African American Presence* (New York: Routledge, 2003).

the South Pacific and the orient/Asia made it an enticing site. As both France and the United States had imperial interests in the Pacific Islands, Hawaii occupied a special place where colonialism and orientalism converged.[4] As colonial ventures in China, Southeast Asia, and the South Pacific intensified, interest in the areas did as well. Orientalism denotes the discursive formation of otherness as well as the "orient" as an imagined "Eastern" culture, typically the confluence of multiple real and imagined influences. Leading scholar of Hawaii's hula culture Adria Imada argues that orientalism's imperial and sexualized dynamics impact how hula and Hawaiian culture are understood.[5] Although one could argue that the "real" Hawaii was far from the "orient," the imagined Hawaii that Baker brought to life at the Casino de Paris slotted neatly into these variations of orientalism.

The desire to watch Wong or Baker play oriental roles is related to colonial aspirations to control particular geographic regions of the world. Those performances helped form the colonial imaginary, which is reflected in the degree to which Southeast Asia and the Pacific Islands serve as reference points for both women's work. Given French political control in Indochina and British control in Malaya and Burma, portrayals such as Baker's "La Tonkinoise," or Wong's "Siamese" dance from *Piccadilly* (1929) were popular. The battles for imperial domination in Southeast Asia mattered; although Thailand (Siam) was never colonized by European powers, it acted as a buffer between British and French colonial interests. By 1893, at the expense of Thailand, the French controlled the Mekong River into Laos, establishing French Indochina (consisting of Laos, Vietnam, and Cambodia) with Hanoi (Tonkin) as the capital in 1902. The French sought to eradicate Sinification (Chinese influence) in eastern Indochina, where recruitment into the state machinery and the ruling class were heavily Sinicized in culture. That gave the French colonial administration added impetus to replace Chinese-inflected power structures and intellectual thought with French language and culture.[6] A Chinese body such as Wong's embodying "La Tonkinoise" could threaten the consolidation of French culture away from Sinification, whereas Baker's body would not.[7]

---

4. Vernadette Vicuña Gonzalez, *Securing Paradise: Tourism and Militarism in Hawai'i and the Philippines* (Durham, NC: Duke University Press, 2013).

5. Adria Imada, *Aloha America: Hula Circuits through the U.S. Empire* (Durham, NC: Duke University Press, 2012), 12.

6. Benedict Anderson, *Imagined Communities: Reflections on the Origin and Spread of Nationalism* (New York: Verso, 1991), 125–126.

7. Patrice Morlat, *Les affaires politiques de l'Indochine, 1895–1923: Les grands commis, du savoir au pouvoir* (Paris: L'Harmattan, 1995); Patrice Morlat, *La repression coloniale au Vietnam (1908–1940)* (Paris: L'Harmattan, 1990).

Even if "L'Hawaïenne" makes more sense as an homage to American imperialism, it played well in Paris because of France's colonial territories in the South Pacific, including French Polynesia and New Caledonia. Part of the French Overseas Departments and Territories (*départements et territoires d'outre-mer*), these territories hold varying legal statuses and different levels of autonomy, although all (except those with no permanent inhabitants) have representation in the French Parliament. Currently 2.7 million people inhabit the French Overseas Departments and Territories, which include islands in the Atlantic, Pacific, Indian, and Antarctic oceans as well as French Guiana.[8] Through Baker's performance of "L'Hawaïenne," the French could imagine their presence in the South Pacific and other tropical islands as normalized and legitimate.

To add another layer of complexity, the American modernity of both women was critical to their ability to thrive in imperial Europe. One of the key aspects of Baker's success in Europe was her American racial modernity: it both enabled her to bring rich African American performing traditions to Europe and gave her an intermediary status that entitled her to perform the exotic without the drawbacks of being an actual colonial subject. The performance of racial difference, in the guise of both jazz and numbers like "L'Hawaïenne," ameliorated the malaise of modernity and naturalized imperialism. Baker's tableaux at the Casino de Paris included not only "L'Hawaïenne" and "La Petite Tonkinoise" but also "The Soul of Jazz." This was distinctly different from the French colonial North African and Caribbean roles that she portrayed in her films such as *Zou Zou* (1934) and *Princess Tam Tam* (1935). What is fascinating is that in her four film performances, Baker portrays neither sub-Saharan Africans nor African Americans. It is in her vaudeville productions such as the ones at the Casino de Paris that she performs a greater range of racial representations. The very comic nature of Baker's colonial performances combined with her frequent costume changes reveal her oriental parts as inauthentic assumed performances. Therein lies the dis-orienting potential of Baker's work.

Like Baker, for Wong American modernity in combination with her racialized otherness held the key to her success in 1920s Europe. Wong's racial Americanized image not only permitted her work to flourish; it also let her be a safe "other." As an American, she was not an immediate colonial subject; therefore, her presence was not a symptom of colonial malfunction such as immigration to the metropole or miscegenation. She was simultaneously dif-

---

8. "Overseas France," Wikipedia, en.wikipedia.org/wiki/Overseas_France (accessed October 22, 2018).

ferently exotic yet safely distant.[9] The door was open for Wong as a diasporic citizen of the world or citizen of nowhere. An analogous formation functioned for Baker. Baker's training in African American performance traditions combined with her dark skin made her irresistible to French audiences. Baker could be simultaneously authentically black and authentically modern. As Baker's cross-racial performances included the oriental as well as Afrodiasporic roles, she had a far greater performance range than Wong, who was almost always cast as some version of the oriental. Wong was continually in danger of having her American modernity not recognized by audiences and being misconstrued as authentically oriental.

By the time Wong watched Baker perform "L'Hawaïenne" in the 1930s, the Parisian cultural climate was changing from the exuberance of the Jazz Age in the 1920s to a more somber Depression-era culture, with fewer American expatriates. Although historian Tyler Stovall has found that the Depression came relatively late to France, it did arrive and reduced disposable income, especially for entertainment.[10] As the Depression whittled down the liveliness of café life, and as the end of Prohibition in 1932 made the United States more appealing, many Americans returned home. Nonetheless, despite the economic cutbacks, the appeal of the performance of the colonial other meant that both Wong and Baker found numerous opportunities for work in France.

Anna Watches Josephine

What does it mean to have Anna May Wong, the leading actress of oriental roles, watch Josephine Baker, one of the all-time music hall greats, portray a Hawaiian? This is a peculiar moment that speaks to the importance of depicting Pacific Islanders, for we would not expect Baker as an African American to play a Hawaiian role. We would instead anticipate Baker's range to go beyond jazz to include African and Caribbean roles, which reference the African diaspora. However, as Noenoe Silva has found, under U.S. imperialism, cartoons racialized Hawaiian Queen Lili'uokalani in ways that

---

9. "Wong's Americanness distances her from the more 'threatening' manifestations of hybridity and miscegenation, resulting from the breakdowns in colonial segregation or from Chinese immigration." Tim Bergfelder, "Negotiating Exoticism: Hollywood, Film Europe and the Cultural Reception of Anna May Wong," in *"Film Europe" and "Film America": Cinema, Commerce and Cultural Exchange, 1920–1939,* ed. Andrew Higson and Richard Maltby (Exeter, UK: University of Exeter Press, 1999), 320.

10. Stovall, *Paris Noir,* 83.

appeared similar to depictions of African Americans.[11] This relationality of racialization between African Americans and Native Hawaiians held in the United States, not just France.

Wong watching Baker's performances in Paris signifies multiple levels of appropriation and displaces the simplistic dynamics of the white straight male gaze that undergirds performances of the primitive and the other under the auspices of modernity. We can imagine, at one level, Wong scrutinizing Baker in a pedagogy of race and dance at the Casino de Paris. Wong observes the acknowledged mistress of race and performance exhibit blackness, yellowness, and the longing for whiteness. We will never know if Wong felt that Baker encroached on her territory. When we consider Wong looking at Baker at the Casino de Paris, Wong as a nonwhite audience member who is also a performer nuances the power dynamics of who watches Baker. Most of the critical work on Baker has presupposed a white audience, not an audience of an Asian American performer.

Wong witnessed Baker's multiple roles in the *La Joie de Paris* in 1932–1933 at the Casino de Paris nightclub. The show was a huge production in two acts with fifty tableaux and numerous performers, all with Baker at the center. In this program, almost all of Baker's roles reflected some aspect of racialized and/or colonial difference. Witness titles such as the dance "L'Exoticisme," performance extravaganzas such as the "Soul of Jazz," "L'Oiseaux des Îles" as well as "L'Hawaïenne" and songs such as "Si J'étais Blanche." *La Joie*'s final number featured Baker as a Water Fairy.[12] "L'Hawaïenne" is one of the biggest numbers of the entire *La Joie de Paris* program. Whereas most of the fifty plus pieces merit one or two lines on the program, the listing for "L'Hawaïenne" fills an entire page complete with creative credits. "L'Hawaïenne" was a highlight of a *La Joie de Paris* revue and did not practice moderation.

When commenting on the entire production of *La Joie de Paris,* French reviewers singled out "L'Hawaïenne" as noteworthy. For example, Gustave Fréjaville in *Comoedia* wrote about the excesses of the production: "Hawaii, where one sees canoes gliding on the rapids and a waterfall gushes at the bottom of the scene in an enchanted atmosphere."[13] In *Le Tempo,* December 1932, Guy LaBorde wrote in his article, "La Revue du Casino de Paris,"

11. Noenoe Silva, *Aloha Betrayed: Native Hawaiian Resistance to U.S. Imperialism* (Durham, NC: Duke University Press, 2004).

12. Program, *La Joie de Paris,* 1932–1933, Anna May Wong Gift Collection, Box 8401, Billy Rose Theatre Collection, New York Public Library, Performing Arts Branch.

13. Gustave Fréjaville, "Au Casino de Paris 'La Joie de Paris,'" *Comoedia,* December 13, 1932, Opèra Folio 1932, Dossier Josephine Baker, 20.

"She [Baker] will not be a female savage after such a new contrasting [role]." LaBorde continued: "In a Hawaiian jungle, where hair tangles with flowers and where the waterfalls sound like human chants. . . . She becomes her dance and entirely the girl of her sky."[14] The set enchanted the reviewers, who saw new possibilities for Baker, including her transformation into a birdlike or angelic figure in the sky.

For Wong, watching Baker was a valuable education in how the oriental could be made marketable in front of French and, by extension, British and European theater audiences. Oriental themes also prevailed among the fifty songs, dances, and tableaux in the *La Joie de Paris*. In this production, as befits a French orientalism that stretches from the Middle East to the South Pacific, additional titles included "La Chinoiserie," "Le Grand Turc," and "La Turquerie" by the composer Sergei Rachmaninoff. In *La Joie de Paris*, "L'Hawaïenne" was thus one among several portrayals of the orient, albeit the most elaborate and the only one starring Baker. Given the quick-change nature of the program and the fact that there were more than fifty numbers meant that some of the shorter skits could last as long as it took one person to get across the stage, whereas show-stopping numbers such as "L'Hawaïenne" would take longer, with far more people involved. Through such a production, Wong learned that portraying the oriental other from a wide range of geographic regions, sometimes in combination, proved popular. These lessons proved invaluable in the creation of her own variety revue that toured France in 1934–1935.

In the same production at the Casino de Paris, Wong observed another example of cross-racial performance. In *La Joie de Paris*, Baker debuted her controversial performance "Si J'étais Blanche" (If I Were White). Wearing a white wig, Baker began her performance singing "I would like to be white. How happy I would be." Using the French conditional tense, Baker makes it clear that she is not actually white, rather, she is imagining what it would be like to be white. Baker had a long history of ambiguous feelings about her skin color, reportedly lightening it with lemon juice and creams, and it is possible to interpret this moment as Baker's desire to be white. A conservative reading of this performance would see it as reinscribing colonial racial power relations. However, it can also be read as a transgression of traditional blackface in which white performers put on black makeup. A black performer assuming whiteface could alarm audiences, for it had the possibility of reversing the power dynamics—the group with societal power traditionally dons the makeup and mimics the other, not vice versa.

---

14. Guy LaBorde, "La Revue du Casino de Paris," *Le Tempo*, December 1932, Opèra Folio 1932, Dossier Josephine Baker, 18.

Contemporary audiences understood the performance of "Si J'étais Blanche" to be whiteface and parody.[15] The comic undertones of Baker's racial play were noted in the press. In a review of "Noire ou Blanche" (Black or White) at the Casino de Paris, it was reported that "Today—o miracle!—the young lady becomes lighter and lighter. Every day, to the astonishment of Henri Varna, her director, she whitens: at present it is the milk that takes over the coffee. What is this mystery? Josephine employs black magic to play for a day 'the white woman'?"[16] Toying with the language of black and white, the writer then asked, did Baker use black magic to portray a white woman? Through such reviews, the press circulated the idea that Baker playing a white woman was a comic gesture, one that riffed on racial authenticity.

What would have been particularly compelling to Wong is that in the Casino de Paris program for *La Joie de Paris,* Baker's Studio Piaz photograph headshot promotes her as a modern performing superstar. Baker gleams; her hair is dressed in ringlets, her eyes look right, and there are flowers in her hair. Her shoulders are bare, lips pursed into a bow with obvious lipstick, even though the photograph is in black and white with no smile or teeth on display. Her fingers are splayed; her hands are crossed and rest on those bare shoulders. The darkness of her eyes and café au lait of her skin mark her as representing the racialized other, but in the most marginal of ways. No longer the performing savage dancer, Baker proves her modern status and is on her way to becoming French. It is precisely because she has become the modern black star that she can play the colonial over and over again. Through Baker, Wong could learn how to embody the colonial and racial other in performance as well as the modern international star in publicity shots. Her career would advance through learning successfully how to display both.

Baker's "La Petite Tonkinoise" and "L'Hawaïenne" renditions can be read as an homage to Wong, which Wong witnessed performed back to her. Baker's oriental performances were crafted later than Wong's. Wong dances a Hawaiian hula in the film *Song/Show Life* (1928), which would have circulated in France by the time Wong saw Baker in "L'Hawaïenne." In fact it is Wong who simultaneously popularized and made into a high fashion object the coolie hat that Baker wore during her performance of "La Petite Tonkinoise." On one level, when Wong watches Baker, she witnesses Baker's staging of the Asian and Pacific Islander colonials and sees a paean to herself

15. Bennetta Jules-Rosette, *Josephine Baker in Art and Life: The Icon and the Image* (Urbana: University of Illinois Press, 2007), 63.

16. Review, "Noire ou Blanche," Josephine Baker Clipping File, Bibliothèque Nationale de France Richelieu, Arts et Spectacles, 4-ICO PER 1326.

as the ultimate oriental referent. Yet she also observes a dancer far more experienced and skilled than herself. Wong, then, could learn how Baker presented "exotic" dances in ways that pleased French audiences, which would have been welcome tutelage in creating her own vaudeville repertoire. Wong and Baker mutually constituted how to play the colonial oriental woman. Of course, these costumes may have been selected by costume designers or directors, the dance moves dictated by choreographers. But the "oriental" look became codified through how Baker and Wong performed their dance poses and wore those ensembles.

Josephine Baker as "La Tonkinoise"

Wearing a coolie hat and feathers, Josephine Baker sings and shakes her head from side to side. The audience howls with laughter. While declaring herself to be a Tonkinese who learns about China and Manchuria, she prances around the stage, pausing on each side to give the audience coy looks. The grand finale, titled "Les Colonies," is the favorite number of the entire evening.

In addition to her role as "L'Hawaïenne," Baker famously performed another oriental role (though not in front of Wong), "La Petite Tonkinoise" (The Little Vietnamese Woman). Both of these numbers reveal how, despite being African American, Baker could portray multiple kinds of oriental roles in Paris. In fact, it was because she was African American, not of Asian descent, that she could effectively play these roles. In variety shows such as *La Joie de Paris,* the sheer volume of personas adopted by Baker through her ability to be a quick-change artist bestowed a playful quality to that range of roles. However, her staging of these roles had both radical and conservative implications.

In the "La Petite Tonkinoise" musical tableau performed at the Casino de Paris's *Paris qui Remue,* Baker sang and danced the role of a Vietnamese consort of a French colonist in Tonkin/Vietnam.[17] Famed artist Paul Colin painted the prologue backdrops. "La Petite Tonkinoise" is the source for one of Baker's most famous anthems, "J'ai Deux Amours" (I Have Two Loves) the singing of which usually sent French audiences into a frenzy because they loved how Baker honored France. As leading Baker scholar Bennetta

---

17. Robert Brisacq called Baker's performance "one of a young intelligence, who sang with malice "Ma Tonkinoise." Robert Brisacq, *La Volonté*, October 11, 1930, *Josephine Baker vue par la Presse Française,* 19, Dossier Josephine Baker [10-5], Opèra Paris, Bibliothèque Nationale de France. See also Krystyn Moon, *Yellowface: Creating the Chinese in American Popular Music and Performance: 1850s–1920s* (New Brunswick, NJ: Rutgers University Press, 2005).

Jules-Rosette astutely points out, "J'ai Deux Amours" was inspired by how "La Petite Tonkinoise" referred to Vietnam under French colonialism.[18] In "J'ai Deux Amours" Baker positions herself as a Vietnamese colonial subject with dual affiliations. Tellingly, the lyrics transmuted. In the new formulation, Vietnam becomes Paris, and the colony drops out of the equation. It is through claiming Vietnam that Baker becomes Parisienne. By portraying the subjects of French colonies, Baker loses her African American heritage, and by playing a Vietnamese colonial woman, she becomes French. In a letter to critic Fréjaville, Baker wrote how much the success of "J'ai Deux Amours" pleased her.[19]

Thinking of "La Petite Tonkinoise" as cross-racial performance instead of yellowface allows us to see it as a performance that disrupts any notion of authenticity. Cross-racial performance, building on the concept of drag in queer studies, gives us the tools to understand the meaning of Baker's performances in *La Joie de Paris* and *Paris qui Remue*.[20] Cross-racial performance means portraying another race while making deliberately obvious your own racial background. Cross-racial performance, then, involves a trace of parody or irony or revelation or discrepancy. In other words, there are elements that expose the dynamics of acting the part rather than the desire to replace an original or to be authentic. This is in contrast to yellowface, when a person of European ancestry assumes "yellow" makeup and taped eyes and uses language and gestures that result in mockery.[21] In yellowface, there is often a desire to pass as authentic. In contrast, in all of Baker's cross-racial acts in *La Joie de Paris,* she is clearly identified as La Bakaire (the Baker), assuming multiple roles. Hence, I would argue that since she is not trying to hoodwink the audience by attempting to portray "authentic" oriental women, she is not playing yellowface but rather is toying with racial categories. In fact, the term "cross-racial performance" highlights the very instability of Baker's blackness, in which she performs a range of roles from an American jazz singer and dancer to a Hawaiian woman. Using yellowface to describe Baker's roles, on

---

18. Jules-Rosette, *Josephine Baker in Art and Life,* 62–63.

19. Josephine Baker to Gustave Fréjaville, Amsterdam, June 14, 1932, Opèra Paris, Bibliothèque Nationale de France.

20. Marjorie Garber, *Vested Interests: Cross-Dressing and Cultural Anxiety* (New York, Routledge, 1991); Judith Halberstam, *Female Masculinities* (Durham, NC: Duke University Press, 1998).

21. See Moon, *Yellowface.* There are numerous excellent studies of race and early Hollywood cinema, including Michael Rogin, *Black Face, White Noise: Jewish Immigrants in the Hollywood Melting Pot* (Berkeley: University of California Press, 1996); and Daniel Bernardi, ed., *The Birth of Whiteness: Race and the Emergence of U.S. Cinema* (New Brunswick, NJ: Rutgers University Press, 1996).

the other hand, would presume some sort of black essence underneath that becomes revealed once the yellow face is effaced.

Baker's cross-racial performances of oriental roles were pathbreaking in complicated and contradictory ways. Jules-Rosette characterizes Baker's performances as "racial transcoding." She argues, "Sidestepping Fanon's modernist imprisonment by colonialist categories of race through her performances, Baker transformed race into a series of costume changes that foreshadowed the desire to be postmodern."[22] Although Baker's performances certified that playing with racial categories could be a costume change, meaning that race was not solely determined by the body, the situation, as Jules-Rosette points out, was more complicated than that. Baker's performances loosened the modernist stranglehold of race, the body, and performance. As literary scholar Anne Anlin Cheng argues, Baker's use of skin as a trope divests the meaning of race from corporeality.[23]

Racial dynamics in the United States at that time help explicate the French ones. In the American context, African Americans playing Asians improved their position. Although historian Krystyn Moon's *Yellowface* mainly examines white portrayals of Asians in theater, her work briefly considers African American yellowface, arguing that "through Chinese impersonations, African Americans were able to ally themselves with whites by marking the Chinese as different from the white norm, as they themselves had been marked."[24] By playing yellowface, African Americans could be brought into the national fold, which in turn excluded Asians. Although I argue that Baker does not play in yellowface per se, as far as nation-state dynamics are concerned, if one substitutes the United States for France there exists an analogous dynamic of being enfolded in the French nation-state when Baker plays "La Petite Tonkinoise."

Baker's performances of "L'Hawaïenne" and "La Petite Tonkinoise" are simultaneously conservative and radical. Given the dynamics of playing the oriental, Baker's portrayal of a Tonkinoise or Hawaiian is really a move of inclusion into France, rather than an exclusion. In other words, this is her way of claiming her French identity even if she is black. In fact, it is precisely because Baker is black that she needs to play other French colonials in order to affirm that she is French. Looking at the broader cultural implications,

---

22. Jules-Rosette, *Josephine Baker in Art and Life,* 65, 66.

23. Anne Anlin Cheng, *Second Skin: Josephine Baker and the Modern Surface* (New York: Oxford University Press, 2010).

24. Moon, *Yellowface,* 133.

instead of blackface or yellowface as a way of attesting whiteness, Baker's "L'Hawaïenne" and "La Petite Tonkinoise" performances uphold the legitimacy of French colonial possessions. Baker is the ultimate Frenchwoman because she can depict so many aspects of being French. She retains the essence of France, a place where in theory the nation supersedes race, because all of the people she portrays are French. There are conservative implications to this in that it nourishes the French colonial mythos around dark women and normalizes France as a colonial imperial center. It made it possible to maintain the French fiction that France was colorblind because what mattered was being French, not skin color, but it did not erase the fact of her blackness.[25] The comic nature of her portrayals revealed that they were performances, not political change. Yet Baker's performances themselves were radical in form and in the way that they unmoored racial categories. Baker's work exposed the inauthenticity and the constructedness of colonial roles.

It is the contrast between the comic colonial performer and the fashionable star that permitted Baker to be both civilized and modern. One interview stated that "Josephine Baker, who is best known as a dancer, reveals her singing and comic abilities. In the final 'The Colonies' Baker directs colonial jazz and amusingly sings the Petite Tonkinoise."[26] The highlight of the evening, "La Petite Tonkinoise," demonstrated how Baker had expanded both the form (song) and the content (comedy) of her performances. The interview picks up on the comedy of Baker's "La Petite Tonkinoise," which is a key performative aspect to Baker becoming modern and claiming French nation-state belonging. It was because she was comic and because she was black and because she was glamourous that she was the ideal person to portray a colonial Vietnamese, for she did not represent the contagion of the colonial subject in the metropole and would never be confused for one. You can see her glamour through a photograph, but you would have needed to witness the actual performance to see the comedy.

Baker's performance of "La Petite Tonkinoise" was concurrent with Paris's Universal Colonial Exposition that opened in May 1931. Not surprisingly, given her portrayals of "L'Hawaïenne" and "La Petite Tonkinoise," Baker was slated to be queen of the exposition until someone scuppered the coronation by pointing out that she was American and therefore not a French colonial

---

25. Crystal Fleming, *Resurrecting Slavery: Racial Legacies and White Supremacy in France* (Philadelphia: Temple University Press, 2017).

26. "La Venus Noire: Josephine Baker," *Eve,* October 12, 1930, Josephine Baker Clipping File, Bibliothèque Nationale de France Richelieu, Arts et Spectacles, 4-ICO PER 1326.

Josephine Baker in ballet costume, by Carl Van Vechten.

(Library of Congress, Prints & Photographs Division, Carl Van Vechten Collection
[reproduction number LC-DIG-ppmsca-07816 (digital file from original photo)
LC-USZ62-93000].)

subject.[27] Instead of having one queen rule over the exposition as was intended by the selection of the racially mutable Baker, the organizers chose representatives from key areas and countries who collectively were grouped as the queens of the outré-mer. Since she could not rule over the Colonial Exposition itself, Baker enacted her de facto queen of the colonies status through her Casino de Paris revues such as *La Joie de Paris* and *Paris qui Remue*. European colonial ventures in Asia and Africa in particular rendered Asian and African racialized bodies both threatening and curious. Baker's formulation of "Paris, c'est mon pays" assured the French that the potentially disloyal disruptive colonial subject was indeed loyal to Paris.

"I Shall Be the Real Thing"

Anna May Wong watches carefully, then copies her instructor's hand movements. She carefully curls each finger in turn, pinkie, ring, middle, index, then thumb. Her arms undulate, fingers unfurling. She takes a bent knee step, this time transfixing her imagined audience with her liquid gaze.

Anna May Wong's dance performances were cross-racial ones costumed in racial drag. As an American, any "oriental" role was a cross-cultural act for Wong. Wong was not known as a singer or an "oriental" dancer in the United States; it was in Europe that she became one. The very imaginative dictates of performance under European colonialism required that she dance. The situation was analogous for Latina actresses in Hollywood.[28] In the film *Piccadilly* (1929), Wong played a "Siamese" dancer, and her dance performances from *Song Show Life* (1928) and *Hai-Tang* (1930) included moves appropriated from hula and other Pacific Islander dances. What is noteworthy about these European films is how Wong's character's oriental provenance is elided. The film settings are not specifically Chinese nor Asian, nor, for the most part, are the supporting characters that surround her. Her costumes mark her as a generalized oriental other.

------

27. Elizabeth Ezra, *The Colonial Unconscious: Race and Culture in Interwar France* (Ithaca, NY: Cornell University Press, 2000); Michael Borshuk, "'Queen of the Colonial Exposition': Josephine Baker's Strategic Performance," in *Critical Voicings of Black Liberation: Resistance and Representation in the Americas*, ed. Hermine D. Pinson et al. (Piscataway, NJ: Transaction, 2003), 47–65; Dana Hale, *Races on Display: French Representations of Colonized Peoples, 1886–1940* (Bloomington: Indiana University Press, 2008).

28. As Priscilla Peña Ovalle argues, for Latina actresses, dance produces "access and agency" while characterizing them as "inherently passionate, promiscuous, and temporary." *Dance and the Hollywood Latina: Race, Sex, and Stardom* (New Brunswick, NJ: Rutgers University Press, 2011), 6.

Most important, Wong herself characterized her roles as cross-racially oriental, explaining to the readers of British magazine *Picturegoer* that she was training in London for the upcoming film *Piccadilly*. She stated: "I have to do a Siamese dance in it; I am taking lessons so that I shall be the real thing."[29] It was while she was in London that Wong learned how to become an "authentic" Siamese dancer; there was nothing innate about Wong's racial background that sanctioned her to "naturally" perform such a dance.[30] It is important to note that Siam/Thailand was not a European colony; therefore, a Siamese dancer was not the role of an actual colonial other.

The significant difference between Baker's excellent dance skills and Wong's mediocre movement played into how their work was perceived by audiences as well as the intervention they made in the construction of racial modernity. Baker's dancing was original, especially as she improvised on well-known dances. Baker's popularity as a music hall artist was well deserved, given the innovative nature of her dance performances. Her style allowed for the comic and disruptive potential to come through. Even though vaudeville performances of the era were typically unrecorded, analogous performances by Baker were captured for posterity in her films and were accessible to an audience beyond those present at her vaudeville revues. Baker's innovative dance style can be witnessed in the French film *Zou Zou,* where she demonstrates her Shadow dance and Charleston. The conceit of the dance scene is that Baker, a washerwoman, is behind the curtain, dancing, and then the curtain rises and she continues without knowing that she has an audience. In her dance, Baker initially imitates animals, moving her head back and forth palms and feet on ground. She then breaks into the Charleston, high kicks, and the knock-kneed portion. At the end of the film, Baker has danced her way to music hall stardom. In real life, Baker's fame, including the banana dance, came from her derivations on the Charleston, that most famous of the jazz age dances.

Despite her "training" as a Siamese dancer, Wong was, at best, passable as a dancer, while the majority of the time she was cringe worthy. Her bad dance performances include her aforementioned Siamese dance in *Piccadilly* in which she undulates and gesticulates in an unconvincing, inharmonious manner. Wong's signature moves in *Piccadilly, Hai-Tang,* and other films are pallid variations on rotating wrists and hula sways. She looks wonderful in her costumes and moves gracefully, but she does not dance well. What

---

29. E. E. Barrett, "Right from Wong," *The Picturegoer,* September 1928, 25.

30. Yiman Wang concurs in "The Art of Screen Passing: Anna May Wong's Yellow Yellowface Performance in the Art Deco Era," *Camera Obscura* 60 (2005): 159–191.

is laudable is the beauty and elegance of her form rather than her ability to dance. The very badness of her oriental dancing provides clues as to its inauthenticity.

Wong's "bad" oriental performances interrupted the fiction that she was an antiquated national Chinese. In films such as *Chu Chin Chow* (1934), Wong parodied and improvised her dances to make them appear Asian. The fact that many male critics adored her dancing speaks to its perceived authenticity or, at the very least, her charms.[31] In *Chu Chin Chow*, which was loosely based on the story of "Ali Baba and the Forty Thieves," Wong's character performs a belly dance in the grand finale in front of the Caliph in order to identify the villain/Ali Baba/Abu Hassan. This is an instance when her "bad" dancing features as a plot device but illuminates, at least symbolically, the inauthenticity of her dances in other films. In her supposedly authentic oriental rendition, her improvised gestures are gauche. The performance is so bad that it becomes apparent that it is not Wong's performance tradition and that she is not supposed to do these dances naturally well. The Caliph's yawn signals to the audience that Wong's performance is a bore.[32] The music that accompanies her dance, a melding of musical pieces evoking such femme fatales as Carmen, Scheherazade, and Salome, provides the musical scales of alterity for the hodge-podge dance.[33] Although the audience may not have understood that her dance performances were inauthentic parody and pastiche, what these performances did do was create fissures in the construction of the colonial and imperial other. In other words, the inauthentic performance of empire, in this case signaling Baghdad decadence to British imperial audiences, could potentially be linked to the cultural "unnaturalness" of empire itself. This is an analogous though not identical dynamic to Baker's wooden clog dance in the Netherlands. So, in one dance Wong embodies the cinematic stereotype and performs it inauthentically so its very badness forms a counteridentification, which potentially provides the grounds for future artists to fashion, to use performance studies scholar José Esteban Muñoz's conceptual

---

31. Hubert Griffith, "Anna May Wong on the Stage: Her Dance the One Perfect Moment in a Play," *Daily Telegraph*, March 15, 1929.

32. A similar dynamic occurred at the 1931 Colonial Exposition in Paris. African dockworkers and other laborers were asked to perform tribal dances that they did not know how to do. James Genova, *Colonial Ambivalence, Cultural Authenticity, and the Limitations of Mimicry in French-Ruled West Africa, 1914–1956* (New York: Peter Lang, 2004).

33. Kathryn M. Kalinak, "Disciplining Josephine Baker: Gender, Race and the Limits of Disciplinarity," in *Music and Cinema, ed. James Buhler, Caryl Flinn, and David Neumeyer* (Hanover, NH: Wesleyan University Press, 2000), 336; Robert Stam and Louise Spence, "Colonialism, Racism and Representation: An Introduction," *Screen* 24, no. 2 (1983), 2–20.

framework, a "disidentificatory work."[34] Like Baker's performances, Wong's performance exposes the inauthenticity and the constructedness of colonial performance.

Yet, despite the disruptions caused by Wong's "bad" dance performances, the significations of her body constrained radical implications. The centering insistence of orientalism pulls Wong in time and time again, continually interpellating her as such. No matter if she is playing Malay or Siamese, Wong is always oriental. Although there should be a layer than can be lifted for Wong to reveal that she is donning a costume and assuming a performative role, that at times she is playing cross-racial roles, she is always oriental, no matter what she does or how hard she tries. There is not the same transgressive effect when she plays a Siamese as when Baker does. The narrow reception of Wong's body impedes other possibilities of playing the oriental. In part this is because of Wong's earnestness in enacting these dances, for which she had little training. Comparing their performing demeanors, namely Wong's facial earnestness versus Baker's comedic wink, Wong's reinforces how audiences might interpret her oriental performances as authentic despite her parodic arm twists. Baker's comic facial gestures demonstrate that she is aware that she is putting on an act and invites the audience to share the joke. Wong's dances provide evidence of her inauthenticity as an oriental dancer, but the supposed racial purity of her body and face, versus Baker's racial hybridity, continually misguide audiences into thinking of her as an authentic oriental dancer.

The convergence of the aesthetics of racial otherness can be traced through the similarities between Wong's and Baker's costumes. In "La Tonkinoise," Baker wears a headdress and ornamental vest that invokes Wong's costume from the British film *Piccadilly* (1929) as well as from *Hai-Tang* (1930). The *New Yorker* magazine writer Janet Flanner discussed how Baker first "looked Harlem; then she graduated to Creole; she has now been transmuted into Tonkinese, or something Eastern, with pagoda headdresses beneath which her oval face looks like temple sculpture."[35] In all likelihood, the headdresses were a legacy from Wong. There is ample evidence that images of Wong in her

---

34. José Esteban Muñoz, *Disidentifications: Queers of Color and the Performance of Politics* (Minneapolis: University of Minnesota Press, 1999), 31. Muñoz argues that "the process of disidentification scrambles and reconstructs the encoded message of a cultural text in a fashion that both exposes the encoded message's universalizing and exclusionary machinations and recircuits its workings to account for, include, and empower minority identities and identifications." In the book's preface Muñoz discusses Jack Smith's performances, which were inspired by B-film characters such as the spitfire (Vélez) and Scherezade (Wong).

35. Janet Flanner, *Paris Was Yesterday: 1925–1939* (New York: Viking, 1972), and *"Paris Journal," 1965–1971* (New York: Harcourt Brace Jovanovich, 1977), xx. See also Jean-Claude Baker and Chris Chase, *Josephine* (Holbrook, MA: Adams Media, 1993), 287.

Anna May Wong Siamese dance.
(Film still, *Piccadilly.*)

Siamese dance costume from the film *Piccadilly* circulated in France. There, *Piccadilly*'s program reveals that Wong received top billing in the film, whereas in England she was listed third.[36] Thirty pictures illustrated the program, including some of Wong in the Siamese dance costume. In France, even those who did not see the film and its program had plenty of opportunities to see Wong in photographs advertising *Piccadilly* because at least fifty different publicity photographs were used to promote it, including a postcard with Wong as a Siamese dancer.[37]

The convergence of oriental exoticism manifested in the leading French cinema magazine, *Cinémonde,* which featured Wong on the January 16, 1930, cover with the text "Anna May Wong dans 'Le Chemin du Déshounneur.'" Wong was depicted in a shiny bikini-style outfit with skirt panels that she wore in the film's main song and dance sequence. This costume resembles Baker's in "La Petite Tonkinoise." Instead of feathers, Wong's outfit bears tas-

36. Program for *Piccadilly,* 4 ICO CIN 12308, Bibliothèque Nationale de France Richelieu, Arts et Spectacles.
37. PHO 04357, Bibliothèque Nationale de France Richelieu, Arts et Spectacles.

sels and lots of looped rhinestones on the headdress, on her top, and on the bottom. Both women hold their right arm up in the air, left down near the side with wrist decor. It is not so much an issue of whether or not Baker copied Wong. Rather, what is noteworthy is that there are iconographic similarities in costuming oriental exoticism.

In her autobiography, Baker deploys the term *gens de couleur* (people of color) as a strategic essentialism, to invoke literary critic Gayatri Spivak's famous term, which served to justify her role as a Tonkinese/Vietnamese.[38] In *Les Memoires de Josephine Baker,* Baker identifies dance performance as a moment of racial identification. As she explains in this autobiography, ghostwritten by Marcel Sauvage, "White people do not know how to dance. Those who wish to know and admire the troubling and profound art of dance must go to Asia or Africa, home of people of color. Only they, the people of color, have kept dance's human and sacred character."[39] Baker's discussion situates her understanding of the significance of race and dance performance. Baker uses *gens de couleur* to conjoin people from both Asia and Africa through dance. Yet, to rework Baker's schema, it is not so much that people whose origins are in Asia or Africa can dance; it is that white Europeans expect them to be able to do so and therefore praise uninspired movements by a racialized other such as Wong because of the exotic aspect of their appearance.

Yet Baker's own words reinforce the construction of a more generalized colonial otherness that collapses national and regional specificity. Doubtlessly in articulating this juxtaposition Baker gives herself permission to play Asian roles. Of course, while celebrating what she sees as people from Asia and Africa having an innate ability to dance, Baker conveniently forgets that she is American. One wonders, then, if under this formulation Baker felt that as a person of African descent she would innately know how to portray dance's sacred character. America and African American performance drop out of the equation. Yet, despite Baker's strategic deployment of geography and dance, she did articulate misgivings about playing "La Petite Tonkinoise." She wrote: "Seeing Noble [Sissle] made me think. I was well aware of his dedication to our people, of the good he had done for colored people and colored theater. But didn't being a *black* star in a *white* show prove something too? Wouldn't it give me more power with which to fight for the cause? Admittedly, when my dresser hurried in with my coolie hat and feathers for the Tonkinese

38. Gayatri Chakravorty Spivak, *Other Asias* (Malden, MA: Blackwell Publishing, 2008), 260.

39. Marcel Sauvage and Josephine Baker, *Les Mémoires de Josephine Baker* (Paris: KRA, 1927), 109. Translation mine.

number and remarked that there were several rhinestones missing from the White Bird's ankle bracelet it made me wonder."[40] The last sentence reveals Baker's misgivings about playing colonial women and animals in *Paris qui Remue.* Despite Baker's wonder, the coolie hat that she wore in "La Tonkinoise" is the same style hat that Wong immortalized when she won her award as best-dressed woman in the world. Through global mass media there is a convergence of how race and exoticism get portrayed.

Each woman employed differing strategies for playing cross-racial roles, which was part of the reinvention of colonial culture in the metropole. Wong and Baker, I argue, not only challenged the binary opposition of primitivism and civilization underlying modernity; they also generated a distinctly new form of the modern. At times the two women mutually informed each other's portrayals of oriental roles, especially in the similarities of their costumes. Yet there were also significant differences. Baker's adoption of oriental roles demonstrates not only that she capitalized on French colonial fantasies but also that she incorporated key facets of the oriental into her version of temporal modernity, which was critical for claiming that she belonged to the modern French nation-state. In addition, their performing demeanors, namely Wong's earnestness versus Baker's comic wink at the audience, effectuate differing strategies for evading or being co-opted by the centering pull of the racialized body. These differences have implications for both the temporality of and supposed authenticity of the performance of racial difference as well as each woman's nation-state belonging.

Anna May Wong in France

One spotlight illuminates the otherwise dark stage, focusing the audience's attention on the actress at the center. She is daringly dressed in men's formal wear, tails, and a top hat. Alone in the light, she addresses an imaginary man.

"Street Girl," performed by Anna May Wong

In France, Wong was a star in her own right. Wong's films enchanted the French public. Paris, alongside Berlin and London, was the third site of Wong's pan-European film productions.[41] Not only did Wong's films circulate; by the time she witnessed Baker's performance of "L'Hawaïenne," Wong's image had

---

40. Quoted in Stovall, *Paris Noir*, 93.

41. Those films included *Song, Pavement Butterfly,* and *Le Chemin du Déshounneur,* known as *Hai-Tang* in Germany and England. This film is also known as *L'amour Maître des Choses,* but I use the title *Le Chemin du Déshounneur* in this section because it is the one that the French film magazines used.

appeared on the covers of the French magazines *Cinémonde* and *Ciné-Mirroir*. Not surprisingly, given her prolific film career in Europe, Wong was highly present in periodicals in France. Between 1928 and 1933, Wong appeared in French cinema and other popular magazines at least fifteen times.

Wong solidified her status as an oriental referent throughout Europe courtesy of her vaudeville revue, which brought her in front of different audiences. Through the development of her repertoire, you can witness her figuring out how her Chinese heritage interfaced with various permutations of nation-state belonging. As Baker was primarily a music hall artist, not a film actress, Wong's music hall performances mark an important site of comparison of how the two women constructed racial difference. In the 1930s, Wong starred in vaudeville variety programs in which she played not only Chinese but also mixed-race roles, which were created chiefly after she witnessed Baker perform in *La Joie de Paris* in 1932. Wong played her vaudeville revue in locales throughout France during her winter tour of 1934–1935.[42]

In Europe, Wong's vaudeville production toured not just in the capital cities but regional venues ranging from Göteborg, Sweden, to Blackpool, England. In her revue, Wong featured dramatic sketches as well as song and dance numbers. For example, in Göteborg she performed eight numbers: "Jasmine Flower (Old Chinese Folk Song)," "Parlez-moi D'Amour," "A Swedish Girl," "Ingenue," "Dragon Dance," "Half-Caste Woman," "Street Girl" (monologue from *Shanghai Express*), and "Encore Number." As Wong stated, one of the appeals of doing vaudeville was that she could change the numbers depending on their popularity and the intended audience. Nonetheless, no matter how the program was changed up, it is evident that Wong played a variety of roles and races, an exercise that could see her move from Chinese to French to "half-caste" with only a change of costume.

Each number demonstrates how Wong depicted racial difference. One of her most famous songs was "A Swedish Girl," which had an adjustable title and lyrics. So, when Wong performed the song in France, the title would be "A French Girl." The lyrics were similarly flexible.[43] In this song, unlike Baker's "Si J'étais Blanche," Wong is not claiming or playing with whiteness nor is she saying that she is French. Rather, she pays homage to the French lady. Wong sings this song in English, which raises all sorts of interesting issues around language and her slippery national signification.

As shown in the vignette that opened this section, "Street Girl," reveals

---

42. Graham Hodges, *Anna May Wong* (New York: Palgrave, 2004), 150.

43. Program, Anna May Wong Gift Collection, Billy Rose Theatre Collection, New York Public Library, Performing Arts Branch.

a fascinating aspect of Wong's repertoire. Based on her character in the film *Shanghai Express,* she plays a prostitute who kills. In this piece, her rage is juxtaposed with her androgynous dress. The lyrics include lines in which she indicates her murderous intentions. Critics proclaimed "Street Girl" to be an "ultra-modern number" in which Wong dressed in "cabaret fashion" in a topcoat and dress hat. The reviewers called it a character study inspired by the cheongsam-clad role she played in *Shanghai Express.*[44] Yet the political nature of the murder and the rape that were part of the film's plot are sidestepped. In "Street Girl," Wong emotes willfulness rather than vengefulness as *Shanghai Express's* avenging angel.

Witnessing Baker's 1932 "Si J'étais Blanche" and other numbers sung in French could have influenced Wong to perform songs in French such as "Parlez-moi D'Amour" ("Speak to Me of Love") or in the Italian language "Parlami d'amore Mariù."[45] Wong's subtle claim to French culture came through when she sang "Parlez-moi D'Amour" in French. Popularized by its original singer, Lucienne Boyer, in 1930, numerous acts have reprised the song. Baker sang a version of this song in the 1950s, but it was not known as part of her repertoire from the 1930s. "Parlez-moi D'Amour" reveals the female singer wanting to hear words of love despite knowing that the lover in question does not mean them. It is the delusion of wanting to believe the words even while knowing that they are lies. Through singing this song in French, Wong positions her character as French, or a French colonial, or as a cosmopolitan woman who can speak French like nobody's business. Wong performed this French chanson during her 1939 Australian visit, signifying its success around the globe.

It is striking that both Baker and Wong sang songs of love in France. The audience can participate in the delusion that the act of colonialism prompts love rather than the hatred of violent coercion. In addition, the colonizer's sexual longing for the dark female colonial body could be made safe through manifestations of her love. Yet Wong's "Parlez-moi D'Amour" sings of love as false and deceptive. So the colonial wants to hear statements of love, despite knowing their false promise. Although this song echoes Baker's "J'ai Deux Amours," it differs in critical ways. Instead of claiming Paris as Baker does, Wong uses the French language while remaining a person of Asian descent who is not French.

---

44. Ibid.

45. Intentionality is difficult to "prove" in a historically responsible manner. However, to take refuge in Judith Butler's theoretical formulation, it is the effect, not the intentionality, that matters. Judith Butler, *Gender Trouble: Feminism and the Subversion of Identity* (New York: Routledge, 1990).

Transnational Divergences

Anna May Wong's and Josephine Baker's divergent paths reveal racialized differences in transnational belonging. Baker exemplifies nation-state belonging, demonstrating how blackness can be incorporated into particular French nation-state narratives, whereas Wong exhibits diasporic belonging, which manifests how Chineseness cannot be subsumed into the French or American nation-state. As postcolonial scholar Ien Ang has argued, "What is particular to the Chinese diaspora, however, is that the extraordinarily strong pull of the 'homeland' colludes with the prominent place of 'China' in the western imagination."[46] Both those factors made Wong, in Western eyes, the ultimate Chinese subject. What was especially noteworthy about Baker was her ability to be enfolded into the French nation-state colonial rhetoric. Baker, though transnational in her performances, was associated with France to the extent that she became a French citizen. The opposite was true for Wong, for no nation-state wholeheartedly embraced her. Although Wong was popular in sites ranging from London and Berlin to Sydney, Australia, in locales such as Australia, Chinese were considered foreign outsiders, and Wong never claimed belonging there. Whereas Baker was location-bounded by France, Wong, like the itinerant character she played in *Song/Show Life,* did not find a real "home" inside or outside of the United States. Like many Chinese Americans, she was considered a sojourner in her own country.

This lack of French or American nation-state belonging reveals itself in the lengthy 1932 piece Wong published in a French periodical, *Revue Mondiale.* Although the subject of "The Orient, Love and Marriage" is interracial marriage, her views on race and nation-state belonging come through as diasporic Chinese belonging. In "The Orient, Love and Marriage" Wong declared, "But if I were to marry a white man, I would remain always Chinese. Because I do not appreciate very much the character of one who changes their nationality." With these statements, Wong conflated race and nationality into a Chinese diasporic citizenship. Yet the very conflation of the two demonstrates how bounded the category of American citizen was with the instability of being Chinese American. The American could always be taken away from her, whereas the Chinese could not. As historian Karen Leong states, "Her U.S. citizenship was always in question because of her racial heritage."[47] She, of course, was American, not Chinese. Wong's remarks reveal another type

---

46. Ien Ang, *On Not Speaking Chinese: Living between Asia and the West* (New York: Routledge 2001), 13.

47. Leong, *China Mystique,* 57.

of change, namely her claiming her diasporic Chinese "nationality" rather than her American one.

By reading the subtext of "The Orient, Love and Marriage," one can see that for Chinese Americans such as Wong, invoking diasporic Chinese belonging was a way to claim geographic space at a time when their country of birth, the United States, gave them the most tenuous form of citizenship and when places like France were not completely welcoming either. In discussing prejudice against mixed-race marriages, Wong brought up her friends at the Chinese school in Los Angeles, who, "like myself, were far away from their own country." Wong meant China as their own country rather than the United States. This was not a surprising formulation, given that anti-Chinese prejudice in the United States was particularly acute for Chinese American women. The 1922 Cable Act stated that an American citizen would lose her citizenship if she married an alien ineligible for citizenship. Therefore, a Chinese American woman such as Wong would lose her citizenship if she married an Asian immigrant. The Cable Act, though not labeled an explicitly anti-Asian marriage act, in effect targeted Asian American women. While the U.S. Constitution's Fourteenth Amendment gave African Americans the right to naturalize, as could European immigrants, the Cable Act deployed deceptively racially neutral language that affected only immigrants of Asian descent as "aliens ineligible for citizenship." "The Orient, Love and Marriage" includes other oblique references to anti-Asian discrimination: Wong mentions one of her friends who "left the country with his young lady." Leaving the country, or at least the state, would have been necessary because of California's anti-miscegenation laws, which made it illegal for Chinese and whites to marry.[48] So for a Chinese American woman such as Wong, American marriage was a fraught topic tied up with citizenship and rights.

In "The Orient, Love and Marriage," Wong used both the terms "Chinese" and "oriental," which indicates that she deployed "Chinese" to refer to language, heritage, and bloodlines. Wong employed "oriental" to denote beauty, as in "cette beauté orientale," rather than Chinese beauty. "Cette beauté orientale" signifies an "Eastern," or "Asian," beauty as a typology that was not as nation-state bound. Such usage demonstrated that for Wong "oriental" was not necessarily a pejorative term. Wong used the term "Chinese" as a modifier for "school," as in "l'école chinoise," to refer to a Chinese-language school. The fact that she selected both terms reveals that she had a different meaning

---

48. Peggy Pascoe, *What Comes Naturally: Miscegenation Law and the Making of Race in America* (New York: Oxford University Press, 2009). In the United States, marriage laws are regulated state by state.

attached to each word. What is most significant is how she used Chinese in a diasporic citizenship sense of the word.

Wong's diasporic belonging dialogued with her sense of belonging in Paris. Despite her success, unlike Baker, Wong did not take to Paris. Although Wong had worked in Paris and vacationed in France, her letters to Fania Marinoff and Carl Van Vechten poignantly state that Paris was an uncomfortable place for her. Two decades after she witnessed Baker's performance, Wong wrote to Marinoff and Van Vechten about her plans for a return trip to Europe, saying "While I'm abroad I thought I would go to Paris (although I have never been at home or could find my way around there)."[49] In a subsequent letter, Wong repeated the motif, writing, "Having spent most of my budget here in London and not knowing my way around Paris."[50] "Not knowing my way around Paris" can literally mean the difficulties of navigating the city, but more importantly it speaks to the cultural alienation that Wong felt from Paris. London was a much more comfortable city for her. Wong, then, could never feel incorporated into the French nation-state. Unlike Baker, who felt at home in Paris to such a great extent that she made France her permanent home, Wong did not share the same affinity.

Baker not only loved France; she epitomized the French nation-state and became a French citizen in 1937. She was not just culturally French, she became a French political symbol. Her French state funeral honored her work as a French patriot during World War II, and she received the French Legion of Honor medal in 1961. When Baker died in 1975, her funeral procession wove through the streets of Paris and ended with a full French military ceremony, complete with a twenty-one-gun salute and official flags. A reported twenty thousand people thronged in front of La Madeline to witness this.[51] Her ability to be enfolded into the French nation-state as a political as well as a cultural icon helped legitimate claims that the French were racially colorblind.

Conclusion

Cross-racially playing the oriental was a product of the interwar period and, more specifically, the 1930s. Hawaiian, Vietnamese, Arab North African, and Siamese roles had much more salience for audiences when colonialism

---

49. Anna May Wong to Carl Van Vechten and Fania Marinoff, August 26, 1955, Carl Van Vechten Manuscript Collection, Beinecke Library, Yale University.

50. Anna May Wong to Carl Van Vechten and Fania Marinoff, London, October 6, 1955, Carl Van Vechten Manuscript Collection, Beinecke Library, Yale University.

51. Jules-Rosette, *Josephine Baker in Art and Life*, 276.

was an actuality, whereas in the era of decolonization after World War II, such roles transformed. In addition, the World War II years shifted the work roles and concurrently the images of both Josephine Baker and Anna May Wong, who in real life aided the war effort, Baker through espionage for France and Wong through China Relief and USO skits.

Could this meeting, this moment of Wong watching Baker play a panoply of racialized roles have happened elsewhere? It definitely could not have occurred at this time in the United States. Racial segregation and the dictates of African American performance would have made it highly unlikely that Baker would play "La Petite Tonkinoise" or "L'Hawaïenne" anywhere in the United States in the 1930s. Perhaps if both performers had remained in the United States they would have met in the New York City salons of Carl Van Vechten. Van Vechten could have been a pivotal bridging figure, for he photographed Wong in the United States and their professional friendship spanned Wong's lifetime. Had Baker remained in the United States, in all likelihood she would have been part of the Harlem Renaissance circle that Van Vechten cultivated in his salons. As far as other European sites as possible meeting grounds, Baker did perform "La Petite Tonkinoise" and other roles in London while Wong was filming *Chu Chin Chow* and *Java Head* there, but Baker's reception in the United Kingdom was lukewarm at best. It was Wong who was the toast of London, not Baker. Berlin is the other place where the two women could have met, especially as imagined on the cover of the German periodical *Simplicissimus*. Although both women had performed in Berlin in the 1920s, the relentless whiteness marked by the rise of National Socialism in the 1930s curtailed performing opportunities for both women during that decade. As one of the main seats of power for colonialism in Asia and the Pacific and as the capital of modernity, Paris operated as a major site for oriental roles. We have seen in this chapter a way to reconsider Baker's oriental portrayals as well as a way to situate France as a significant site for Wong's performances.

New York, 1932: Her arm hurts but she keeps it steady as she holds the cocktail glass in her hand, looking wistfully to the side. She experiments with different angles for tilting her head. The camera clicks, capturing each of the nuances. The pain is temporary and will be worth it. She knows that this will be one of the best photographs of her. Ever.

4

Glamourous American Moderns

Anna May Wong and Lupe Vélez

I prefer the profile D-19 to any of the others.[1]

In the 1930s, Anna May Wong co-created her own image in portrait photography. With such favorable evaluations as the one in the quotation above, from a letter to her friend the photographer Carl Van Vechten, she not only shaped how she was imaged but also influenced modern photography and modern art. Although Wong had affected her image throughout her career, the medium of photography was one that gave her a particular kind of authorial control. Working with Van Vechten, she repeatedly critiqued the photographs he took of her, giving him feedback on what she liked and what she did not. Photography in the 1930s created new opportunities for how race and gender were portrayed, such as in the chapter-opening Van Vechten photograph. However, many examples, especially the Edward Steichen portraits, disclose the historical legacies of oriental images. In contradistinction, in these Van Vechten portraits Wong worked in conjunction with her friend to create the modern photographs that she preferred.

This portrait of Wong reveals her as the quintessential modern woman. There is a wistful yearning quality to this 1932 Van Vechten photograph, as if

---

1. Anna May Wong to Carl Van Vechten and Fania Marinoff, July 31, 1932, Carl Van Vechten Manuscript Collection, Beinecke Library, Yale University (hereafter, CVVMC).

Anna May Wong's favorite photograph, by Carl Van Vechten.

(Library of Congress, Prints & Photographs Division, Carl Van Vechten Collection
[reproduction number LC-USZ62-121312].)

Wong had stepped aside during a cocktail party to contemplate a point or to get some quiet time by herself. She is not thinking about pleasing or seducing her audience. As the audience, we feel that we are witnessing a stolen moment. The subject is lit from the right, and you can see the light gleam on the back of her neck and head. Her cocktail dress has cap sleeves and a bowtie at the neck. There is not a hint of the oriental in her dress or costuming. Instead she represents the contemporary woman, especially with the cocktail in her hand.

The portrait is saying both that Wong is a glamourous, sophisticated, and self-reliant woman and that she knows the symbolic traps of traditional femininity and can step out of them at will. The perspective of the low camera angle aggrandizes the power and importance of the subject portrayed. The main object of visual attention is her neck, a sensual and eroticized element in the picture. The beam of light reaches one of the leaves on the background and a corner of the glass in her hand. The photograph highlights and establishes a symbolic connection between Wong, the leaves (a stylized representation of nature), and the drink (desire). She therefore inhabits some of the traditional associations of femininity with nature (reproduction) and sensuality but does so in such aestheticized and minimalist ways that all become redefined as an artistic performance that only a refined and sensitive artist could accomplish. This image is modernity at its most sophisticated, deploying traditional symbols through allusion in order to both critique them and use their capital.[2]

It is precisely the aesthetic moves of glamour to the surface that created the space for Wong to be a key figure in shaping modern images. Courtesy of film and photography, in the 1930s glamour became a dominant mode of aesthetics, infusing art, politics, and advertising. As literary scholar Judith Brown argues, glamour "transcends any simple structure of the commodity, rising into the realm of formal aesthetics, modern philosophies of space and time, the shifting lines of identity, and the dazzling effects of the surface."[3] Glamour has been correlated with whiteness; film stars such as German-born Marlene Dietrich and Swedish-born Greta Garbo are widely known for embodying modern glamour. What differentiates my argument in this chapter from previous scholarship on glamour is that it considers non-whiteness— race and glamour—through the figures of Wong and Mexican actresses Lupe Vélez and Dolores del Río in order to unveil the development of race, ethnicity, and photography as relational.

---

2. I thank Adrián Pérez-Melgosa for pointing out these aspects of the photograph.

3. Judith Brown, *Glamour in Six Dimensions: Modernism and the Radiance of Form* (Ithaca, NY: Cornell University Press, 2009), 5.

After having focused on Europe in Chapters 1–3 of this book, we now cross the Atlantic to the United States in order to scrutinize the nexus of race, glamour, Hollywood, and commodification in one of the most significant nodes in the creation of global images. First, I consider the intersection of glamour and race through the iconic portraits of Wong, del Río, and Vélez shot by famed artist Edward Steichen in art photographs as well as photos featured in the Condé Nast publications *Vanity Fair* and *Vogue.* Second, I examine how Wong intervened in how she was racialized. Wong's correspondence with Van Vechten demonstrates how she molded her own image. In these Van Vechten photographs, Wong deployed a glamour that incorporated the modern and the Asian.[4] Third, I look at advertisements, which register the differences in commodification and glamour between Vélez and Wong. Unlike Wong, Vélez starred in mainstream American advertising campaigns for Lux Soap and Coca-Cola. Chinese American and African American bodies did not wield the same power as commodities.

Race, Gender, and Changing Images

Photography presented a whole new way to understand racial and gendered difference, both with its claims on visual reality and its reproducibility and circulation. Nicéphore Niépce and Louis Daguerre in France and William Henry Fox Talbot in England developed the photographic medium, which was subsequently revealed to the world in 1839 and codified by name in 1855.[5] Many early photographic representations reiterate elements that were circulating in American culture beforehand. However, the photographic and cinematic culture industries produced a dramatic shift in these already-in-motion processes. As argued throughout this book, modernity denotes the changes in self and society as manifested in the central organizing principles of racial and sexual difference, which were normalized as well as contested through the circulation of motion pictures, images, and the commodification of the body.

Photography played a central role in the development of modernity as part of the encounter with everyday life.[6] A century after its development, the medium reached its zenith in the 1930s because it became an accessible and democratic art available to millions through print journal circulation, it

---

4. The concept of primitive glamour comes from Brown, *Glamour in Six Dimensions,* 126. Brown does not actually analyze orientalist primitive glamour in her book.

5. Alan Trachtenberg, *Reading American Photographs: Images as History, Mathew Brady to Walker Evans* (New York: Hill and Wang, 1990), 3.

6. Nicholas Mirzoeff, *An Introduction to Visual Culture* (New York: Routledge, 2009), 65.

used ordinary people as subjects, and it lacked a "unified tastemaking elite."[7] Dorothea Lange, Walker Evans, and Margaret Bourke White were just some of the photographers who became famous for depicting ordinary Americans, and those pictures circulated widely. This era signified opportunities in photography that empowered Wong to create images with Van Vechten that were distinctly different from the portraits of racialized difference from the turn of the century.

By the time Wong was photographed by Van Vechten and Steichen in the 1930s, historical legacies of earlier photographic conventions lingered. Before the ascendance of Wong, del Río, and Vélez, exploitative photography such as images of Filipino colonial subjects and lynching photographs of African Americans dominated nationally circulating images of racial difference. Asian American studies scholar Nerissa Balce points out that through colonial photography sanitized photographs of the docile Filipino body obfuscated the violent realities of colonial warfare.[8] The most famous photographs of Chinese Americans at the turn of the century, Arnold Genthe's Chinatown portraits, promoted an exoticized Chinatown.[9] Historian Jack Tchen has found that though these photographs seemingly present a "realistic" and "objective" portrait of the Chinese in San Francisco, the majority of them were doctored and altered.[10] Given these visual regimes of racial control, it is important that Wong sought to create and present a particular type of image to the greater public.

Wong's importance to American photography bears historical antecedents: Chinese women who migrated to the Americas were the first group as a whole to be singled out for U.S. governmental photographic regulation. Historian Anna Pegler-Gordon has researched that U.S. government photographic identity documents were used first and exclusively on Chinese migrants, begin-

---

7. John Raeburn, *A Staggering Revolution: A Cultural History of Thirties Photography* (Urbana-Champagne: University of Illinois Press, 2006), 2.

8. Nerissa Balce, *Body Parts of Empire: Visual Abjection, Filipino Images, and the American Archive* (Ann Arbor: University of Michigan Press, 2016).

9. Anthony Lee, *Picturing Chinatown: Art and Orientalism in San Francisco* (Berkeley: University of California Press, 2001); Thy Phu, *Picturing Model Citizens: Civility in Asian American Visual Culture* (Philadelphia: Temple University Press, 2012); Emma Teng, "Artifacts of a Lost City: Arnold Genthe's Pictures of Old Chinatown and Its Intertexts," in *Re/collecting Early Asian America: Essays in Cultural History,* ed. Josephine Lee, Imogene L. Lim, and Yuko Matsukawa (Philadelphia: Temple University Press, 2002), 54–77.

10. Jack Tchen, *Genthe's Photographs of San Francisco's Old Chinatown* (New York: Dover, 1984).

ning with Chinese women in 1875.[11] The 1875 Page Law, which theoretically targeted a broader swath of Chinese migrants but in reality targeted Chinese women as a group, as they were suspected of prostitution, prompted this scrutiny of Chinese migrant women. "Visual regulation" became a central means of controlling migrants, with Chinese women being controlled first. As the only other groups forced to submit to U.S.-government-issued identity photographs at this time were criminals or deported immigrants, de facto Chinese migrants were criminalized.[12] Yet, as Pegler-Gordon has found, the Chinese American community resisted this visual regulation by creating their own alternatives. Wong working with Van Vechten on her photographic image is part of the broader history of a Chinese American community in which not only were women singled out for photographic scrutiny but also resistance to official regulation by fashioning one's own image was part of one's relationship to the American nation-state.

Around 1890, demeaning consumer advertisements that confirmed those images of alterity, especially of African Americans and Chinese Americans, began to circulate widely in the American public sphere. In these advertisements, race and otherness become a major theme through what historian of advertising Jackson Lears terms "theatrical exoticism."[13] The circus roots of displays of the exotic led to the association of racial otherness with new products. For example, Fleury's Wa-Hoo Tonic advertisement utilized an infantilized Chinese man holding chopsticks with a cat preying on a rat. This caricature of a Chinese immigrant from roughly 1890 can be traced back to the violence of the gold rush era and the subsequent Chinese immigration exclusion laws that resulted in the 1882 Chinese Exclusion Act. These legacies made representations of African American and Chinese American bodies especially freighted, as would be reflected in Edward Steichen's 1931 and 1935 photographs of Wong published in *Vanity Fair*.

The new era in images and advertising signified by Steichen's art photographs of Wong and Vélez as well as Vélez's Lux Soap and Coca-Cola advertisements was prompted by changes in racial images and gender roles and consumer culture. As bodies under modernity became distinguished by racial difference, they also became marked by sexual difference. Women's reconfigured sexual, familial, and public roles made them the main subjects of the newly emerging consumer culture. Consumer culture became a hallmark of

11. Anna Pegler-Gordon, *In Sight of America: Photography and the Development of U.S. Immigration Policy* (Berkeley: University of California Press, 2009), 24.

12. Ibid., 38.

13. Jackson Lears, *Fables of Abundance: A Cultural History of Advertising in America* (New York: Basic Books, 1995), 142.

Fleury's Wa-Hoo Tonic advertisement, circa 1890.
(Warshaw Collection of Business Americana, Archives Center,
National Museum of American History, Smithsonian Institution.)

the New Woman, which made the female film star's role as the embodiment of glamour especially pronounced. As Stephen Gundle writes in *Glamour: A History,* "The female body carried special connotations for societies that practiced sexual repression. It was the source of fantasies that could be deployed to excite interest, sell goods, and provide entertainment."[14]

What is noteworthy is that the image of the New Woman expanded to categories of otherness as represented in film by Swedish "foreign" actress Greta Garbo or Mexican-born Vélez and del Río or Wong.[15] The Depression-era ethos signaled changes in glamour and racialized standards of beauty in the United States. In 1933, *Photoplay* magazine declared del Río to have the most perfect figure.[16] Del Río was an upper-class Mexican criollo, highly educated, could speak English without an accent, and, with her first marriage to Cedric Gibbons, had married into Hollywood's "aristocracy." As

14. Stephen Gundle, *Glamour: A History* (New York: Oxford University Press, 2009), 12.

15. Lucy Fischer, *Designing Women: Cinema, Art Deco, and the Female Form* (New York: Columbia University Press, 2003), 18–19, 33–40; Yiman Wang, "The Art of Screen Passing: Anna May Wong's Yellow Yellowface Performance in the Art Deco Era," *Camera Obscura* 60 (2005): 167; Linda Hall, *Dolores del Río: Beauty in Light and Shadow* (Palo Alto, CA: Stanford University Press, 2013); Joanne Hershfield, *The Invention of Dolores del Río* (Minneapolis: University of Minnesota Press, 2000), 7–9; Rosa Linda Fregoso, "Lupe Vélez: Queen of the Bs," in *From Bananas to Buttocks: The Latina Body in Popular Film and Culture,* ed. Myra Mendible (Austin: University of Texas Press, 2009), 55.

16. Hershfield, *The Invention of Dolores del Río,* ix; *Photoplay,* February 1933, 74.

Anna May Wong in "On the Spot," by Joseph Grant.
(National Portrait Gallery, Smithsonian Institution;
gift of Carol Grubb and Jennifer Grant Castrup.)

historian Linda Hall writes, "Her very beauty and social class diminished the significance of her Mexican background."[17] In films such as *Flying Down to Rio* (1933) she could be perceived as white, albeit South American, but in others, such as *Bird of Paradise* (1932), she played a Hawaiian exotic. These different racialized roles made del Río both a desired and racially uncomfortable presence in Hollywood.

17. Hall, *Dolores del Río*, 6.

After her triumphs in Europe, Wong returned to the United States a star, playing the lead role in Broadway's *On the Spot*. In addition, Wong's fashion savvy was recognized in 1934, when, as noted in previous chapters, the Mayfair Mannequin Society voted her the best-dressed woman in the world. Based on her introduction of the coolie and mandarin hats in London and Paris, fashion experts in London, New York, Berlin, Paris, Vienna, and Stockholm ranked her the most sophisticated woman on both sides of the Atlantic. Wong did not merely reflect current fashion trends; she determined them. Her ability to be a modern hybridized cosmopolitan woman gave her more class and clout than being elite Chinese or working-class American. It is striking that, in back-to-back years, these racial minority actresses were considered more beautiful than their European American counterparts. These women exemplified Hollywood's and the general American public's absorption with gendered ethnicity and racialized otherness. The aesthetics of the era valorized racial minority actresses as the epitome of glamour.

Edward Steichen

American cultural fascination around the oriental was exhibited vividly in Edward Steichen's photographs of Wong. Although Wong inspired modern philosophers such as Walter Benjamin, the subject of Chapter 1, and Steichen, both men relied on oriental paraphernalia to enhance her racialized body, evincing the imbrication of modern art and orientalism. Over time, the aesthetics of the Steichen photographs of Wong developed from disembodied Art Deco in 1930 to oriental fantasia in 1935.

Edward Steichen (1879–1973) has been hailed as one of the leading art photographers of the twentieth century as well as an innovator in advertising photography and celebrity portraits. Born in Luxembourg, Steichen spent most of his professional life in the United States. With artist Alfred Stieglitz, he founded the Photo-Secession, a group of photographers who wished to elevate photography to the same status as established fine arts such as painting and sculpture. Steichen was a pioneer in photography alongside other modern and avant-garde artists such as Paul Cézanne, Pablo Picasso, Henri Matisse, Gertrude Stein, and Auguste Rodin. Before World War I, the influence of the impressionist painters is evident in Steichen's atmospheric photographs of Rodin and his sculptures in Paris as well as the Brooklyn Bridge and the Flatiron Building in New York City. In this era, Steichen took portrait-style photographs of well-known figures such as financier J. P. Morgan, President Theodore Roosevelt, and ex-president William Howard Taft. In my opinion,

Steichen created some of the most beautiful art works of the twentieth century, which makes his rendering of Wong all the more disquieting.

After World War I, although Steichen continued to work on photographing ordinary objects such as raindrops and flowers so that they took on artistic dimensions, he began a significant shift to celebrity photographs. In 1923 Steichen agreed to take on the portraiture of prominent people for *Vanity Fair* and fashion photography for *Vogue*.[18] Steichen not only photographed celebrities; through his work with luminaries such as Garbo, Paul Robeson, and George Gershwin, he was instrumental in creating the celebrity portrait genre. It is highly significant that he photographed Wong, Vélez, and del Río for the upper-class magazine *Vanity Fair* as well as for art photographs. Starting in 1929 and continuing into the mid-1930s, he created numerous iconic portraits of all three women. However, as was the case for Benjamin, Wong's racial difference became the ruling trope for how Steichen saw her. Wong's Chinese features guided Steichen's costuming and props.

Steichen's art photographs of Wong as well as Vélez are part of his experiments in form and photography. What stands out is that although the photographs are aesthetically interesting, even beautiful, both women are fragmented.[19] The photograph entitled "Anna May Wong. New York. 1930" is the most striking of the Wong portraits. Though the fragmentation is disturbing, the overall aesthetics are sculptural and dramatic. All you see of Wong is her head situated in the upper left corner of the photograph, sideways with her left cheek on a dark table. Right next to her head, on the right and slightly below, is a large white flower, a peony, which, with the plum blossom, is a symbol of China. The top right of the photograph has a light background, the rest of the photograph is dark so that the flower and, to a lesser degree, the right side of Wong's face that points to the ceiling, pop out to the viewer. There is a reflection of both the flower and Wong's face on the table below. The qualities of the photograph are sculptural and aesthetically beautiful. Wong's lack of facial expression and closed eyes emphasize the planes and angles of her face, which make her like a sculpture rather than a breathing, living person. The fragmentation is rendered artistic rather than alarming. Placing the horizon line vertically adds to the photograph's induced discombobulation, for it makes the viewer feel as if the photograph should be rotated ninety degrees. This is Eros and Tanthos together, reflected on the seamless slick surface of modernity.

---

18. Edward Steichen, *A Life in Photography* (New York: Doubleday, in collaboration with the Museum of Modern Art, 1963), chap. 7, 1. Because this book does not include page numbers, I use page numbers by chapter.

19. Here I refer to "Lupe Vélez and Conrad Veidt. Hollywood. 1929."

Anna May Wong, New York, 1930, by Edward Steichen.

Two brief comments by a photography scholar and a Steichen museum curator, respectively, uncover how complicated it is to evaluate this photograph. On the one hand, photography historian John Raeburn's one-paragraph analysis of the photograph argues that it contains an orientalist subtext ("Wong's eyes do not look back at the viewer") and that its "inscrutability". . . heightened the sense of the strange and exotic to correspond to the most commonplace cultural attitudes about Wong's race."[20] On the other hand, in the introduction accompanying a catalog of Van Vechten photographs, curator Keith Davis contrasts this Steichen photograph with the Van Vechten photograph of Wong in a tuxedo sipping champagne. He writes, "The result is abstract and static: the subject as an elegant Brancusi-like work of sculpture."[21] Taken together, both remarks highlight the power of this photograph. It is an aesthetically compelling portrait with potentially orientalist undertones in which Wong is rendered literally a beautiful object. But one can complicate Raeburn's assessment by looking at the photograph's minimalist composition, with complex planes and surfaces, as one that furthers modern, not orientalist, aesthetics. We can see elements of Man Ray and surrealism in this photograph. If it is an exemplar par excellence of Art Deco with its Asian motifs, then those particular aesthetics deign Wong a notable subject. But, in light of Steichen's later photographs of Wong for *Vanity Fair* in 1931 and 1935, this one is not overtly marked with oriental cues. Yet, no matter what the photograph, Wong's body emblematizes the racial difference thematized by modern photography.

Although such a practice seems commonplace to contemporary observers, this was the era when actresses first became major bodies around which commodification occurred. This held true in both glamour and art photography. Stemming from the tradition of wealthy people having their portraits painted, glamour portraits' first subjects were socialites, and this expanded to film stars and other noteworthy cultural figures. Steichen discussed "the portrait series I had planned to make of distinguished artists in Europe. I hoped to included painters, sculptors, literary men, and musicians."[22] His photograph of Garbo turned her into an icon for American audiences. It was at this time that celebrity and luxury became linked. The aim of such magazines as *Vogue* and *Vanity Fair* was to "bring together advertisers selling luxury goods with consumers rich enough to buy them."[23] Not only was

---

20. Raeburn, *A Staggering Revolution,* 78.
21. Keith Davis, *The Passionate Observer: Photographs by Carl Van Vechten* (Kansas City, MO: Hallmark Cards, 1993), 24.
22. Steichen, *A Life in Photography,* chap. 2.
23. Raeburn, *A Staggering Revolution,* 64.

Steichen considered the "most successful commercial photographer of the 1920s and 1930s," with his work appearing in almost every mass-circulating magazine in the United States; his celebrity portraits also made him "the most admired and widely seen American photographer."[24] The manner in which Steichen racialized Wong matters: these images appeared in influential and widely circulating forums.

In the 1930s, Steichen created celebrity portraits of del Río, Vélez, and Wong for *Vanity Fair*, a magazine that epitomized modern glamour, Wong in 1931, Vélez in 1932, and both Wong and del Río in the same March 1935 issue. A pioneer of celebrity portraiture, Steichen's photographs of Wong are an anomaly within his oeuvre. As Patricia Johnston, one of the leading Steichen scholars, argues, "He developed an iconography for celebrityhood that traced surface beauty and created the appearance of character. Beauty is treated like any fine possession; it is a material asset for display. . . . Steichen's portraits may be more honest. They do not promise more than loving description of the surface, and this can be recognized as a picture of the sitter's public image, not the sitter's inner life."[25] Johnston's characterization of Steichen's work dovetails with literary scholar Judith Brown's parsing of the iconography of glamour in its focus on surfaces, simplification, and public image.[26] For the portraits of Vélez and del Río, Johnston's analysis holds true. However, I find that in the case of Wong, Steichen's portrait promised much more than a "loving description of the surface." As was the case for Benjamin, for Steichen, Wong's race mediated how he saw her. She then becomes an exception to the tenets of both Benjamin's and Steichen's artistic practice of translation, or "loving description of the surface."

A Steichen glamour portrait of Vélez that appeared in *Vanity Fair* in June 1932 demonstrates how he developed his "iconography for celebrityhood that traced surface beauty." Vélez poses as a modern film star. She sits in evening wear on a sofa, eyes staring straight at the camera, and she does not smile. The camera is positioned above, looking down at Vélez. She is heavily made up, with her eyebrows arched and eyeliner swooping upward. Her arm is extended, displaying the bangles on it, and her other arm is crossed in front of her chest with her hand resting on the upper arm. The dark and high-contrast chiaroscuro shadows make her face, leg, and arm pop out. Vélez is the emblem of a modern socialite or film star.

---

24. Ibid., 62. See also Patricia A. Johnston, *Real Fantasies: Edward Steichen's Advertising Photography* (Collingdale, PA: Diane Publishing, 1997); Steichen, *A Life in Photography*, 1.

25. Johnston, *Real Fantasies*, 202.

26. Brown, *Glamour in Six Dimensions*.

It is apparent that Steichen crafted favored looks for each particular star, the crossed arms in the case of Vélez, the peony above and to the side of the head for Wong. Yet the snake-like bracelet at the forefront of the image, the long fleeces of her minimal dress, the boa-like posture and hypnotic look could indicate that he is racializing Vélez as an "exotic savage" or perhaps connecting her with the snake of biblical resonance and Eve-like femininity.[27] Wong and Vélez wear jewelry that marks them as decorations themselves on the larger body of the modern West. Both are connected to symbols of nature and fertility—peonies for Wong, snakes for Vélez. They are performing as they pose.

Steichen did not always employ nature symbols or exoticism in photographing Mexicans. In the 1929 Steichen photograph of Dolores del Río published in *Vogue* three years earlier, she was portrayed as the pinnacle of modern glamour. As *Vogue* was a leading high-fashion magazine, image making for it can be considered a blend between art and commerce. In the *Vogue* photograph, del Río is enveloped in a light-colored fur-lined wrapper. She wears a long gown and leans against a column. The lightness of her dress and wrapper make her dark hair and eyes stand out. She wears a diamond-jeweled pointed choker around her neck. She does not smile but looks wistfully up and to her right (the viewer's left). Her hands are crossed, clutching the wrapper close to her. This is the epitome of a high-class fashion photograph without a trace of exoticism or foreignness in her clothing, hairstyle, or props.[28]

In contrast, Steichen's portraits of Wong in *Vanity Fair* are far more exoticized than those of Vélez or del Río. A Steichen photograph accompanied an article on Wong, simply titled "Anna May Wong," in the September 1931 issue. Providing a narrative for the photograph as much as the photograph provided a visual narrative for the article, the text highlighted the cosmopolitanism Wong acquired during her years in Europe.

> After an absence of three years Anna May Wong has returned to the Hollywood she left in the days of silent films to play in *Daughter of the Dragon* for Paramount. She is hardly new to talkies, however, having recently starred in them in England, Germany and France, an international experience unrivalled by any of our Caucasian film luminaires. She is a person of great charm and culture, speaks four

---

27. I thank Adrián Pérez-Melgosa for pointing out these aspects of the photograph.

28. On other occasions del Río performed ethnicity and race, especially in connection with her films *Ramona* (1928) and *Bird of Paradise* (1932). Hall, *Dolores del Río*.

Anna May Wong in *Vanity Fair,* 1931, by Edward Steichen.
(© 2018 The Estate of Edward Steichen/Artists Rights Society [ARS], New York.)

languages fluently, and is a native of California. She appeared last season on Broadway in Edgar Wallace's crook melodrama, On the Spot, and in London in an ancient Chinese drama. Vienna saw her in a musical revue; in fact the only place to which Miss Wong has never been is China.[29]

Yet without the caption a reader might believe that Wong was a Chinese national based on the photograph alone.

Steichen's portrait for the article skillfully aestheticizes the antiquated oriental. It is a visual and textual play on light and shadow. Wong appears to be seated, although we see only the upper half of her body. She wears a high-necked oriental gown, presumably silk or satin, with details at the neck. She looks off to the viewer's right, her left. Her right hand gestures in front, Buddha-like, so that it is at the center of the photograph. Her hair is pulled back in a bun, with bangs framing her face. Not a hair is out of place, and her hair is plastered to her skull in a very round shape. A peony, the same type of flower associated with China and featured in the 1930 Steichen photograph, appears again in this one. This time the flower is above her head, as if floating, with stem and leaves visible. Yet the setting, the composition, and the lighting are minimalist and very modern. Wong's ethereal presence flows right under the peony, a spectral figuration that grounds the point of excess. This is like the redoubling of spheres in the Steichen art portrait of Wong, where her head becomes doubled in the peony and again in the reflection. The doubling, the mirroring, the reflection allude to the multiplicities of Wong, an actress with multiple facets, Asian and modern.

After shooting the 1931 oriental modern photograph of Wong for *Vanity Fair*, Steichen created an oriental fantasy in his 1935 portrait. This intensified racialization was not extended to all of his photographs, for the one he took of del Río in the same March 1935 issue pared down any exoticist representation. These differences in racialization between Mexicans and Chinese Americans are stark. The del Río portrait retains its "loving description of the surface." Del Río's body faces to the side, her face toward the camera and the audience. She wears a black, thin-strapped top with no visible adornment. Her hands are on her hips, with her right hand displaying a ring. Her head is slightly tossed back, a smile on her face and her teeth gleaming. The simple costuming emphasizes del Río's smile and face. The lighting is such that the background appears dark except for a spotlight on her face and chest. This simplicity is in keeping with Steichen's modern aesthetic in photography.

---

29. *Vanity Fair,* September 1931, 43.

Dolores del Río in *Vanity Fair*, 1935, by Edward Steichen.

The simplicity in this del Río portrait is diametrically opposed to Steichen's photograph of Wong that appeared in the same March 1935 issue of *Vanity Fair*. With a caption that reads: "Anna May Wong, An American Oriental," the photograph projects excessive oriental fantasia. The copy under the caption reads: "At present on a personal appearance tour of Europe, she returns this spring to Hollywood and the films." The caption does not match up with the photograph, for there is nothing American about it, except for the American imagining of the orient. In the photograph, Wong wears a large dark headdress, its central jewels framed by enormous white peonies. The headdress extends out past her head on either side. It looks like a huge mortarboard anchored by an extended crown. She wears an elaborate high-necked silk or satin shiny robe with long sleeves, light colored, with dark piping details. Her left arm rests on a table, and, elbow bent and hand extended to the ceiling, she holds a small oriental lantern with tassels dangling. Lest the viewer miss the orientalizing signifier of the peony, Steichen includes the unambiguously oriental lantern. The lantern confirms that Steichen liked to photograph Wong with a pale object near her head, revealing it to be a signature motif: it appears in the same location and in the same size as the white peony did in 1931. Once again, like the previous *Vanity Fair* photograph, Wong's right hand is splayed in front of her chest and occupies the center of the photograph. Out of all of the Wong photographs or films that I have ever seen, this is one of the most excessively oriental in costuming. It is striking that Steichen portrays Wong in this manner, for it is not as if he has placed a sombrero on del Río's head, castanets in her hands, or a rose between her teeth. At least the caption acknowledges that Wong is American. Unlike in his work with other celebrities, Steichen failed to see past Wong's race.

Despite the problematic orientalizing image making reflected in the Steichen photographs for *Vanity Fair,* these images allowed Wong to pander to Hollywood expectations and thus the possibility of finally winning a leading A-list role. With both photographs, Wong publicizes in a mass-circulating periodical that she can play the oriental better than anyone else. This was especially important vis-à-vis European American actresses such as Helen Hayes, who won the leading role of a Chinese woman in *The Son-Daughter* (1932) over Wong. In both the 1931 and 1935 photographs, Wong's Chineseness is presented as a restrained modern oriental with high-class standing. She is not a prostitute, nor is she the laundrywoman. For Wong herself, this photograph was a performance of how an American woman could portray an oriental; there was status to be gained by doing so in a convincing manner. Yet appearing in elaborate Chinese costume was not enough to gain her the starring role of O-lan in MGM's instant classic about Chinese peasants, the *Good Earth* (1937), which was cast in 1935, the same year as the second Steichen photograph. Western conceptions of Chineseness at times confined Wong into a narrow set of professional possibilities, especially in venues such as *Vanity Fair,* an elite high-class magazine appealing to upper-crust European Americans or those who strove to emulate them.

Although all forms of orientalism share commonalities in defining other groups of people, what is particular about this American form of orientalism versus the European versions discussed in Chapters 1–3 of this book are the political implications. When Wong appeared on the covers of the London magazines *Tatler* and *The Sketch,* she was misidentified as being a Chinese national. Here in *Vanity Fair,* she is identified as American, but, through the costuming and props, she is placed outside of the American nation-state in antiquated time. As anthropologist Johannes Fabian has found, the West asserts its geopolitical power by castigating other peoples and cultures as temporally backward.[30] The historical American national image of the Chinese as alien, non-American, and antithetical to the nation-state, leading to the passage of anti-immigration and racial segregation laws, is reaffirmed. Unfitness for inclusion in the modern nation-state is reinforced anew. These photographs prove that, despite many changes in images and glamour during this era, in 1935 American interest in the oriental was alive and well.

It is tempting to dismiss these *Vanity Fair* photographs as separate from Steichen's artistic oeuvre or to attribute them to the magazine's production staff rather than to the man as an artist, but that would not be accurate. Although Steichen is responsible for the lighting and pose, it is possible that *Vanity Fair*'s art director chose the props and the clothing. However, Steichen's name appears below the photograph on the bottom-right corner, indicating that he took artistic credit for the photograph. When Steichen was first hired, Condé Nast's editors told him that he did not have to sign his *Vogue* magazine portraits. Not only had he already done fashion photography in 1911; he said, "If I made a photograph, I would stand by it with my name"—that is, he would stand by its artistic merit.[31] Steichen saw continuities between his art and commercial fashion photography and assumed creative credit for both.

In response to the oriental fantasia projections that resulted in the 1935 Steichen *Vanity Fair* photograph, Wong subsequently sought to control her

30. Johannes Fabian, *Time and the Other: How Anthropology Makes Its Object* (New York: Columbia University Press, 1983).

31. Steichen, "Fashion Photography and Fabric Design," in *A Life in Photography,* chap. 7, 1.

visual representation through her photographic work with Van Vechten. As these types of nonmodern portrayals were dominant tropes for representing Asians in this era, it was doubly important that Wong created modern portraits of herself, such as the Van Vechten ones, for wider circulation.

Anna May Wong and
the Carl Van Vechten Photographs

Anna May Wong's work with Carl Van Vechten stands in contrast to her sessions with Steichen, for she co-created the images. Through their correspondence and the photographic record, one can witness Wong, as the putative photographic subject, turn herself into the author of her own image.

Van Vechten famously proclaimed, "My first subject was Anna May Wong."[32] As one of Van Vechten's pioneering photography subjects, Wong was a primary vehicle through which he would become an eminent celebrity photographer. In addition to Wong, in his first year as a photographer Van Vechten captured images of author Eugene O'Neill; painters Frida Kahlo and Diego Rivera, Henri Matisse, and Georgia O'Keefe; and composer George Gershwin. As his biographer Edward White found, "The discipline of portrait photography was tailor-made for Van Vechten. It indulged not only his voyeurism but also his fascination with exceptional people and the immense pleasure he took in being in their company."[33] Van Vechten's selection of Wong as his "first subject" indicated their close working relationship as well as his confidence that the quality of photographs with her would attract other famous sitters. Like Benjamin as well as Steichen, Van Vechten found Wong to be a compelling medium through which he could work out his ideas on modern art and modernity.

Van Vechten has been a controversial figure. Writer W.E.B. Du Bois condemned Van Vechten's novel, *Nigger Heaven* (1926), for its primitive and licentious images. Though Van Vechten had his detractors, he also had influential African American supporters. In an era when most African American artists had white patrons, Langston Hughes, Zora Neale Hurston, and others saw Van Vechten as a champion of black arts and cultures. A lifelong correspondent and friend of Van Vechten's, Hughes dismissed Du Bois's stance of racial

---

32. Edward White, *The Tastemaker: Carl Van Vechten and the Birth of Modern America* (New York: Farrar, Straus and Giroux, 2014), 261. Van Vechten then would state that his second subject was Eugene O'Neill. Even if these statements were not strictly true, the larger point, as White points out, was that he was indicating that he photographed famous people.

33. Ibid., 263.

uplift as bourgeois and old fashioned, advocating that African American writers should promote the black working class.[34] Van Vechten and his wife, the actress Fania Marinoff, were famous for throwing interracial parties attended by artists such as Hughes, Clara Smith, Paul Robeson, and Hurston. Van Vechten turned to photography in 1932, creating more than twenty thousand photographs of celebrities such as Billie Holiday, Joe Louis, Aaron Copeland, and Marlon Brando, with special interest in photographing distinguished African Americans.[35] The most productive way to think about Van Vechten is as a prominent person who provided an entrée for certain artists of color and intervened in racializations.

Wong's correspondence with Van Vechten and Marinoff reveals the negotiations through which she crafted herself as a modern cosmopolitan woman. They began writing in 1929 with Wong's visit to Berlin and stopped only on her death in 1961, sending each other birthday cards, holiday cards, and news updates, resulting in around three hundred pages of correspondence from Wong. In her letters regarding the photographs, Wong decisively tells Van Vechten which photographs she prefers and which ones she dislikes. I have matched her opinions to the actual Van Vechten photographs in order to demonstrate the nuances of her deliberate self-fashioning. These findings refute the critics of mass culture who consider stars to be mere cogs in the Hollywood studio machine and in part explain the changes in how Wong was imaged from the late 1920s through the 1930s.[36]

Wong's comments on the Van Vechten photographs reveals what she valued in her own image as a modern film star. In the Van Vechten portraits, Wong is not costumed in the orientalist robes and headgear that marked Steichen's photographs for *Vanity Fair,* but she is dressed and accessorized as a contemporary woman. Beginning in 1932 with the first photographs, Wong wrote to Van Vechten regarding the publicity shots he took of her. Note her decisive language. "However, I think some of them are very good. I prefer the profile D-19 to any of the others, although I like C-F and C-16 very well. I don't like C-12; it looks too 'mausoleumesque.' Nor do I care for the ones

---

34. Langston Hughes, *Remember Me to Harlem: The Letters of Langston Hughes and Carl Van Vechten,* ed. Emily Bernard (New York: Vintage, 2002), xxi.

35. Emily Bernard, *Carl Van Vechten and Harlem Renaissance* (New Haven, CT: Yale University Press, 2012), 15.

36. For insightful work on the power of stars as discursive formations, see Richard Dyer, *Stars* (London: British Film Institute, 1998); and Richard deCordova, *Picture Personalities: The Emergence of the Star System in America* (Urbana-Champaign: University of Illinois Press, 2001).

in the tuxedo—do you?"[37] Wong's clear judgment reveals a woman actively invested in shaping her modern persona.

In keeping with the aesthetics of glamour as the emblem of a surface rather than a deep or inner being, Wong selected poses and costuming that revealed her not as a hybrid or primitive oriental but as the epitome of racially unmarked glamour. Broadcasting her goal to appear as a modern sophisticated woman, Wong states explicitly, "I prefer the profile D-19 to any of the others."[38] Wong refers to the portrait of herself with the cocktail in her hand that opens this chapter. In these photographs, Wong's costuming with overt Asian signifiers dropped out of the composition, leaving her own body as the only signifier of racial difference. With its attention to surfaces, the aesthetics of glamour offer the possibility of decoupling the corporeal from essentialized racial subjectivity.[39] Reading Wong alongside del Río and Vélez, women who get characterized as "dark," the aesthetics of glamour render them beautiful and figures to be emulated. This particular form of glamour that Wong invoked is the pinnacle of the modern.

The photographs that Wong disliked reveal that she preferred a modern feminine appearance. The tuxedo portraits that she disdained were part of the larger trend of actresses of the era such as Josephine Baker and Marlene Dietrich wearing menswear to highlight their femininity. In one such tuxedo photograph, Wong looks directly at the viewer. She holds a cocktail glass in her hand. Her hair is tucked up into the top hat and is visible only as it sweeps above her ear. She is wearing makeup, clearly marking her as female. The top hat dominates the upper portion of the photograph, her face the middle, and her hand, with its long elegant nails curving around the cocktail glass, the bottom. Her lips are together but appear to curve up a bit on the viewer's right. The tilt of the hat brim down on the viewer's right and the slightest curve of the lip up on the same side give her a slightly off-kilter, rakish air. This is actually quite an appealing photo of Wong, and I would argue that the menswear accentuates her femininity. Yet Wong wrote: "Nor do I care for the ones in the tuxedo—do you?"[40] This tuxedo photograph is the one that has received attention from scholars and curators. It is the only one of Wong

---

37. Anna May Wong to Carl Van Vechten and Fania Marinoff, July 31, 1932.

38. Ibid.

39. Anne Anlin Cheng, "Shine: On Race, Glamour, and the Modern," *PMLA* 126, no. 4 (2011), 1039. Cheng explores how Wong's body "might operate subjunctively rather than materially" and concludes that fascination with Wong is due to "extravagance of style, rather than the fulfillment of embodiment."

40. D-12 tuxedo photograph from Library of Congress collection; comment by Anna May Wong to Carl Van Vechten and Fania Marinoff, July 31, 1932.

Anna May Wong in a tuxedo, by Carl Van Vechten.
(Library of Congress, Prints & Photographs Division, Carl Van Vechten Collection
[reproduction number LC-USZ62-42509].)

that appears in White's biography of Van Vechten, the only one that appears in Raeburn's cultural history of 1930s photography, and the only one in the Hallmark Collection's Van Vechten photographic exhibition catalogue. However, Wong's own words demonstrate that it was not in keeping with how she wanted to appear. Since Raeburn categorizes it as a sexualized portrait, her dislike could mean that she does not care to present herself as such.

Wong's letters to Van Vechten reveal her awareness of how beauty and art are staged and constructed categories heavily dependent on the subject (Wong) to create it. As Wong wrote to Van Vechten and Marinoff, "To tell the truth, I had much rather pose another time when I am either not feeling so happy or when I look more fit. I'm afraid I wasn't particularly interesting as a subject for your new art."[41] Note that Wong calls herself a subject, not an object. Wong uses collaborative pronouns to characterize the work she and Van Vechten did together: "If possible let us wait before giving out too many; our next sitting will probably be much more satisfactory."[42] With those words, Wong stipulates that she preferred quality over the proliferation of images not up to her standards. Through her letters, Wong reveals her awareness that beauty is not natural but is a cultivated attribute, writing, "Wish you could make some pictures of me now. I look much better and am much easier on the lens these days after enjoying a grand rest."[43] Typically, Wong was careful not to comment on her own appearance in personal terms. However, in one letter from 1940 she demonstrates that she is fully cognizant of her appearance: "Does that sound conceited to say that one is beautiful."[44] Otherwise, Wong used phrases such as "like a sculpture," "best portraits of me," without directly referencing her beauty or lack thereof, or without discussing other appearance-related issues such as aging.

In the "Anna May Wong in white" Van Vechten photograph, Wong deploys non-Asian racial signifiers by dressing in metaphorical whiteface. This racial cross-dressing suggests that Wong did not believe race to be innate but instead saw it as an act or a masquerade, to paraphrase Judith Butler, as a performance to be donned off and on.[45] Although Wong did not approve of most of the photographs from the 1932 sitting, in one that she did endorse she appeared in all white. She stated: "I like . . . C-16 very well."[46] One of the most noteworthy features of this photograph is that everything is white, from the white feathery wig on Wong's head to the pale shiny cloth in the background that bears small hints of the oriental. This fabric reflects currents of what was in fashion. If it has any bearing on Wong's Chineseness, it is in relation to all the whiteness around her. She holds a white flower (a peony like the Steichen photographs) in her hand, with its edge in her mouth. Her bracelet and ring stand out. Wong looks up, to the viewer's left. Wong herself occupies the right

41. Anna May Wong to Carl Van Vechten and Fania Marinoff, July 31, 1932.

42. Ibid.

43. Anna May Wong to Carl Van Vechten and Fania Marinoff, September 21, 1932, CVVMC.

44. Anna May Wong to Carl Van Vechten and Fania Marinoff, December 30, 1940, CVVMC.

45. Judith Butler, *Gender Trouble: Feminism and the Subversion of Identity* (New York: Routledge, 1990).

46. Photo no. 22 C 16, Carl Van Vechten Photographs, Beinecke Library, Yale University; Anna May Wong to Carl Van Vechten and Fania Marinoff, April 20, 1932, CVVMC.

Anna May Wong in white, by Carl Van Vechten.

half of the photo, with a shadow of her profile larger on the left side. The whiteness emphasizes her eyes, although because of the shadows across her face, they are not exceedingly prominent. This artistic photograph, unlike the others, "had" to have hints of the oriental because so much was done to bleach it and whiten it out. These "oriental" touches are very subtle, unlike the Steichen *Vanity Fair* photographs. Like the 1930 Art Deco Steichen art photograph of Wong, her shadow is a crucial part of the composition. Differentiating it from the 1930 Steichen photograph are her open eyes and actual embodiment, which give the photograph a human quality.

Commodified Glamour and Racial Cross-Dressing

Beginning in the 1920s, Lupe Vélez appeared in another form of commercial glamour photography and artwork: print advertisements for the likes of Coca-Cola, Lucky Strikes, and Lux Soap that also served as promotional material for particular Hollywood films.[47] In a departure from how racial minorities had previously been portrayed in advertisements such as the Fleury Wa-Hoo Tonic I discussed earlier in this chapter, Vélez starred as an all-American beauty. Vélez became an ideal figure through which to embody numerous contradictions in American society, especially the anxieties around immigrants, the status of women, and class. Vélez was commodified in the United States in a way that Wong never was and to a far greater extent than del Río. I have yet to come across a single national American advertisement featuring Wong in the 1930s that was not for a film, play, or vaudeville production, although I do showcase her 1957 Qantas advertisement in the Epilogue. The fact that Vélez starred in chiefly B-list Hollywood films as well as appeared in advertisements for mainstream corporations demonstrates that she had the ability to be enfolded into the commodified American marketplace. In some ways, Wong's inability to be commodified speaks to the strength of yellow journalism against "orientals" as well as to the virulence of the anti-Chinese sentiments that had resulted in laws that banned Chinese migration. These were not lifted until 1943 and only in the most token of ways. The miscegenation laws that forbade Wong to marry a European American for the most part deemed Mexicans white and able to marry European Americans.[48] As historian Peggy Pascoe finds, regarding the anti-miscegenation case *Kirby v.*

---

47. Clara Rodriguez, *Heroes, Lovers, and Others: The Story of Latinos in Hollywood* (Washington, DC: Smithsonian Books, 2004), 69.

48. Peggy Pascoe, *What Comes Naturally: Miscegenation Law and the Making of Race in America* (New York: Oxford University Press, 2009).

Kirby (Arizona, 1922), "Mexicans are classed of the Caucasian race."[49] Unfettered by anti-miscegenation laws, Vélez's stardom was augmented by dating celebrities like Gary Cooper and her marriage to Johnny Weissmuller. Vélez, then, under the guise of ethnicity rather than race, was much more likely to be provisionally incorporated into the American nation-state. Since, historically, advertisements for commodities used highly charged stereotypical images of African Americans and Chinese Americans, it would signal a significant break in visual culture to use an actress like Wong to nationally market products such as Coca-Cola or Trans World Airlines (TWA). Looking at Vélez in national mass-circulating advertising campaigns reveals not only a broader range of her star iconography in a mainstream context but also a fascinating fluidity in ethnicity and racializations. These campaigns demonstrate how certain Mexican and Mexican American bodies could be intermeshed within the categories of ethnic immigrant whiteness and Americanness.[50]

Vélez's Asian and Pacific Islander Hollywood starring roles paved the way for her commodification. This was an era when Mexicans such as Ramón Novarro (del Río's cousin) starred as Tom Lee in *The Son-Daughter* (1932), a film that both Vélez and Wong hoped to star in but that was cast with European American actress Helen Hayes instead.[51] Portraying East Asian and Pacific Islander characters permitted Vélez's exotic racial ambiguity to be referenced, while ultimately delivering the message that she was a glamourous ethnic white. Through her playing these cross-racial roles, the anxiety-producing spectrum and specter of Mexican racial identity could be both addressed and assuaged. One such production, *East Is West,* was a longstanding vehicle with multiple iterations. It was first a Broadway play in 1919. Then Constance Talmadge played Ming Toy in the silent film *East Is West* (1922) under the auspices of Constance Talmadge Productions, complete with a Frances Marion screenplay (Marion also authored *The Toll of the Sea* [1922]).[52] Finally, in 1930 Vélez glamourously portrayed the role. As Asian American studies scholar Karen Kuo elucidates, in the film Vélez wears minimal makeup and is lit in such a way that she appears whiter and lighter than

49. Peggy Pascoe, "Miscegenation Law, Court Cases, and Ideologies of 'Race' in Twentieth-Century America," in *Unequal Sisters: An Inclusive Reader in U.S. Women's History,* 4th ed., ed. Vicki Ruiz and Ellen Dubois (New York: Routledge, 2008), 307.

50. For more on European immigrants and whiteness, see Matthew Frye Jacobson, *Whiteness of a Different Color: European Immigrants and the Alchemy of Race* (Cambridge, MA: Harvard University Press, 1998).

51. Ernesto Chávez, "'Ramón Is Not One of These': Race and Sexuality in the Construction of Silent Film Actor Ramón Novarro's Star Image" *Journal of the History of Sexuality* 20, no. 3 (September 2011): 520–544.

52. The trailer is available on YouTube and shows the comic nature of the film.

the cast around her.[53] Director Josef von Sternberg similarly used this lighting technique on German actress Marlene Dietrich to heighten her glamourous whiteness, including in her film with Wong, *Shanghai Express* (1932).

In both *East Is West* (1930) and *Honolulu Lu* (1941), Vélez's characters' deliberate racial ambiguity enabled Hollywood to manage her non-whiteness, which ultimately enhanced her glamour and stardom. In the case of *Honolulu Lu,* Vélez playing the title role whitened American claims to Hawaii. As bearers of the Hawaiian spirit of aloha, hula dancers demonstrate what Adria Imada calls "the imperial repertoire," which normalizes colonialism and, in the case of Hawaii, makes it warm and welcoming.[54] In the case of Ming Toy, Vélez depicts a Chinese who is ultimately unveiled as white, which alleviates the threat of interracial marriage. This film, one of many of the era in which the Asian partner is revealed as white, preempts Wong as a potential lead, for she could never be unmasked as white.[55]

Velez's comic gifts undercut racial typecasting in all of her roles. Film scholar Ana López's classic article "Are All Latins from Manhattan?" argues that Vélez not only inhabited the stereotype but also exaggerated it to such a degree that she obliterated it.[56] In her Asian and Pacific Islander performances in which her whiteness was affirmed, Vélez demonstrated the absurdity of cross-racial performance. Vélez heightens her racial impersonation, which makes obvious the performativity of her roles. With her wink and exaggerated gestures, Vélez invites us to be in on the joke, implicating us in her performance. She is not deceiving the audience but bringing them around to her point of view. In B-list films such as the *Mexican Spitfire* series, Vélez shares with Josephine Baker comic gifts that make her racial cross-dressing a toying with categories. Unlike Baker, she is not portraying another race while making deliberately obvious her own racial background. Instead she uncovers the humor in portraying *any* race, therefore exploding the stereotype.

Vélez's Coca-Cola and Lux soap advertisements represented a new facet in race and American advertising. U.S. marketing struggled to find a way to connect the power of sex without "staining" the moral superiority of the white

---

53. Karen Kuo, *East Is East and West Is East: Gender, Culture, and Interwar Encounters between Asia and America* (Philadelphia: Temple University Press, 2012), 46–47.

54. Adria Imada, *Aloha America: Hula Circuits through the U.S. Empire* (Durham, NC: Duke University Press, 2012), 10–11.

55. Gina Marchetti, *Romance and the "Yellow Peril": Race, Sex, and Discursive Strategies in Hollywood Fiction* (Berkeley: University of California Press, 1993), 4.

56. Ana López, "Are All Latins from Manhattan? Hollywood, Ethnography and Cultural Colonialism," in *Unspeakable Images: Ethnicity and American Cinema,* ed. Lester Friedman (Urbana-Champaigne: University of Illinois Press, 1991), 406–407.

Lupe Vélez in *Mexican Spitfire.*
(Film still, *Mexican Spitfire.*)

woman. What these advertisements show us is that Vélez was the outsider who could be sexualized without being charged with corrupting the image of white America. Given the historical legacies of Chinese prostitution and the then current Chinese immigration exclusion act, Wong could not be deployed in similar roles. It is not so much that one would prefer that Wong be used to sell Lucky Strike cigarettes, rendering the Asian American body visible to consumer society. Rather, commodification raises interesting points about the racialized body and inclusion or exclusion in the consumer's republic of the United States.[57]

The question becomes, why Vélez? Why use someone marked as Mexican and female to promote mainstream consumer products in the United States? The companies could have picked anyone, male or female, of any race, to promote them. As Roland Marchand has argued in his foundational work, advertising "reflects needs and anxieties" not actual circumstances.[58] The answer lies in the way that Vélez's race could be incorporated into whiteness and American ethnicity.

57. Lizbeth Cohen, *A Consumer's Republic: The Politics of Mass Consumption in Postwar America* (New York: Borzoi Books [Knopf], 2003); Nancy Tomes, *Remaking the American Patient: How Madison Avenue and Modern Medicine Turned Patients into Consumers* (Chapel Hill: University of North Carolina Press, 2016).

58. Roland Marchand, *Advertising the American Dream: Making Way for Modernity, 1920–1940* (Berkeley: University of California Press, 1985), xxi.

It is significant that advertisers used Vélez to represent a company such as Coca-Cola, seeing as agencies figured out the target audience for their clients carefully. As both historian Jennifer Scanlon and art historian Patricia Johnston have documented, such an ad would be designed to appeal to the majority of American consumers.[59] This confirms that Vélez was used for her mainstream appeal. Vélez's 1932 Coca-Cola advertisement depicts her as an all-American beauty. In it, Vélez poses as a Southern California film star, for she is photographed standing next to an outdoor swimming pool while holding a bottle of Coca-Cola, toasting the sky. Her face is in profile, head tilted slightly back, teeth uncovered in a pleasant smile (nowhere near as huge as in her caricatures).[60] Clad in a plaid bathing costume with low-heeled shoes, Velez has one hand on her hip, while the other holds the bottle. In this advertisement from a 1932 issue of *Photoplay,* one can see how Hollywood and Coca-Cola mutually reinforce each other.[61] Advertising's earlier practice of placing movie star portraits in cigarette packages is apparent in the way this advertisement is constructed, especially in the slogan and the listing of Vélez's upcoming film, *The Broken Wing.* The film lends the advertisement date and time specificity. "Wholesome cheer" is the phrase used in the advertising copy, and Vélez's facial expression indicates her vivacity. Although Vélez's legs and arms are exposed, her pose is not provocative. There is nothing in the copy or photograph to indicate that Vélez is Mexican. The Coca-Cola advertisement mirrors MGM studios' publicity shots of Vélez. Like the advertisement, her studio portfolio features photographs of her posed around her pool.

Even more surprising, Vélez's image was interjected into the most hallowed grounds of whiteness, namely soap advertisements. Soap has been ground zero for metaphors of whiteness.[62] If, as cultural historian Jackson Lears has found, "national advertisers remained wedded to its principal strategy: the promise of magical self-transformation through the ritual of purchase," then soap has signified to immigrants and working-class Americans

---

59. Johnston, *Real Fantasies,* 50. Johnston's material comes from Mr. J. Esty, "On the Duplication of Magazine Circulation," "Minutes of the Representatives Meetings," July 21, 1931, 3, J. Walter Thompson Archives. See also Jennifer Scanlon, *Inarticulate Longings: The "Ladies' Home Journal," Gender and the Promise of Consumer Culture* (New York: Routledge, 1995), 221–222.

60. For Lupe Vélez caricatures, see her New York Public Library file, Performing Arts Branch.

61. *Photoplay,* Lupe Vélez Coca-Cola ad (Sydney Fox on cover), May 1932, 22.

62. Timothy Burke, *Lifebuoy Men, Lux Women: Commodification, Consumption, and Cleanliness in Modern Zimbabwe* (Durham, NC: Duke University Press, 1996).

the promise of whiteness and becoming American.[63] As historian Matthew Frye Jacobson argues in *Whiteness of a Different Color,* Jewish Americans, Irish Americans, and Italian Americans were only provisionally white before World War II. Afterward, those groups, which had previously been considered to be American ethnics, became white.[64] It is entirely possible that Vélez was used to display how buying a consumer product increases whiteness. The "Cupid Talks It Over with Lupe Vélez" campaign for Lux soap ran in national venues such as the mass-circulating magazine the *Ladies' Home Journal.* In it, Vélez's skin, key to her romantic appeal, was the subject of banter between Vélez and the matchmaker Cupid. The language used in the advertisement is evocative: "fragrant, white" soap, "the kind of skin men adore," "you have such devastating skin." Lupe's skin was not too dark for national emulation, in fact, it was considered quite ideal. Since soap has been associated with purity and innocence through using young girls and babies as spokesmodels, it is significant that the Lux soap advertisement emphasizes Vélez's sexuality through her appeal to men. This ad appeared in the *Ladies' Home Journal* in 1934, a magazine noted for its "use of advertising in defining the American woman," who was "female, middle class, and white."[65] Vélez, who was not securely white, made a living off of her exaggerated Mexican accent, and came from the working class, disrupted some of those main tenets of idealized American womanhood and opened up the category to define American women in broader terms.

Vélez's off-screen persona as a woman for all American women to emulate is especially significant, given that leading scholars have found that her film characters' roles transgressed normative American culture.[66] In "Lupe Vélez: Queen of the Bs," film scholar Rosa Linda Fregoso argues that "In the embrace of sexual liberalism, financial independence, and personal meaning derived from something other than motherhood, Vélez subverted the prevailing gendered framework."[67] Vélez's cinematic roles might assault American middle-class culture, but her commodified advertising persona reinforced it. Her visibility as a spokesmodel for Coca-Cola and Lux Soap made American middle-class culture Mexican and female. Vélez's commodification as an icon for mainstream America can be ascribed to the racializations of this era.

---

63. Lears, *Fables of Abundance,* 139.
64. Jacobson, *Whiteness of a Different Color.*
65. Scanlon, *Inarticulate Longings,* 198.
66. Victoria Sturtevant, "Spitfire: Lupe Vélez and the Ambivalent Pleasure of Ethnic Masquerade," *Velvet Light Trap,* no. 22 (Spring 2005): 23.
67. Fregoso, "Lupe Velez: Queen of the Bs," 55.

For Vélez, as a light-skinned Mexican woman who dated famous European American actors, it would seem that her ethnicity as Mexican was read as equivalent to that of Italian Americans.

Unexpectedly, Vélez's Coca-Cola advertisement appeared before the 1933 Good Neighbor Policy took effect. The Good Neighbor Policy has been cited by many scholars as a major reason why the portrayal of Latinos in Hollywood improved in the 1930s.[68] The policy was articulated by U.S. president Franklin Delano Roosevelt in April 1933 as a corrective to the Monroe Doctrine and as a means to open up Latin American markets to U.S. control. Looking at the scholarship on film and Latinos instead of the advertisements themselves, one would assume that the commodification of a Mexican actress such as Vélez would date from after the Good Neighbor Policy was instituted.

Wong as Spanish Señorita

If Mexicans or Spanish actresses could play Asians and Pacific Islanders, then why not have a Chinese American play a Spanish role? In the 1936 Van Vechten photographs, Wong posed in a series of "Spanish" señorita costumes, and her comments indicate that she would be willing to be cast as one. Wong remarked, "The Spanish ones I think are frightfully interesting and if I do not get a job as a Señorita on the strength of those, then the film producers won't know what a Señorita is all about."[69] Wong's words were made ironically, since film producers had shown a marked reluctance to cast Wong in non-Asian roles. Regardless, these comments uncover the contrast between Wong's performative understanding of race and ethnicity versus the producer's essentialist casting preferences. Wong could not be cast as a señorita at this time since her obvious racialization as Asian would pollute the image of America, even "Spanish" America, as white. Although Wong did not receive any señorita roles on the strength of those photographs, it is noteworthy that she even broached the subject. As someone who played exotic though chiefly Asian roles, Wong did not think that playing a señorita role was racially outside the bounds of possibility. Wong was fully aware that people of all races, including Mexicans, played oriental roles. But as Steichen's *Vanity Fair* photographs did not render del Río or Vélez "Spanish," with a fan or a lace mantilla, one could conclude that high fashion and art photography precluded such a staging of señorita photographs.

---

68. López, "Are All Latins from Manhattan?," 406–407.
69. Anna May Wong to Carl Van Vechten and Fania Marinoff, March 14, 1936, CVVMC.

Anna May Wong as a Spanish señorita, by Carl Van Vechten.
(Library of Congress, Prints & Photographs Division, Carl Van Vechten Collection
[reproduction number LC-USZ62-135272].)

The 1936 Van Vechten Sittings—
Glamour and Modernity

In contrast to the unsatisfactory photographs taken in 1932, Anna May Wong and Carl Van Vechten created a terrific set of portraits together in 1936 that pleased her. On March 14, 1936, Wong seized the opportunity to comment on another set of Van Vechten photographs, many of which she liked and some about which she raved. Wong had very few negative things to say about these photographs, whereas earlier she had had qualms about most of them. Working with Van Vechten and having a longstanding relationship with him gave her far more artistic control over the creation of her image. Unlike the Steichen photographs, where Wong's Chinese heritage collapsed into nation-state historical signifiers and China and the Chinese become subsumed to temporal noncoevalness, these 1936 Van Vechten photographs placed Wong squarely in contemporary time and arguably in avant-garde time.[70]

Wong preferred the photographs that tended toward high art, "like a sculpture," and those in which she looked modern and stylish. Wong reserved her highest praise for four of them, two of which were among "the most wonderful profiles I have ever had. They are like a sculpture."[71] In one of those "wonderful profiles" that are "like a sculpture," Wong poses sideways against a web-like background that looks like a series of wavy lines that are organized into a square-ish shape.[72] With her geometric striped dress, Wong's profile stands out against the lines of the background as well as the dress. "Like a sculpture" is a good way of describing it and constitutes high praise from Wong. Akin to the 1932 cocktail glass portrait, it is a terrific photograph of her. This modern style of clothing emerged during the Depression, and that streamlined fashion privileged a body with "small hips, broad shoulders, and a slim yet shapely torso," all of which Wong had.[73] Wong's clothed body fit the aesthetics of the time, which was reflected in the power of these photographs.

Wong's preferences for an artistic, modern image are especially pronounced when she makes different comments about different photographs in the same sequence. She lauds, "two of the best portraits I have ever seen

70. Fabian, *Time and the Other*.

71. "The ones I particularly like are: XXIII 2, 5, 16, and 17." Photo no. XXIII 16, Carl Van Vechten Photographs, Beinecke Library, Yale University; Wong to Van Vechten and Marinoff, March 14, 1936.

72. Photo no. XXIII 16, Carl Van Vechten Photographs, Beinecke Library, Yale University.

73. Deborah Cohen, "The Way We Look Now," *The Atlantic,* May 2014, 100–111.

of myself," in which she is dressed in a black costume, wearing a hat and a starburst pinwheel brooch.[74] These two "best portraits," according to Wong, are matching photographs in different poses. In them, Wong wears the same outfit, and the photographs share the same backdrop. The difference is in her gaze toward the camera and the viewer. In the one I designate "mysterious glamour," Wong looks pensive, she looks down and to the viewer's left, her right. The lighting is dramatic, Caravaggio-like chiaroscuro (light and dark), which highlights her left cheek and her nose, and the contrasting lighting throws much of her face into the shadows, especially her eyes. You see the fine molding of her nose, chin, and mouth. Her bangs settle across her forehead, but are slightly feathered on the left side. There is the merest hint of a gloved hand by her neck. The mood is mysterious. Comparing this image to the Steichen art photograph in which she is a beautiful disembodied head next to a peony, both share sculptural elements that highlight her bone structure. But in the Van Vechten photograph she is not disembodied, although one could make a case that the starburst brooch represents an abstract peony.

Matching up the photographs with the commentary in the letters reveals Wong's impeccable taste in glamourous presentation. By contrast, in a photograph that Wong disliked, which I identify as "non-mysterious glamour," the lighting is much more even and direct.[75] Instead of the Caravaggio-style chiaroscuro, her entire face is lit and visible. Although her cheekbones create shadows, none of her features are obscured as they are in the mysterious glamour photograph. She is pensive, looking off to her right, the viewer's left. A gloved index finger extends past her crossed arms. Her head is not as bent as it is in the mysterious glamour photograph. The mysterious glamour shot is far more interesting than the non-mysterious glamour shot: its composition demonstrates greater visual complexity in terms of, for example, shadow and depth.

What is so interesting about these Van Vechten photographs is the degree to which Wong exhibited her modern hybridity in fashion. This glamourous hybridity was evident in her winning the Mayfair Mannequin award as well as in her outfits in Paramount B films such as *King of Chinatown* (1939). Rather than adopting across-the-board American or Western styles, she brought "Asian" cultural influences and Western tailoring together in contemporary time, negating the "exotic" "ancient" costumes that served to mark Asians as

---

74. Wong writes, "For the series of XXII, 23, 25 (two of the best portraits I have seen of myself)." Photos nos. XXII 25 and XXII 23 (mysterious glamour photograph), Carl Van Vechten Photographs, Beinecke Library, Yale University.

75. Carl Van Vechten Photographs, Beinecke Library, Yale University, XXII 23 (non-mysterious glamour photograph), XXII 25 (mysterious glamour photograph).

Mysterious glamour, by Carl Van Vechten.

backward and nonmodern. In *King of Chinatown,* leading Hollywood clothing designer Edith Head concocted glamourous hybrid clothing for her. In
every scene, Wong dazzles in a different costume. Postmodern pastiches of
both the primitive and the civilized, her hats and jackets are the latest Western fashions with Chinese accents. Her elegant wearing of Chinese-accented
American clothing made such fashions acceptable and desirable in mainstream circles. These Van Vechten photographs reflect a heightened version
of her modern style.

"The World's Most Beautiful Chinese Girl": *Look* magazine, 1938

My final example of Wong's role as a glamourous modern icon comes from
her 1938 *Look* magazine cover and photo spread. Although Wong had graced
the cover of many film magazines around the world, this marked the first
time that she appeared on the cover of a general-interest magazine. As "The
World's Most Beautiful Chinese Girl," Wong embellished the cover of the
March 1938 issue. Founded in 1937 and now defunct, during its heyday *Look*
boasted a circulation of two million and a price of ten cents an issue. The
cover of *Look* magazine crowned Wong's status and featured her as a hybrid
Chinese American film star.

In *Look* magazine, the pages devoted to Wong highlight her glamour,
clothing, and, not surprisingly, given the moniker "The World's Most Beautiful Chinese Girl," her physical attributes. The captions and photographs in
Look magazine display both Wong's Chinese ethnicity and American citizenship. Underneath a still photograph of Wong from the British movie *Chu
Chin Chow* (1934), the pictorial's text explains that Wong had only recently
visited China and that, despite her appearance, she was American born. In
case the point was not understood, the next picture clarifies Wong's nationality as a sophisticated American citizen. The words proclaim: "An American
citizen, she has given up plans to retire to China." A picture of Wong wearing
a modish Western ensemble—a long striped tunic belted over a dark skirt
with a jacket whose lining and length matched the tunic, accessorized with
a dark hat tilted at a rakish angle and black high-heeled pumps—beautifully
illustrates the caption.

Look's feature confirms Wong as the icon of modern hybrid Chinese
American culture. One caption reads, "Umpire Wong," as in umpire for the
quintessential American game, baseball. For the game, Wong is dressed in a
dark cheongsam with white wavy lines on it as a pattern. Although the text
calls her all-American, given her outfit, the photograph suggests a redefinition

of that term. The caption and photograph expand the concept of American-ness by presenting a visible ambiguity that evokes wholesomeness. Such a portrait of Chinese American identity works to assuage anxiety over race and acculturation. The Chinese and the Western co-exist and cosignify each other.

Look magazine emphasized Wong's global fame. It reproduced Alfred Eisenstadt's 1928 photograph of Wong with Marlene Dietrich and Leni Riefenstahl in Berlin discussed in Chapter 1. The magazine proclaimed that "she is very popular in England, where she has made a number of pictures. She first visited China in 1935, was received there like a princess." American audiences are informed about Wong's transnational reach and expertise. The caption and photo herald Wong's international prominence. Association with Dietrich, dazzling costumes, being received like a princess, and travels to Britain all signify woman-of-the-world glamour and a moneyed lifestyle. This Look magazine cover marked the apex of her Hollywood B-list career. Wong had found a way simultaneously to embody a Chinese and an American in a modern way that increased her fame.

Conclusion

Race and glamour have had a vexed relationship, allowing Anna May Wong, Dolores del Río, and Lupe Vélez to catapult to fame. But race could also be used to typecast. Steichen's shots of Wong demonstrate how race is fully imbricated in modernist aesthetics such as photography. To counter this, Wong worked to shape a different image in the Van Vechten photographs. Her fame reached its height when she was featured on the cover of Look magazine.

Geographically this book continues westward across the Pacific in Chapters 5 and 6, following Wong on her journeys to China and Australia. As the ultimate diasporic Chinese woman, Wong searched for belonging in the world as she continued to play oriental roles. Chapter 5, "'My China Film,'" focuses on one of Wong's finest moments as a cultural worker. In 1936, Wong traveled to China for the first and only time to see the "native land" of her parents. Through these materials crafted by Wong, one can see her framing of the dynamics of race, nation, and travel.

5

"My China Film"

Scene 2: The Chinese Tailor Shop in Shanghai

Setting: The scene opens inside a tailor shop that specializes in cheongsams, the traditional garment of Chinese women newly revived by modern women. Flanked by the tailor and a member of her entourage, Wong places herself at the center of the frame in her strikingly chic and contemporary ensemble. Wong flings off her close-cut coat to reveal the elegant clothes that conform to the lines of her greyhound-lean body. Like a queen extending a hand to be kissed by her subject, she holds out her arm for measurement. The tailor moves expertly around his regal client, measuring her with a simple rope, an archaic yet efficient technique. As he translates her body into a series of knotted lengths, Wong poses for the camera, slightly tilting her head and coyly directing her eyes away. She is the perfect mannequin; the tailor unwittingly takes on the role of Hollywood designer. As the camera swivels, the rest of the workshop, where workers—men and children— sew piles of cut silk by hand, comes into view. In a later scene, Wong costumes herself in one of these garments to portray a Chinese villager when she visits her family's ancestral home.[1]

---

1. "My China Film," by Anna May Wong. The film itself does not contain numbered scenes. I have added them for greater clarity.

The moment depicted above is a scene in the film that Anna May Wong created to counteract Metro-Goldwyn-Mayer's award-winning film about Chinese peasants, *The Good Earth* (1937).[2] Infamously, Wong auditioned for the leading role in *The Good Earth*, only to be passed over in favor of a white European actress who would play the role in yellowface. Immediately after that casting rejection, Wong traveled to China for the first and only time, in 1936, to see the real China. Ever ingenious, Wong arranged to have her experiences there filmed by cinematographer H. S. (Haisheng) "Newsreel" Wong in order to make her own movie about China. In contrast to *The Good Earth*, "My China Film" is the result of a Chinese American actress seizing the means of production. It is seductive to believe that Wong, at long last, took full charge of her artistic medium.

In a consciously staged shot during the opening sequence to "My China Film," Wong holds the camera while capturing scenes in the street. There are no technicians or crew in sight, just Wong filming daily life in urban China. As she herself is being filmed, self-fashioning clearly operates. This image of Wong in control of the camera, making her own film about China, is evocative. Words from the film such as "I was particularly anxious to get these pictures and I'm glad I did" reveal that she had definite ideas about what she wanted to include in her film and what types of scenes would make for good cinema. No slouch on the publicity front, she wrote a series of articles about her journey to China for the *New York Herald Tribune*. Her impetus to control how she was perceived in "My China Film" can be seen as a continuation of the work she had done in shaping her photographs with Carl Van Vechten. In both the film and her sessions with Van Vechten, she demonstrates her desire to frame the dynamics of race, nation, and image.

The film serves as autobiography, self-fashioning, and image making for through it, Wong created her Chinese American self. Rather than being a straightforward documentary travelogue, "My China Film" reflects differing agendas and multiple Chinas. Wong showed her audience the New China of the 1930s, one that existed in contemporary time to the making of the film. This China had a semicolonial relationship with the West. Nostalgia and family reunification with her father (Sam Sing) are prominent themes in the film.[3]

---

2. Wong's "My China Film" is available at the UCLA Film and Television Archive, Los Angeles, California. Titled "Native Land," it was broadcast as part of the *Bold Journey* ABC television documentary series on February 14, 1957.

3. For travel movies made by immigrants' children, such visits are forensic and "attempt to substitute a spatial for temporal migration." Peter Feng, *Identities in Motion: Asian American Film and Video* (Durham, NC: Duke University Press, 2002), chap. 4.

Wong worked hard to bring "My China Film" to the American public, and she succeeded when it finally aired in 1957 on television as part of a series entitled *Bold Journey.*

The existing film footage dates from the 1930s, whereas Wong's voice-over comes from the thirty-minute 1957 television broadcast. These discrepancies in time make the film both fascinating as a product and tricky to analyze. In "My China Film," Wong does a fluid voice-over during the entire production, displaying a fine sense of humor and a narrative gift for storytelling, rendering her ability to frame it in retrospect even more evocative. As might be expected, her tone is relentlessly upbeat, frequently that of a curious tourist. Wong is supposed to be an insider, guiding American audiences through her "native land" or, to be more accurate, the supposed native land of her parents, but every gesture confirms her outsider status. The voice-over from the television broadcast uncovers her own nostalgia for her younger self on the screen as well as for her father, who had passed away.

The meaning ascribed to such historical material is complex. One should not be naïve enough to believe that Wong's China film demonstrates her complete control over her career. Strong arguments can be made that no historical source is an authentic representation of a person's intent. In a twentieth-century world structured by modernity, it is difficult to claim that any one individual has complete free will over her or his life. Yet, compared to the other artifacts Wong has left us, such as her European and Hollywood films—within which she interprets her roles and star persona, in her China film and writings, she constructs the overall vantage point and narrative that she wants the world to know. "My China Film" and her writings about the journey are still produced from within the confines of her "star image," to use film scholar Richard Dyer's phrase—the roles she performs in public, and the ones others expect her to play.[4] Yet she claims ownership, calling the product "my film." Since the movie does not have an official title, I have titled it "My China Film" because Wong repeatedly calls it "my film" in her letters to Van Vechten and his wife, the actress Fania Marinoff. It is crucial to recognize that, despite Wong's "authorship," her motion picture and writings are creations intended for the outside world. I argue that the most accurate way to view this film and her writings about her travels are as Wong's mediation of her public persona. Taken as a whole, they speak volumes as to how Wong wanted to be perceived.

Ironically, Wong's "My China Film" and her writings about it demonstrate her Americanness and her modern Western self as they reveal her dis-

---

4. Richard Dyer, *Stars* (London: British Film Institute, 1998).

tance from Chinese cultural practices such as theater and tailoring. In contrast to Berlin, as I analyze in Chapter 1, a site where she found "my Chinese soul coming back to claim me," or her Chinese ambassadorial persona in Australia as I discuss in Chapter 6, Wong's China film showcases her lack of "authentic" Chinese culture. Her motion picture reveals her craftsmanship as an American actress learning to play a Chinese by equipping herself to perform the role of a transnational Chinese.

Although "My China Film" is the heart of this chapter, its larger significance comes from its impact on the trajectory of Wong's Hollywood career. The chapter is bookended by a discussion of Wong's career before and after her trip to China. The China trip marked a turning point for Wong. *The Good Earth* casting rejection prompted her visit to China, but upon her return she won a Paramount Pictures contract for four B-list Chinese American–themed films.

Hollywood, Yellowface, and *The Good Earth*

Anna May Wong's 1936 film about her journey to China stands as a counterpoint to Hollywood cinema's construction of China and Chinese Americans. In the 1930s, Asia, especially China, loomed large in the American imaginary, and Hollywood made films to express those fantasies and anxieties. Although that did result in Wong gaining leading roles, she fought continually against the typecasting that placed European Americans in starring Asian roles. Indeed, Wong's failure to land a major part in *The Good Earth* (1937) was the main reason she decided to travel to China and to make her own film of that trip. In the initial stages in 1935, it was widely known that Metro-Goldwyn-Mayer (MGM) intended *The Good Earth* to be an important film: it had been allocated one of the largest budgets in cinematic history, two million dollars.[5] A film that celebrated resilient Chinese peasants, *The Good Earth* was created in order to resonate with Depression-era American audiences. It has been argued that the book was a major impetus for shifting American opinions from demonizing the Chinese to allying with them during the Sino-Japanese War (1931–1945), especially after its author, Pearl S. Buck, won the Nobel Prize in literature in 1938.[6] The Sino-Japanese War, triggered in 1931 by Japan's invasion of Manchuria, resulted in greater sympathy for China and Chinese Americans. The United States sided with

---

5. *The Good Earth*, MGM, 1937.
6. Harold Isaacs, *Scratches on our Minds: American Images of China and India* (New York: Routledge, 1980), 157.

China, which also signaled a turn in how Hollywood portrayed race and boosted the value of Hollywood films about the "good" Chinese.

To many, Wong was the logical choice for the leading role of O-lan. However, MGM thwarted Wong's hopes of starring in an "A" film feature by casting Luise Rainer, the European actress who would land back-to-back Academy Awards for Best Actress, including one for O-lan. MGM invited Wong to screen test as Lotus, the second wife who ruins the family. Conflicting reports from her letters versus newspaper stories manifest the complexity of race and Hollywood casting. Wong reportedly repudiated the role because she did not want to be the only Chinese American cast in a leading role as the film's only negative character. As she stated in the *Los Angeles Times:* "I'll be glad to take a test, but I won't play the part. If you let me play O-lan, I'll be very glad. But you're asking me—with Chinese blood—to do the only unsympathetic role in the picture featuring an all-American cast portraying Chinese characters."[7] Despite feeling insulted, Wong took a number of screen tests for the "unsympathetic" part of Lotus. Those remarks reported in the *Los Angeles Times* were most likely part of her literally and figuratively face-saving self-fashioning strategy: as historian Karen Leong states in the *China Mystique,* casting notes from two different screen tests revealed that Wong was not considered beautiful enough for the role.[8] Viennese actress Tilly Loesch won the role of Lotus. Wong's *Los Angeles Times* condemnation of playing the role of Lotus echoed the 1931 interview titled "I Protest," in which she denounced evil portrayals of the Chinese in *Daughter of the Dragon* as "so wicked." It was striking that Wong's face-saving comments censuring MGM's desire to cast her as an evil Chinese instead of as the heroic O-lan appeared in Hollywood's hometown, broadly circulating newspaper.

Wong's report in her letter to the Van Vechtens dated December 16, 1935, evinced a radically different view of the *Good Earth* casting process than the *Los Angeles Times* article. As she wrote: "Have made two tests for the 'Lotus' part. From all appearances Miss Rainer is definitely set for the part of Olan. No use backing up against a stone wall. Practically everyone, including my friends, seem to feel that I should take the Lotus part 'if there is enough money in it.'"[9] This letter indicates that, at least in private, Wong took a pragmatic attitude in considering playing Lotus. Reports also surfaced that

7. *Los Angeles Times,* 1935. Also cited in Graham Hodges, *Anna May Wong* (New York: Palgrave, 2004), 152.

8. Karen Leong, *China Mystique: Pearl S. Buck, Anna May Wong, Mayling Soong, and the Transformation of American Orientalism* (Berkeley: University of California Press, 2005), 76.

9. Anna May Wong to Carl Van Vechten and Fania Marinoff, December 16, 1935, Carl Van Vechten Manuscript Collection, Beinecke Library, Yale University (hereafter, CVVMC).

Wong was not offered the part because she looked too old. MGM's refusal to headline her in such a high-profile movie is significant: the opportunity would have increased Wong's visibility in Hollywood and beyond. Between five hundred and two thousand thespians, many of whom but not all were Chinese American, worked as extras on *The Good Earth,* including Wong's sister Mary, but not Los Angeles's most famous actress of Chinese descent.

MGM's casting of European American actresses in the *Good Earth* was not an anomaly but the norm. Wong had previously encountered the problem of not being the right kind of Chinese at that studio. In 1932 she stated: "I made a test at Metro Goldwyn Mayer studio for the leading role in the *Son Daughter,* the Chinese play David Belasco produced years ago with Leonore Ulrich. I guess I look too Chinese to play a Chinese because I hear Colleen Moore is going to do it, although no definite decision has been made."[10] With these words, Wong verified that she understood the racial politics of Hollywood casting. Under the ethos of yellowface, a person of European descent could play a Chinese role more palatably than a person of Chinese descent.[11] Like the African American equivalent, blackface, yellowface functioned to explore otherness in a racially safe way while sanctioning whiteness. It is not surprising that Wong did not win the MGM role in *The Son-Daughter.* David Belasco's theatrical productions had a long history of casting European American women in Asian roles, notoriously Blanche Bates as Cho-Cho San in *Madame Butterfly* and as Yo-San in *The Darling of the Gods.*[12] Even if theater impresario Belasco did not have anything to do with the MGM film production of *The Son-Daughter,* the legacy of yellowface casting in his plays would have set the historical precedent for MGM to do the same in selecting Helen Hayes or Luise Rainer instead of Wong.

In order to understand the magnitude of Wong's accomplishment as a cultural worker in making her own film, it is important to comprehend the sheer dominance of Hollywood studios in American filmmaking. In the early part of the twentieth century, the film industry consolidated and moved to Los Angeles. By the 1920s, the major studios, known as the Big Eight, controlled 90 percent of the films made. The studios monopolized big stars such as Mary Pickford and Charlie Chaplin and controlled movie theaters to such an extent

---

10. Anna May Wong to Carl Van Vechten and Fania Marinoff, September 21, 1932, CVVMC.

11. Mexican American actress Lupe Vélez auditioned for the same lead role in *The Son-Daughter,* which was won by European American actress Helen Hayes, and Mexican American actor Ramón Novarro played a leading role in it.

12. Mari Yoshihara, *Embracing the East: White Women and American Orientalism* (New York: Oxford University Press, 2003), 79–87.

that they could block book seventy or eighty films a year into theaters around the country.[13] The 1930s have been considered the golden age of Hollywood studio production for the films' quality as well as quantity. Although African American filmmakers such as Oscar Micheaux and Lincoln Pictures made "race" movies intended for black audiences, there were no such alternatives for Wong as an Asian American.[14] As shown in this book's previous chapters, Wong had already explored the main alternative to Hollywood film production, making films in Europe. Limited as it was, major studio film work in Hollywood or Europe was her only moving picture work option outside of her own initiatives.

Anna May Wong, Modernity, and Modern China

Anna May Wong's China film reveals not only her own lack of Chinese culture but also her fascination with Chinese modernity. Although many Americans held Western colonial ideas of China as antiquated and backward, Wong's China film, to the contrary, uncovered a China imbued with the modern. What becomes abundantly clear in the film is that China becomes a foil for Wong's own modernity.

During the introduction to "Native Land," the 1957 live television broadcast of "My China Film," host John Stephenson asked Wong about her impressions of China, and she reported on the up-to-date Chinese tea-drinking habits. American common knowledge would have been that tea drinking was the ultimate traditional Chinese custom, but in reality it proved to be quite the opposite. Wong stated in the film's introduction, "Well, I have always heard about the Chinese taking their time and sipping tea and spending hours at the ceremony so I said, At long last a cup of real Chinese tea in China. So when I arrived at the Park Hotel, the Chinese hotel, I said I'd like some tea please. So up they rush with a tea bag."[15] Wong explained that the hotel had provided a modern American tea bag because the Chinese kitchen had closed. Rather than being an antiquated land, Wong found that China fully utilized up-to-date American innovations.

Wong's letters about her trip to China played with Western notions of authenticity and modernity, including her own. She wrote, "Have been to

---

13. Lary May, *Screening Out the Past: The Birth of Mass Culture and the Motion Picture Industry* (Chicago: University of Chicago Press, 1980), 177–178; Neil Gabler, *An Empire of Their Own: How the Jews Invented Hollywood* (New York: Anchor, 1989).

14. Pearl Bowser and Louise Spence, *Writing Himself into History: Oscar Micheaux, His Silent Films, and His Audiences* (New Brunswick, NJ: Rutgers University Press, 2000).

15. *Bold Journey,* "Native Land."

Canton, which is to-date the most Chinese City I have visited. The surrounding country was simply heavenly. As you know Shanghai and Hong Kong are much too international to be called China. Will be returning to Shanghai via the 'President Coolidge' arriving March 25th and will be stopping at the Park Hotel, Shanghai for two months."[16] Like many Westerners, for Wong, the taint of Western colonialism made Shanghai and Hong Kong less authentic than other Chinese spaces farther removed from the West. But she still availed herself of Western-style amenities such as her choice of the Park Hotel.

What is particularly striking about Wong's film is that it demonstrates her eagerness to place China in contemporary time. As we saw in Chapter 2, London theater audiences and critics reflexively placed Wong's roles and costumes in antiquated time, and, in Chapter 4, photographer Edward Steichen did so as well. Wong reveals a diametrically opposite vantage point—in her motion picture she corroborates that China itself is temporally modern. In the streets of Shanghai, the camera shows a young girl, and Wong comments on "Little Missy Shanghai with the latest in haircuts." In the film footage focused on a blind traveling musician, Wong narrates that in China the flag he carried denotes a blind person, which she points out is the same as "our blind here with their canes." In this case, Wong uses "our" to signify her fellow Americans, exhibiting how she situates China as having practices analogous to those of the United States.

It is not surprising that Wong enjoyed discussing the modernity of the Pacific Rim—the recounting of her stop in Honolulu on her China voyage conveys her clear understanding of authenticity and the modern. In the newspaper account of her visit, she explained that Honolulu is "exceedingly modern" and "I knew better than to expect any grass huts; I remembered hearing of a Hollywood company that went to Honolulu to take South Sea village scenes, and then discovered that the only grass hut there was in a museum. Even the hula skirts, someone said, are now imported from Iowa."[17] Wong's insider knowledge of what it takes to make a Hollywood film provided her with a lens through which she could understand modernity and the changing world. Wong's example demonstrates the dynamics of the colonial economy, where the metropole could produce "authentic" products such as hula skirts to be sold back to the colony. Hawaii, a territory de facto colony of

---

16. Anna May Wong to Carl Van Vechten and Fania Marinoff, March 14, 1936, CVVMC.

17. Anna May Wong, "Anna May Wong Relates Arrival in Japan, Her First Sight of the Orient," *New York Herald Tribune,* May 24, 1936, sec. 2, pt. 2, 1.

the United States since 1898, did not become a state until 1959. Contrary to Hollywood's depiction, Wong refused to put colonial Hawaii in primitive time.

Wong was fascinated with not only Chinese and Pacific Rim modernity; most importantly, her journey to China highlighted her own modernity. Early in the film there is a scene with Wong flanked by two women at a market in the streets of Shanghai, with crowds following her. This scene immediately preceded the one in the Chinese tailor shop. Wong reported: "Wherever I went in China, I heard Chinese remarking, who is that foreign-looking or Chinese-looking lady, I should say, in foreign dress."[18] Wong's slip of the tongue and readjustment is telling. The phrase "foreign looking" conveys her inability to pass as a Chinese national and indicates her Western appearance. She corrects her phrase to reflect that she looks Chinese, but is clad in foreign clothes. That continued marking as foreign, meaning not Chinese, bothered Wong to such an extent that she decided to make changes. As Wong narrates in her China film, "Well, I thought I ought to do something about that so Mrs. Wong took me to the leading silk shop, Lau Kai Fouks in Shanghai, where I chose materials for my first Chinese dresses." She then brought this material to the Chinese tailor shop. The consummate actress, Wong's comments attest that a change of costume can do wonders for one's ability to play a role, in this case, that of a Chinese woman. As Sean Metzger argues in *Chinese Looks,* a close examination of clothing such as the cheongsam or *qipao* can show how Chineseness was theorized at particular historical moments.[19] This moment encapsulates one of the most important themes of Wong's film, her alienation from "authentic" Chinese culture as well as the pedagogy of her learning how to become Chinese. Wong's China film confirms that there is nothing inherent about transnational Chinese belonging.

Wong's visit to the Chinese tailor is one of the most charming moments in the film. It is also possibly the most culturally revealing, for it promulgates Wong's Western film star fashion status. At the Chinese tailor Wong wears a black beret; a big polka-dotted, light-colored shirt; a belt; and a narrow, perfectly fitted skirt suit. She looks every inch the movie star. She takes off her jacket, undoes her scarf, and holds out her arms out for the tailor's measurements. She poses for the tailor, holding her arms out so he can access her, instantaneously turning herself into a mannequin. In this vignette, all of her experiences of being fitted for film costumes come to life for the viewer.

---

18. *Bold Journey,* "Native Land."

19. Sean Metzger, *Chinese Looks: Fashion, Performance, Race* (Bloomington: University of Indiana Press, 2014), 25.

This moment evokes Wong's own modernity. As she poses, the Chinese tailor uses a string to measure her. She explains in the film voice-over, "Although he wanted to come to me at the hotel, I was particularly anxious to get these pictures, and I'm glad I did because his way of measuring is he takes a piece of string and he ties a knot for each measurement." One knot represents the arm length, another the neck measurement, and so forth. Revealing her verbal dexterity, Wong chortles, "Now how he can tell which knot is what knot I know not." Displaying her Western expectations of tailoring, she exclaims, "And they never pin you up when they fit you either ". . . and it fits perfectly. I don't know how they do it." Chinese tailoring was as much a mystery for Wong as it was for her American audience. This moment underscores that for Wong, her true "native land" was in the West.

From a contemporary perspective, one of the most daunting aspects of the scene at the tailor is the use of child labor to make the clothing. When Wong says "they never pin you up when they fit you either," the camera uncovers shots of a child working alongside the adults. Wong's voice-over mentions "busy little hands" but does not display alarm at child labor being an integral part of the manufacture of her exquisite clothing. Presumably the children are part of a larger family-labor system in a hand-sewing business, much as there was an overt family-labor system in the United States before child-labor protection laws were put into place with the Fair Labor Standards Act (1938). Wong and her siblings had participated in such a family economy in their laundry business.

During a journey to the temples in the Western Hills, Wong exhibits her pleasure in being a Chinese American who successfully passes for Chinese. For her visit Wong dons "native" dress: very chic versions of the coolie hat and coolie top and pants. She appears gleeful that her outfit successfully transformed her into an "authentic" Chinese character. Not only had she determined the correct costume for her visit; she asserted her movie star and American privilege, for coolies conveyed her in a sedan chair. She stated, "After that first stay in Peiping I was exhausted with all these new impressions that I had to take off to the temples in the western hills to meditate and digest what I've seen. But I am not used to going on foot." Wong regally portrays the grande dame sitting in a sedan chair carried by four bearers on her way to the temple. But, as she tells the audience, indignity of indignities, she was eventually forced to walk: "The sedan chair refused to take me any further because they don't like to climb steps." The camera documents Wong, spry on her feet, bounding up stone stairs to the temple. Even in her Chinese-style attire, she cannot pass for a peasant. With its high-quality materials, wide brim, and the rakish angle at which she wears it, the coolie hat beautifully frames Wong's artfully made-up face. Everything about Wong's stylish ensemble marks her as the class opposite of a coolie, a comparison underscored by her proximity to the Chinese male peasants who wear the traditional coolie hats.

Despite her forays into wearing a "native" costume, the next scenes confirm that Wong's gait, makeup, and unbound feet all mark her as modern and Western. Her narration continues, "So I was unceremoniously dumped out," meaning out of the sedan chair. Note the colloquial American language and sense of humor displayed in that phrasing. After being summarily ejected from her seat, Wong walked up to the temple to find that her visit coincided with the day of ancestor worship. Wong exclaims: "Here's a wonderful old lady. See her little bound feet." It could be argued that Wong herself employed the ethnographic gaze in emphasizing the "little bound feet."[20] The wonderful old lady has wrinkles, no makeup, is tiny and modestly dressed. The camera then cuts to a close-up of Wong, her skillfully applied eyeliner and makeup apparent. Wong's youth and beauty are at their height, and the camera makes that very visible. The differences between Wong and the "wonderful old lady" are palpable, for Wong is tall, elegant, and chic. Numerous moments make it abundantly clear that Wong's feet are not bound, for the camera measures their full size as she briskly bounds up the stairs. In a later shot, she lounges while drinking tea, with her feet tucked up beside her, clearly large and flat in her chic satin beribboned athletic shoes. During this visit to the temple, Wong's words, unbound feet, and costume in comparison with an elderly Chinese woman continue to emphasize her photogenic image as a Western film star.

Chinese cultural insularity is called into question when Wong's motion picture exhibits a Chinese bride's procession. It is a typical Chinese street scene, complete with the pageantry of the wedding procession. However, notions of Chinese authenticity and timelessness are shattered in the next instant. Wong explains, "She is supposed to be weeping [but she is not]. . . . This is an American-educated bride." Despite the overwhelming nostalgia and sentiment attached to such a cultural moment, the actual evidence reveals the cultural complexity of the Chinese diaspora.

Scene 6: School of Drama in Peiping (Beijing)

Setting: The scene opens on an outdoor courtyard in the middle of Peiping's renowned drama school, where a male teacher instructs a class of young girls in the

---

20. I thank my anonymous reader for this insight.

language of the fan. A bobbed-haired student imitates his every move, fluttering her fan and taking mincing steps with toe shoes that create the effect of bound feet.

Wong's Voice-over: "These are the only scenes ever made of the famous School of Drama in Peiping, where they take children from poor families who have talents for theater, acting, and dancing ". . . [who are] given a two month's trial, and after two months if they show no further talent, they are relegated to being Chinese musicians. . . . This instructor is a famous female impersonator. Now this is very amusing. He is showing the girls how to be girls."

What is particularly poignant in "My China Film" is Wong's interest in Chinese theater and what it reveals about China in particular and about gender more broadly. It gives her a space for imagining an alternative life for herself as an actress in China. But it also discloses how that imagined alternative in China could not mirror or even come close to her Western career—leading roles in Chinese theater were played by female impersonators. The young girls she saw at the drama school were training for minor roles. Wong could not have been a leading theatrical actress in China; therefore, it could never have been a true homeland for her unless she gave up her chosen profession. Wong's visit to the School of Drama demonstrates her keen interest in self-fashioning and her eagerness to learn how to personify women in Chinese theater. This moment proclaims that, for Wong, playing oriental roles in any geographic location constitutes racial drag; in China, it is both national and gendered impersonation.

In a series of quick shots, Wong reveals the pedagogy of female impersonation, herself becoming a student in the process. A female impersonator is introduced, uncostumed, as he throws and catches sticks in the air. Another moment features a demonstration on how to create bound feet, called lotus feet. A young male actor transforms into a female character through pinning on long hair in five different sections. The camera then reveals the actor who plays the role of the Spirit of the White Snake in full glory as a female and depicts portions of the Dance of the White Snake. Wong sits down at a makeup desk with another actor, watching him intently while he applies the makeup that will transform him into a female character. Just as the instructor taught the girls how to be girls, this young man is teaching Wong how to be a Chinese female actress. This moment beautifully exemplifies the cultural and social constructedness of gender. As Judith Butler has famously argued, gender is not innate but performative.[21] This scene certifies that even the

---

21. Judith Butler, *Gender Trouble: Feminism and the Subversion of Identity* (New York: Routledge, 1990).

most famous actress of Chinese and oriental roles still has much to learn about how to perform female Chinese roles. Since all of the theater and opera performers were men, the instruction was about stylization not just absolute mimicry. Tellingly, Wong's favorite actor was not a female impersonator but a young man who played male prime minister roles, or, as Wong translated, the peacemaker parts.

In addition to her lessons in female impersonation, Wong is in need of further basic cultural instruction on how to behave around Chinese actors. She explains to the film viewers, "The Chinese actors are very superstitious about your touching their beards. I once tried one of the beards on and I nearly had my ears pinned back." Presumably, Western actors were much more informal with their props. With that remark, Wong conveys her Western film star assumptions and her outsider status—she did not know Chinese superstitions. Wong further translates cultural lessons, explaining to the American viewers that Chinese theater operates through inference: the audience works "almost as hard as the actors exercise their own imagination."

Uneasy Modernity

Given her status as the most famous global actress of Chinese descent, who drew crowds and accolades from audiences around the world, one would reasonably expect Chinese film critics, government officials, and Chinese crowds to be devoted to Wong. That was not the case. Although the West frequently identified Wong incorrectly as a Chinese national, many in China did not embrace her. The China visit discloses how Wong was a touchstone for critiques and negative opinions about Chinese modernity, hinted at in "My China Film" when Wong wryly admitted that some people thought she was "foreign-looking" or a "Chinese-looking lady in foreign dress." Press coverage brought forth overt critiques of Wong as a representative of Western racial modernity. Wong's visit to China intermeshed with China's fraught relationship with the West, which, in part, explains the disquiet with her visit.

During the live studio broadcast of "My China Film," Wong glosses over her role as an uneasy representative of racial modernity. Instead, echoing her language in describing Berlin, Wong characterized Shanghai as cosmopolitan. When asked if, as a Hollywood leading actress, she was known in China, Wong invoked the language of modernity in terms of cosmopolitanism, explaining: "Well, [I was known] in the big cities like Shanghai where [the people] are more cosmopolitan. Back in the countryside they thought that I was a robot or a legendary figure that a machine made move, meaning that they didn't think I was a living person. I was just a picture, a flicker personality."[22] According to Wong, for naïve country audiences, films were not based on the real.

Literary scholar Leo Ou-fan Lee confirms Wong's characterization of the city as cosmopolitan. He states that from 1927 to 1937, the end of which coincided with Wong's visit to China, was the era when cosmopolitanism flourished in Shanghai. In *Shanghai Moderns,* he categorizes "the phenomenon of Chinese writers eagerly embracing Western cultures in Shanghai's foreign concessions as a manifestation of a Chinese cosmopolitanism, which is another facet of Chinese modernity."[23] To extend this example to film, in this era, Hollywood productions flourished in China, often surpassing Chinese-made movies in popularity. For example, Chinese magazines such as *Linglong Funü tubhua zahi* (*Lin Loon Lady's Magazine*) rated the top ten films in the December 6, 1933, issue, and nine out of ten were Hollywood or Western ones. The January 31, 1934, issue was filled not with Asian actors but with Hollywood stars who have made cameos in this book, such as Dolores del Río, Greta Garbo, and Marlene Dietrich.[24]

What Wong optimistically described as cosmopolitan might be better characterized as semicolonialism. With the nineteenth-century Opium Wars and the subsequent forced opening of the treaty ports in China to Westerners, China was marked with semicolonial spaces in ports such as Shanghai. Literary scholar Shu-mei Shih makes a convincing case for terming this relationship between China and the West as one of "semicolonialism," arguing that modernism circulated between China, Japan, and the West. Shih writes that "Chinese semicolonialism registered a set of cultural politics and practices different from formal colonialism."[25] Given Japan's influence in the region, the West was not the only source of modernism in China; therefore, the relationship between China and the West was more complex than one of metropole and colony—hence, the concept of semicolonialism. Compared to an actress of European descent, Wong's Chinese heritage put her in the complicated position of having imagined herself and been treated as a person of Chinese descent her entire life, yet having been fully molded by the West.

Not surprisingly, numerous groups in China reacted to these Western semicolonial incursions in ways ranging from uneasy to hostile. During the making of "My China Film," cosmopolitanism was on the wane. Wong ar-

---

22. *Bold Journey,* "Native Land."

23. Leo Ou-fan Lee, *Shanghai Modern: The Flowering of a New Urban Culture in China, 1930–1945* (Cambridge, MA: Harvard University Press, 1999), 313.

24. Lee, *Shanghai Modern,* 86–87.

25. Shu-mei Shih, *The Lure of the Modern: Writing Modernism in Semicolonial China 1917–1937* (Berkeley: University of California Press, 2001), xi.

rived in a Shanghai where the Chinese "Modern Girl" was a prominent figure who had reached her heyday. As scholar Madeline Dong has researched, the Modern Girl was often depicted in Western clothing as a career girl. She was an appealing figure for some women to emulate because she blurred class boundaries and the adoption of her look served as a means for female social mobility. Images of the Modern Girl appeared after China began propaganda efforts to get Western support in the face of Japanese imperialism. Yet the Modern Girl was a contested figure. Some believed that she was an index of colonialism and all things foreign. There was backlash against women who exemplified her. For example, the "Brigades of Destroyers of the Modern" patrolled and actually slashed women's clothing if they appeared too modern.[26] In addition, some Chinese feminists felt that the frivolity of the Modern Girl pulled the movement back. After Wong's departure from China, though not in response to it, the backlash against the Modern Girl triumphed, and women who represented her were no longer as visible in Chinese culture.

Even before her arrival in China, Wong had received strong negative criticism from the Chinese press. The rising new conservatism that condemned the Modern Girl and films such as *The New Woman* (1935) created an unwelcoming atmosphere. According to biographer Graham Hodges, magazines questioned Wong's character and whether or not she should be welcomed into China.[27] Some Chinese saw Wong as Western and as having capitulated to the worst of Hollywood typecasting. It is not surprising that Wong's China film did not reflect this disjuncture, instead demonstrating nostalgia for an imagined China. For some, Wong was a touchstone that underscored ambivalence toward modernity and colonialism. Film scholar Yiman Wang argues that Wong was not considered any more Chinese than the white actors who played Chinese roles and was castigated by the Chinese press for not presenting the "state-sponsored image of modern China."[28] Over time, opinions did improve, and the press eventually mustered up some warmth toward Wong. After she raised money for United China Relief and the Kuomintang Party (KMT), the KMT invited her to a special reception, which contributed to Wong's loyalty to the nationalists.[29]

---

26. Madeline Dong, "Who Is Afraid of the Chinese Modern Girl?," in *The Modern Girl around the World: Consumption, Modernity, and Globalization,* ed. Modern Girl around the World Research Group (Durham, NC: Duke University Press, 2008), 215–216.

27. Hodges, *Anna May Wong,* 159–160.

28. Yiman Wang, "Watching Anna May Wong in Republican China," *American and Chinese-Language Cinemas: Examining Cultural Flows,* ed. Lisa Funnell and Man-Fung Yip (New York: Routledge, 2014), 173–174.

29. Hodges, *Anna May Wong,* 168–171.

All of these changing attitudes toward modernity and the West, along with the difficulties Wong had in gaining acceptance in China, made it hard for Wong to get misty eyed about the present-day Chinese, and, as she wrote to Marinoff and Van Vechten, caused her to jettison any notion of a future in China. What this negative press in China indicates is how much of Wong's "star text," to use Dyer's phrase, was not just her films but all of the press, advertising, newsreels, and fashion spreads surrounding her.[30] In China, except for the elites such as those in the KMT who were educated in Britain, the United States, or Japan, nonelite people would not have had access to her star text in English or in European languages. Wong's glamour and exoticness did not work in the same way in China as it did in Berlin or Sydney or London. Even though Wong's "My China Film" paraded China's modernity, local protests around her visit to her family's ancestral village revealed her as a polarizing representative of modernity.

Scene 7: The Wong Family's Ancestral Village

Setting: At an urban train station, Wong, in a Western coat, climbs aboard a long steam train with her brother Richard and her sister Ying. As the Chinese countryside flashes past out of the train window, she compares it with California and the Philippines, familiar reference points for the American-born actress. After their long journey, they arrive at her family's ancestral village, where her father has returned for a visit. For her grand entry, Wong unveils one of her new cheongsams. Wong's stylized face, with pale radiant skin and perfect teeth, appears in stark contrast to her father's dark, weathered visage and his gap-toothed grin—the movie star and the peasant.

Wong's Voice-over: "Now for the great adventure to see my father. . . . People curious and come from miles around to see what a movie star looks like. . . . This is one of my favorite pictures of my father. He was so happy that day to be surrounded with his family from the West and the East. . . . Although I have been to many, many places in the world, this first and only trip I made to China was the most meaningful."

"My China Film" footage of Anna May Wong's visit to her ancestral village confirms how she was suspended between the two worlds of China and the United States. Wong begins the final segment of her film by gaily announcing, "Now for the great adventure to see my father." Wong's father lived in

---

30. Dyer, *Stars*.

California, not China, where he was visiting. During this visit, a longing for an imagined ancestral place and past that Wong never knew comes out in full force. Wong's Chineseness grows as the train journey to visit her father in their ancestral village progresses. Tellingly, the film footage displays her in a Western-style coat as she embarks on her journey, but wearing a dark Chinese cheongsam as she disembarks. As she and her brother Richard and sister Ying walk from the train station to the village home, Wong's dark cheongsam popping out against Richard's and Ying's white outfits, Wong exclaims, "There is our old pappy!" who is also dressed in all white.

Yet, underlying this feel-good moment, there is no indication of the protests and unrest that stymied Wong's initial visit to the village. Nor is there any sign of her father's own alienation from China that comes through in Wong's letters. According to Hodges, the first time that Wong attempted to visit the ancestral village she was greeted with anger and protests, something not apparent in the film.[31] The conditions were so hostile that Wong had to abort that trip and try again later. Only her second trip, however, was memorialized in her film. In discussing whether or not she was known in China during the introduction to the televised broadcast of the film, she tells the audience, "I remember when I first went to the village to visit my father I was dressed in a white dress and the children all ran to the mothers and said oh here comes the white devil." So within the heartwarming visit to the ancestral village there was a moment of nonwelcome, one that did not appear on camera. The term "white devil" typically refers to European Americans as foreigners; thus we might infer it did not refer to Wong's white dress. Such a remark indicates that Wong did not code as a local or as Chinese to the children. In that scene from her second visit to her father's ancestral village, which is shown toward the end of "My China Film," Wong is dressed in one of her dark, not white, "native" costumes, presumably one of the cheongsams she had made for her in Shanghai. Despite the fact that she was not dressed in white during the second visit, her carriage, makeup, accessories, shoes, and the accompanying film cameras all still marked her as an outsider, a "white devil" to the children. In her voice-over corresponding with the actual film footage, she omits any mention of herself as the "white devil," noting instead, "People curious and come from miles around to see what a movie star looks like."

Sentimentality is at its heaviest in the final scene with Wong and her father. She tells the television audience, "Favorite pictures of my father. Surrounded with his family from the West and the East." In the final, pastoral

---

31. Hodges, *Anna May Wong*, 166–167.

clip, with her brother and sister excised from the scene of reunion, only Wong and her father have tea together. Then, in the finale, which foreshadows the film *Gone with the Wind* (1939), Wong and her father stand, backs to the camera, in the sunset, looking over the fields and the village. The footage put together by Wong displays her as the central child within the family for she takes command and is at the center of all of the activity. The movie ends as Wong finishes her narrative statement with the revelation: "Although I have been to many, many places in the world, this first and only trip I made to China was the most meaningful." You can almost hear the orchestra music swell as Wong and her father gaze over the ancestral land.

Yet that supposed tie to an ancestral China shown in "My China Film" was largely illusory. Not only were Wong and the younger generations of Chinese Americans alienated from Chinese culture and customs; the older generations who had left their motherland for the United States found themselves similarly estranged. As Wong wrote to Marinoff and Van Vechten in reference to her father's 1932 visit to China, "After all the wear and tear of returning to California to see my father off to the old country, he has changed his mind. I am rather pleased as I am convinced he would feel like a fish out of water, not having been to China for years and years."[32] According to Wong, being Chinese and comfortable in China is not innate or biological, but the result of culture and habit. This correspondence expressed that Wong hoped that her father would avoid the disappointment of feeling alienated from China. So although the film places her father comfortably in China, Wong's written words communicate otherwise.

Rather than being a fish out of water like her father, Wong explained her own familiarity with China as one based on story and legend. She wrote: "I am going to a strange country, and yet, in a way, I am going home. I have never seen China, but somehow I have always known it. My father and his friends passionately loved their native country, and I was brought up on stories of tree-shaded villages set on the edge of old canals; of Buddhas seated on gold-leafed lotus flowers; of the kitchen-god who is burned with much ceremony every year after his mouth has been rubbed with sugar, so that when he ascends in smoke he will report only good things to the heavenly authorities."[33] For her father and her father's generation, "native country"

---

32. Anna May Wong to Carl Van Vechten and Fania Marinoff, September 21, 1932, CVVMC.

33. Anna May Wong, "Anna May Tells of Voyage on 1st Trip to China," *New York Herald Tribune,* May 17, 1936, sec. 2, pt. 2, 1, 6.

meant China, not the United States. Hearing stories like that, Wong would have been familiar with the China of her father's generation, not the contemporary China she planned to visit.[34] The older generations' stories offer a form of nostalgia rather than an accurate depiction of how life really was. Wong wrote: "Chinese in the United States suffer from a lifelong homesickness, and this somehow is communicated to their children, even though the children know nothing about their ancestral homeland."[35] Wong is indirectly pointing to the Chinese Exclusion Acts that made travel between the United States and China a fraught process. Wong's framing of her film's story as one of nostalgia and family reunification would prove to be critical to her ability to get it aired on national television in 1957.

Hearst Newsreels

A fascinating contrast to Wong's "My China Film" is the Hearst Metrotone News newsreel "Anna May Wong Visits Shanghai."[36] What is striking is that the two films display completely different footage of her trip. As the titles imply, "My China Film" revealed the geographic range of her visit to China, whereas the newsreel exhibited only Shanghai. More importantly, Wong's film comes across as her personal pilgrimage, the newsreel as a star's promotional tour. The Hearst newsreel depicts a Hollywood version of Wong's trip, complete with press conferences and visits to film locales and leading hotels. In the newsreel, the labor of a film star is made visible, whereas, for the most part, in her own film this labor is erased. Movie theaters screened newsreels before the main feature and, in an era before television, were an important way for audiences to get a visual story about contemporary events. The fact that a Hearst newsreel was made of Wong's time in Shanghai signifies that her visit there was newsworthy to American audiences.

"Anna May Wong Visits Shanghai" opens with a shot of Wong standing on a boat on the Huangpu River surrounded by roughly twenty reporters who are chiefly white and male, but also included are some Asian male and white female journalists. The media apparatus around her public persona

---

34. For more on transnational Chinese families, see Madeline Hsu, *Dreaming of Gold, Dreaming of Home: Transnationalism and Migration between the United States and South China, 1882–1943* (Stanford, CA: Stanford University Press, 2000); Mae Ngai, *The Lucky Ones: One Family and the Extraordinary Invention of Chinese* America (New York: Houghton Mifflin Harcourt, 2010).

35. Wong, "Anna May Tells," 1, 6.

36. Available at the UCLA Film and Television Archive.

is made visible. Wong's ensemble befits a Western film star with a dark fur coat, hat, and gloves, and she wears her signature hairstyle of bangs with a bun at her nape. Extensive newsreel footage depicts a flurry of reporters taking notes, snapping pictures with their cameras, and Wong being filmed. Although the version housed at the UCLA Film and Television Archive does not have sound, Wong is shown at the center of the coverage, listening to and answering the reporters' questions.

Depicting a day in the life of a movie star, the next scene in the Hearst newsreel assemblage focuses on a street in Shanghai with a luxury car pulling up to the famous Park Hotel. Wong descends from the car and enters the doorway of the hotel. From here on out Wong wears several different "native" costumes. The newsreel captures Wong in the street, clad in a white cheongsam with a fur wrap (probably fox) with the tails trailing over her shoulders. Later she admires Chinese calligraphy. The newsreel shows her on a Chinese film set wearing a darker cheongsam with a jeweled fastening, watching intently the actors being filmed. Wong then strolls around an outdoor flower market, and in the next scene she holds the treasures discovered there in the form of a bouquet and a little basket. Throughout this coverage American audiences could view Wong as the glamourous great lady visitor to China. Since Wong's "My China Film" would not air for the American public for another two decades, the Hearst newsreels provided an opportunity for American and global audiences to witness her time in Shanghai.

Suspended between Two Worlds

Wong's journey to China revealed how she found herself caught between China and the United States, not finding acceptance in either place. Wong's written account of her visit to China published in the *New York Herald Tribune* evocatively declared, "I am suspended between two worlds."[37] Her visit to her ancestral village in particular underscores that liminal position. Although this suspension between two worlds refers to Wong's ocean voyage, it makes a striking metaphor for her lack of acceptance in the United States and alienation from China.

Wong was not the only Chinese American who felt suspended between two worlds, the United States and China. In what Gloria Chun calls the Great Debate of 1936, the Ging Hawk Club of New York sponsored a nation-

---

37. Ibid.

wide essay contest that asked, "Does My Future Lie in China or America?"[38] In one of the noteworthy essays, "American" values and principles are compared with "Chinese" ways and thought. Numerous essay contestants pointed out the pervasiveness of racism in the United States and the inability of Chinese Americans to find full employment, yet many described themselves longing for Chinese recognition even though they felt alienated from China and Chinese customs. Although this younger generation worked to find a place of belonging, for many, neither option was ideal.

In "My China Film" Wong adopted what I call a cultural ambassador position between the United States and China, translating Chinese culture for Americans. This stance gestures to her trying out her Chinese transnational persona. In the articles she wrote about her voyage to China, Wong seized the opportunity to explain to an American audience her understanding of American race relations. She wrote, "In America, the Chinese often are isolated, not because of any deep prejudice, but because Americans regard them as a dark mysterious race, impossible to understand."[39] For a broad newspaper audience, Wong's articulation of American attitudes toward the Chinese lets Americans off the hook of "deep prejudice." However, European and Hollywood typecasting as well as that era's alien land laws, anti-miscegenation laws, and racial segregation, in addition to the anti-Chinese violence and race riots that marred her childhood, would have given Wong ample evidence that American race relations were about not just prejudice but structural inequalities. In an era marked by the Sino-Japanese War, Wong's comments in the *New York Herald Tribune* could be intended to differentiate between the Chinese and the Japanese: "They do not realize that, despite important differences, the Chinese are closer to Americans in mental make-up than any people of the East. They are both ambitious, home-loving, anxious to give their sons and daughters every educational advantage, and blessed with a strong sense of humor."[40] According to Wong, the Chinese share some of the best characteristics of the Americans. Wong, then, feels she has to present China in the best light to Americans.

The confusion caused by Wong as a Chinese American in China arises directly in "My China Film." Prompted by Stephenson, who asked, "So you

---

38. Gloria Chun, "Go West ". . . to China," in *Claiming America: Constructing Chinese American Identities during the Exclusion Era,* ed. K. Scott Wong and Sucheng Chan (Philadelphia: Temple University Press, 1998), 170.

39. Anna May Wong, "Anna May Wong Relates Arrival in Japan, Her First Sight of the Orient," *New York Herald Tribune,* May 24, 1936, sec. 2, pt. 2, 1.

40. Ibid.

are going to go native?" Wong declared, "It was a grand time going native, I must admit." "Going native" meant for Wong in this instance a form of play, a form of acting and adopting costumes such as the cheongsam. The remark is multilayered because of Wong's Chinese racialized appearance and heritage, all the more incongruous because of her being an American of Chinese heritage. Despite being taken for Chinese in Germany or the United States or later in Australia, in China itself, Wong could never be mistaken for a "native."

In her writings for the *New York Herald Tribune* about her trip to China, Wong explained that "native country" to her meant the United States: "I am very proud of being an American; for years, when people have asked me to describe 'my' native country, I've surprised them by saying that it is a democracy composed of forty-eight states."[41] Wong reveals that she confounds people's racialized and orientalizing expectations in claiming the United States as her country. This use of "native country" to signify the United States stands in contrast to the potential confusion caused by the title of her television segment, "Native Land," through which an inattentive viewer could mistakenly assume that Wong's native land was China. Wong explains her awareness of her Chinese heritage: "But I've always been aware of another country, in the background of my mind, just as I have never forgotten that my real name is Wong Liu Tsong, which means 'Frosted Yellow Willow.'"[42] This is another moment of Wong's self-fashioning. Wong demonstrates being suspended between the two worlds of this ingrained double consciousness.

Wong's reportage of her trip to China highlights her sly sense of humor through her deployment of language. In many ways, these formulations convey her greater comfort with American culture. She wrote, "During my stay in Shanghai I will most likely be making many trips, especially to Nanking, Hangchow, Foochow and a few other 'Chows.'"[43] By using the phrase "a few other 'Chows,'" Wong is playing on Western perceptions of the unintelligibility of the Chinese language with its seemingly endless repetition of sounds and syllables. Such a pun demonstrates Wong's colloquial American perspective on the Chinese language. As with "Ching-chong Chinaman," language has been one of the ways that the West has castigated people of Chinese descent as different and strange.

Wong's journey to China was significant for her personal sense of self. As she stated for the *Bold Journey,* "Native Land," viewing audience, "I am very glad I am of Chinese extraction shall we say." The trip enabled her to develop

---

41. Wong, "Anna May Tells of Voyage," 1, 6.
42. Ibid.
43. Wong to Van Vechten and Marinoff, March 14, 1936.

a newfound pride in her Chinese heritage. At the same time, she gained a more realistic view of the tensions between tradition and the modern, especially surrounding gender roles in China.

Paramount Chinese American Roles

Anna May Wong's return from China marked her new status as a leading actress: she was offered starring Chinese American roles at Paramount Pictures. Although these were in low-budget "B" films, they are nonetheless significant in that she played parts such as a surgeon in *King of Chinatown* and a gallery-owner detective in *Daughter of Shanghai*. Rather than the showgirl ingénue or scheming Chinese harridan roles of her earlier Hollywood career, these were respectable Chinese American characters, and in these films she was clothed by Paramount's designer-to-the-stars, Edith Head.

Although I have previously written elsewhere about these films and their importance in establishing Wong's cultural citizenship, re-examining them in light of her letters and her trip to China gives them new meaning. These letters and "My China Film" place the Paramount films in the broader context of her championing her Chinese heritage as well as her own understanding of her evolving career. As she reported in a letter to Van Vechten and Marinoff during the development stages of the proposed Paramount B-list films, "Arthur has probably told you about my offer to do a series of lady detective pictures. At present, they are running into a few snags, due to difficulties in obtaining a proper release." Wong hoped the opportunity would work out for her, as she reported, "Haven't done a stroke of work professionally since my return [from China]."[44] Wong framed the opportunity to star in the series of lady detective pictures in terms that show the resignification of China. She wrote, "It's a grand idea, it if goes through, and would really give me the opportunity to do something really constructive for China, and worthwhile for myself."[45] This valorization of her Chinese heritage, at least in the 1930s, is in keeping with American patriotism, for she uses the term "China" to refer both to China the country and the image of Chinese American subjects in the United States. What is noteworthy about Wong's Chinese American

---

44. Anna May Wong to Carl Van Vechten and Fania Marinoff, March 4, 1937, CVVMC. For more on the Chinese American Paramount movies, see Shirley Jennifer Lim, *A Feeling of Belonging: Asian American Women's Public Culture* (New York: New York University Press, 2006), chap. 2; and Sean Metzger, "Patterns of Resistance? Anna May Wong and the Fabrication of China in American Cinema of the Late 30s," *Quarterly Review of Film and Video* 23 (2006): 1–11.

45. Wong to Van Vechten and Marinoff, March 4, 1937.

films is that, for the first time, they broadcasted Chinese Americans as loyal Americans who worked for causes that helped China. Casting Wong in this type of patriotic Chinese American role contested Hollywood's reliance on yellowface such as MGM's casting for *The Good Earth*.

Filming the first of these lady detective pictures, *Daughter of Shanghai* (1937), unleashed a flurry of activity. As Wong wrote to Van Vechten, "Please forgive my seeming negligence in not having written but life seems to have been fraught with this and that ever since my arrival—immediate activity with 'Daughter of Shanghai' my first Paramount picture, a siege of bronchitis, younger sister Mary's arrival from war torn Shanghai,—now the second picture 'Dangerous to Know' (Edgar Wallace's 'On the Spot')."[46] As indicated in other letters, Wong's life as an actress entailed feast or famine. Either she faced a rush of work or long periods of inactivity during which she was worried that new work would not be forthcoming.

Perhaps these films appealed to Wong because they provided plot twists novel to her career. What is particularly telling is that the production notes for *Daughter of Shanghai* reveal that, as initially scripted, the main character initiated very little action, but once Wong committed to the movie, the screenwriter rewrote her character, Lan Ying, so that she instigated the major plot sequence.[47] Referring to the Paramount films, one newspaper stated, "The idea is her own, and will establish her as a sort of feminine counterpart of 'Charlie Chan.'"[48] Charlie Chan, played by European American Warner Oland, was a successful detective series that featured in supporting roles Asian American actors such as Keye Luke, who played the Number One Son. Having an Asian American female lead would be noteworthy. Given the success of the Charlie Chan series, clearly Paramount Pictures hoped for equivalent popular success with Wong's film.

As a Chinese American female heroine, Wong's character Lan Ying in *Daughter of Shanghai* ingeniously restores justice to her world. The basic plotline of the movie is that Ying tracks down the bad guys and, at the end of the movie, marries her fellow detective. The day after her father's assas-

---

46. Anna May Wong to Carl Van Vechten and Fania Marinoff, December 4, 1937, CVVMC.

47. *Daughter of Shanghai* Production Notes, Paramount Pictures files. I thank Cynthia Liu for calling my attention to this point. Cynthia Liu, "When Dragon Ladies Die, Do They Come Back as Butterflies? Re-Imagining Anna May Wong," in *Countervisions: Asian American Film Criticism*, ed. Darrell Hamamoto and Sandra Liu (Philadelphia: Temple University Press, 2000), 23–39.

48. Louise Leung, "East Meets West," *Hollywood*, January 1938, 40, 55, Anna May Wong Clipping File, Billy Rose Theater Division, New York Public Library, Performing Arts Branch.

sination, Ying takes over her father's business and vows to bring the assassins to justice. Traveling to Central America, she cleverly infiltrates the crime ring's business without arousing suspicion. She escapes the Central American island by dressing like one of the Chinese male workers, in black pants and shirt with her hair tucked underneath a large straw coolie hat. Working with Kim Lee, a detective on the case played by Korean American actor Philip Ahn, they capture the wealthy female European American illegal alien smuggler and bring her to justice.[49] *Daughter of Shanghai* ends with the promise of Wong and Ahn's future marital bliss, restoring heterosexual harmony to their world.

Wong was enthusiastic about the potential commercial success of this series of "lady detective pictures," despite her qualms about their artistic excellence. On January 3, 1938, she wrote to her fellow actress Marinoff: "'Daughter of Shanghai' was released at the Criterion and I think it will be a money maker although it's just plain hokum 'mellerdrammer.'"[50] The use of the words "hokum" and "mellerdrammer" in quotation marks highlights Wong's fine sense of the absurd. To this letter, Wong added, "PS ". . . Am glad you approved of the 'Daughter of Shanghai' performance."[51]

Playing a Chinese character blurred the distinction between cinema and reality, and Wong's real life mirrored some aspects of her cinematic life. On January 3, 1938 (her birthday), she wrote to Van Vechten and Marinoff, referring to China relief for the Sino-Japanese War: "Please don't think that I neglected you at Christmas in not sending you some message but the need is so great out in China that I felt all my friends would understand when they know that my remembrance to them this year is in aid of a good cause. I turned over all my Christmas money to Dr. Margaret Chung in San Francisco who is doing some fine work in gathering funds to send out medical supplies to China."[52] Just as her character in the Paramount film *King of Chinatown* (1939) (in which her role was based on the life of Dr. Margaret Chung) sent money and medical supplies to China to assist with humanitarian relief, the real-life Wong did the same. Wong's cinematic heroine was linked to actual Chinese American situations. Just as it was within the bounds of American

---

49. Hye Seung Chung, *Hollywood Asian: Philip Ahn and the Politics of Cross-Ethnic Performance* (Philadelphia: Temple University Press, 2006).

50. Anna May Wong to Carl Van Vechten and Fania Marinoff, January 3, 1938, CVVMC, Beinecke Library, Yale University.

51. Ibid.

52. Ibid. For more on Dr. Margaret Chung, see Judy Tzu-Chun Wu, *Dr. Mom Chung of the Fair-Haired Bastards: The Life of a Wartime Celebrity* (Berkeley: University of California Press, 2005).

patriotism for Wong herself to visit and provide aid to China, so it was for her cinematic character to do likewise.

Wong's Chinese American roles that followed the creation of "My China Film" were part of not only her newfound pride in her Chinese origins but also the shifting Hollywood racial and gender mores of the late 1930s. Although Wong's early success in films and as a cultural icon can be attributed to Western imperialism's fascination with the other, her later ability to play Chinese American film roles needs to be evaluated in the context of a changing Hollywood that contributed to newly emerging possibilities for all racial minorities. Film scholars have argued that Depression-era Hollywood, especially with regard to race and gender, was ahead of American society.[53] Wong's ability to align American patriotism with Chinese patriotism and to play a role that might previously have gone to a male actor meant that once Paramount Pictures green-lighted Chinese American–themed films, she would be the one that would win the starring roles, thus contributing to the race and gender realignment of Hollywood.

Scholars of African Americans and Latinos in film have discovered, as was the case for Chinese Americans, an overall trend of more film roles as well as more "positive" portrayals in them during this era. The films of Oscar Micheaux, for example, featured all-black casts in detective stories and dramas, and his stories expanded the types of roles that African Americans could play.[54] The 1930s thus were a turning point for African Americans in mainstream movies in that they gained more prominent roles of all types.[55] Though Hollywood continually typecast Hattie McDaniel and Butterfly McQueen as mammies and maids, the actresses won critical recognition for their acting, most notably McDaniel's Best Supporting Actress Academy Award for her portrayal of the problematic role of Mammy in *Gone with the Wind* (1939). Lena Horne also gained prominence in mainstream Hollywood.[56] Moreover, when African Americans did not like film portrayals, protests ensued.[57] Similar "positive" roles were available for Latino/a actors and actresses. Scholar

53. Thomas Cripps, *Slow Fade to Black: The Negro in American Film, 1900–1942* (New York: Oxford University Press, 1993), 5.

54. Bowser and Louise Spence, *Writing Himself into History*.

55. Cripps, *Slow Fade to Black*.

56. Arthur Knight, *Disintegrating the Musical: Black Performance and American Musical Film* (Durham, NC: Duke University Press, 2002).

57. Ed Guerrero, *Framing Blackness: The African American Image in Film* (Philadelphia: Temple University Press, 1993); Anna Everett, *Returning the Gaze: A Genealogy of Black Film Criticism, 1909–1949* (Durham, NC: Duke University Press, 2001); Valerie Smith, *Representing Blackness: Issues in Film and Video* (New Brunswick, NJ: Rutgers University Press, 1997).

Ana López has found that the film roles of Latinos in Hollywood improved, in part due to the U.S. Good Neighbor policy toward Latin America in the late 1930s.[58] Hence stars such as Dolores del Río, Lupe Vélez, and Anthony Quinn enjoyed Hollywood success.

News about Wong's playing a new Hollywood crime-stopping Chinese American heroine was publicized in the Chinese American community. A major Chinese American newspaper, *Chinese Digest,* divulged that Wong had signed a three-year contract with Paramount.[59] In a later edition, it reported that she "has played the villainess for so long now she would enjoy a nice role for a change."[60] The community understood that Wong felt positively about these new "nice role" Chinese American motion pictures, work that would align her newly developed Chinese transnational persona with Hollywood's political culture.

Conclusion

Anna May Wong's "My China Film" and her writings about her trip to China can be construed as a turning point in her career and, more importantly, in her sense of self, which reflect larger trends in the relationship between China and the West. That journey would be Wong's one and only visit to China. "My China Film" reveals the complex dynamics between her citizenship and her ethnicity, highlighting her Americanness, even as it confirms her distance from Chinese cultural practices and the everyday realities of actual Chinese people that she encountered who become essentially extras in her movie about her China reverie. The shifting images of Wong offer a window into how racial categories of nation-state belonging mutated into the embodiment of transnational modernity. As an Asian American perpetually excluded from the American nation-state, Wong knew that her ties to the American nation-state were unstable. It is precisely because of those tenuous ties that in her life, body, and career she could come to epitomize transnational racial modernity. The Epilogue of this book continues the story of "My China Film" through

58. Ana López, "Are All Latins from Manhattan? Hollywood, Ethnography and Cultural Colonialism," in *Unspeakable Images: Ethnicity and American Cinema,* ed. Lester Friedman (Urbana-Champagne: University of Illinois Press, 1991), 406–407.

59. *Chinese Digest,* May 1937, 12. For more information on the history of Chinese community newspapers in the United States, see Karl Lo and Him Mark Lai, *Chinese Newspapers Published in North America, 1854–1975* (Washington, DC: Center for Chinese Research Materials, Association for Research Libraries, 1975); Him Mark Lai, "The Chinese Vernacular Press in North America, 1900–1950: Their Role in Social Cohesion," *Annals of the Chinese Historical Society of the Pacific Northwest* (1984): 170–178.

60. *Chinese Digest,* July 1937, 8.

the 1957 television broadcast that Wong worked so hard to make happen, which indicates a different historical context and understanding of the end of her career.

Chapter 6, "Anna May Wong in Australia," examines her final journey across the Pacific Ocean, this time in 1939, to Sydney and Melbourne, Australia, to star in a theatrical variety revue. There, Wong would strategically deploy her new authority as a China expert and cultural ambassador.

6

Anna May Wong in Australia

If the rest of my stay in Australia will be as pleasant and happy as today has been, then I know that I shall enjoy every moment of it.

—ANNA MAY WONG,
Fox Movietone News Australia newsreel, Sydney, 1939

The visiting actress is delighted by the fact that members of Australia's Chinese community have given her such a whole-hearted welcome. She has had many letters from them, and yesterday when the train arrived in Sydney deputations from the New South Wales Chinese Women's Relief fund and the Young Chinese League were there to meet her.

—*Sydney Morning Herald,* July 18, 1939

A nna May Wong's final international journey brought her back across the Pacific, this time to Australia. This chapter uses Wong's 1939 visit to Australia as a touchstone to examine the various meanings of Chineseness in the late 1930s both from the perspective of mainstream Australian society as well as that of Chinese Australians. Fascination with her visit to Australia was so great that Fox Movietone News Australia, mainstream newspapers such as the *Sydney Morning Herald,* and Australian magazines covered her visit. Chinese Australians in particular showed great devotion, with fans meeting her when she arrived, writing her letters, and demanding her autograph throughout her stay. Unlike Wong's time in Berlin (Chapter 1) or Paris (Chapter 3), this focus on Australia offers a settler-colonial racial dynamic analogous to that of Wong's birthplace, California, with Wong as a symbol of settler-colonial racial modernity.

Australian national identity at this time centered on the exclusion of the Chinese from both immigration and citizenship. Historian David Walker's *Anxious Nation* has explored Australia's spatial and racial anxieties around Asia.[1] In addition, scholar Helen Irvine has argued that at the heart of

---

1. David Walker, *Anxious Nation: Australia and the Rise of Asia 1850–1939* (St. Lucia, Australia: University of Queensland Press, 1999).

Australian federalism, "the function played by the Chinese [was that] of identifying a community by what it is not. The white populations of Australia metaphorically became British together."[2] Australia's role in the transnational reception of Asians and Asian Americans in global popular culture is a critical one, impinging on the core of Australian conceptions of national being. I have found that these meanings exhibit both the historical ambivalence about the Chinese as explicated by Walker and Irvine yet point to a new politics of engagement with Asia in general and Chineseness in particular.

Wong's visit to Australia in 1939 verifies both the contemporary as well as the historical importance of the Chinese in transnational racial formations. During the great oceanic migrations of the nineteenth and twentieth centuries, fifty million Chinese, the same number of Europeans, and thirty million South Asians migrated. Although humans have continually migrated, what is unprecedented is the sheer scope and distance. What is of particular interest to this project is that these migrations raised issues of race, citizenship, and rule resulting in, to use W.E.B. Du Bois's formulation, the modern color line. Building on colonial routes, British colonial ones in particular, the modern global color line was a transnational phenomenon in the creation of whiteness from South Africa to North America to Australasia. A transnational facet of modernity, the global color line's actions and language were expressed in nationalistic and racial terms. As Marilyn Lake and Henry Reynolds have persuasively argued, "the masculine democracies of North America and Australasia defined their identities and rights in racial terms: the right of Anglo-Saxons to self-government and the commitment of white workers to high wages and conditions, against those they saw as undermining their new-found status."[3] In the case of Australia as well as the West Coast of the United States, Chinese functioned as the antithesis to the Anglo-Saxon. In fact, miners in the Australian gold-mining region of the British colony of Victoria (Melbourne) followed the example of anti-Chinese agitation in California; indeed, some had participated in it.[4] The first (anti-Chinese) immigration restriction act in Victoria passed in 1855. As in the United States, white male working-class identity was formed against and within racial difference. As was written in Australia in 1879, "'As an

---

2. Helen Irving, *To Constitute a Nation: A Cultural History of Australia's Constitution* (Melbourne, Australia: Cambridge University Press, 1977), 114.

3. Marilyn Lake and Henry Reynolds, *Drawing the Global Colour Line: White Men's Countries and the International Challenge of Racial Equality* (London: Cambridge University Press, 2008), 7.

4. Ibid., 18.

object of public interest and public dread' the Chinaman has no equal."[5] That racial dread of the "unassimilable Chinese" fed the concept of white racial homogeneity as the basis of a healthy settler-colonial (and potentially national) life. Protests and counterprotests attest that this equation of whiteness and Australian settler colonialism was continually battled. In Australia under colonialism, race trumped being a British subject; in other words, a British colonial subject of Chinese origin was not welcome as an Australian settler colonial. Thus racial conflict broke the belonging of empire—the universal rights of a British subject across empire—and paradoxically paved the way for the nation-state. Under Australian federation, these formations against the Chinese were consolidated. By the time Wong arrived in Australia, China stood as the historical and contemporary specter to white Australia, a specter suited to settler-colonial narratives because it maintained the fiction that white Australians were the "original" Australians. However, as Wong's arrival came decades after the formation of Australia as a white nation, it also coincided with the dawning of a potentially new era, namely the thawing of relations at the start of World War II in the Pacific. Indeed, her visit can be read as part of the potential change in sentiments of Australians toward a Chinese ally in the Pacific.

Absence marks the historiographical record regarding Wong's visit to Australia. In Graham Hodges's biography, Wong's visit merits half of a page. Karen Leong's excellent chapter on Wong as an "accidental" transnational covers Europe and China but not Australia.[6] This chapter does not seek to correct those absences in the historiography through the mere recitation of Wong's presence. Rather, Wong's visit shows us Chinese racialization within Australia. Much like Wong, Australia was also caught between the United States, China, and imperial Europe. Wong's time in Australia therefore affords insights into the dynamics of hybrid culture. What is striking, after the visit to China discussed in Chapter 5, is how comfortable Wong was with slipping between her Chinese and American identities.

As part of the growing interest in Asian Australian studies, I discuss the critical markers of Wong's racialization and reception in Australia, among both "mainstream" society and Chinese Australians. To what degree was she understood as American, modern, Chinese, European-trained, or all of those categories? How did these categories mesh with Australian racializations and

---

5. Ibid., 34, quoting John Wisker, "The Coloured Man in Australia,' *Fortnightly Review,* July 1, 1879, 82.

6. For an artistic response to Wong's 1939 visit to Australia, see Derham Groves, *Anna May Wong's Lucky Shoes: 1939 Australia through the Eyes of an Art Deco Diva* (Ames, IA: Culicidae Architectural Press, 2013).

modernity? As the source of so many pertinent questions, Wong's visit to Australia provides a rich case study for understanding the negotiation of race.

Wong's Australian visit was particularly charged because Australia's national identity was formed through and against the Chinese. However, Wong's embodiment of modernity posed a challenge to any simplistic formulation of her Chinese authenticity. The artifacts generated by her visit show that blended or hybrid notions of race and nation emerged. Wong adopted the mantle of cultural ambassador, graciously translating Chinese society and culture. Finally, Wong's visit highlights the Chinese Australian community's performance of cultural citizenship as a response to a racially stratified society. In the 1930s, Chinese Australians worked to resignify the meaning of China in Australia.

Anna May Wong in Australia

Anna May Wong's ability to portray glamourous racialized modernity, a glamour that made her more visible and more palatable as a racial minority subject, was the reason why she was brought to Australia in 1939 to perform on the Tivoli Theatre circuit in Sydney and Melbourne. When she arrived in Australia, Wong was in the twilight of her film career, for she had completed the majority of her sixty-plus films. However, she was building up her theatrical repertoire and had been a vaudeville star throughout Europe, and a theatrical actress in the United States and England. As revealed in other chapters, Wong's glamour had been well established worldwide. The cover of the Tivoli program portrayed her as "Anna May Wong famous star of stage and screen."[7] In Melbourne, the revue commenced on June 12, 1939, with matinee and evening performances produced by Wallace Parnell. The vaudeville show began in Sydney on July 20, 1939.

Highlighting Wong was an effective advertising ploy because, for over a decade prior to her visit, audiences throughout Australia had attended Wong's films. In 1927, there were 1,250 film theaters in Australia, 110 million admissions, and a population of 6 million—meaning that every person in Australia made an average of eighteen cinema visits per year, one of the highest rates in the world.[8] Looking through the regional Australian press, it is clear that Wong's films had wide circulation. As reviews and publicity

---

7. Tivoli Theatre Program, The Arts Centre, Performing Arts Collection and Research Library, Melbourne.

8. Graham Shirley and Brian Adams, *Australian Cinema* Sydney, Australia: Currency Press, 1983), 77.

notices published in newspapers around the country affirm, almost all of her major films, including more recent hits such as *When Were You Born* (1939) and *King of Chinatown* (1939), played in Australia.

Categories of nation-state citizenship and belonging in white settler-colonial societies such as Australia and the United States are unstable. Their boundaries are continually tested and redrawn in a number of forums, including musical theater. As scholar Jill Matthews has found, forms of urban entertainment were key to modernity in Australia.[9] The performance of racial difference has been a critical part of Western modernity in the twentieth century. What is particularly striking about the interwar era is how global racial categories were refracted through American modernity, a modernity mediated by both racial mixing and by Hollywood and other entertainment industries, which created a historically specific cosmopolitan culture. Settler societies such as the United States were critical to racial formations, and sites such as Australia were nodes in the transnational performance circuit.

The Tivoli Theatre producers' appetite for Asian American and African American performers underscores Australia's shared interest in American racial modernity. Onstage, Wong's racial play in performing mixed-race and Chinese women drew in audiences, whereas offstage her elegant cosmopolitan persona attracted crowds. The Tivoli Theatre circuit was a site for the performance of race and difference, and its producers sought out performers from England and the United States. For example, in 1908, Jack Johnson, the celebrated African American boxer, headlined the Tivoli, and in the 1930s the African American singer Bob Parrish was brought to the Tivoli as was "dusky" Nina May McKinney, who had played opposite Paul Robeson in "Sanders of the River."[10] While at the Tivoli in 1939, Wong was part of a larger variety program entitled "Highlights from Hollywood" that included Alfredo and Delores, "Cuban Dancers," Jack Lane, "America's Young Comedy Star," and Bugs Wilson, "The Radio Racketeer."

Wong came to the Tivoli Theatre to perform a vaudeville act she had perfected in Europe (see Chapter 3), in which she performed not only Chinese but also mixed-race roles. Through the development of her repertoire, you can see her working through issues of how her Chinese heritage interfaced with various permutations of nation-state belonging. As Wong stated, one of the strengths of doing vaudeville was that she could change up the num-

---

9. Jill Matthews, *Dance Hall and Picture Palace: Sydney's Romance with Modernity* (Sydney, Australia: Currency Press, 2005).

10. *The Tivoli Story: 55 Years of Variety* (Melbourne, Australia: Victory Publicity, 1956), 4, 10, Australian National Library, Canberra.

bers depending on their popularity. Australia's complex relationship with the Chinese did not preclude her acting in Chinese roles. Far from it: the Tivoli Theatre program cover promotes Wong wearing a blue cheongsam, and the program lists her stage persona as Lao Chen.[11] The *Sydney Morning Herald* explained that in its initial variation, Wong's revue was in four parts. "First she came in wearing an Oriental coat and a high headdress and sang a Chinese folk-song. Next, she gave some impressions of an Australian girl."[12] As had been the case in France, typically Wong performed a song with adjustable lyrics. She could insert the name of the country in which she performed, resulting in lines that proclaimed that she was a girl from Australia or a girl from Denmark. The *Sydney Morning Herald* noted, "After that came Noel Coward's 'Half-caste Woman.'" That piece, which saw Wong portray a Eurasian woman lamenting her fate of being between two cultures, was frequently the highlight of her vaudeville productions around the world. Wong's finale was called "At the Barricade." As the review explained, "This sketch dealt with the present situation in Tientain.'"[13] The newspaper lambasted it as "unexceptional propaganda," which as drama, "seemed very poor indeed." The review was not all bad, however: "'Half-caste Woman' gave Miss Wong opportunity for some harsh and intense acting. In the rest of her material, she was agreeably decorative."[14] Other reports presented a slightly different account of her extravaganza: "Typically, Wong began with a Chinese folk song, then sang a Basque love song and also had a satirical tribute to Australian women."[15] Other accounts suggested that she sang a French chanson, in all likelihood "Parlez-moi D'Amour" ("Speak to Me of Love"). In Wong's rendition of "Parlez-moi D'Amour," she is not playing with whiteness or claiming French belonging. Rather, she portrays cosmopolitan French culture without being French. Nonetheless, no matter how the revue was changed up, it is evident that Wong played a variety of roles and races, an exercise that could see her move from Chinese to Australian to "half-caste" with only a change of costume.

In Australia, Wong engaged with cross-cultural performance. The audiences could be amused by a woman who was clearly of Asian descent singing in French. The disjuncture between the construction of French racial whiteness and a Chinese face could be farcical or uncanny, reinforcing Wong's

11. Tivoli Theatre Program, The Arts Centre, Performing Arts Collection and Research Library, Melbourne.
12. *Sydney Morning Herald,* July 21, 1939, 13.
13. Ibid.
14. Ibid.
15. Hodges, *Anna May Wong,* 198.

seemingly essential Chineseness. However, such racial play could question assumptions about nation-state and race, thus creating doubt about essentialist racial categories. Wong performed Australianness while singing that she was "An Australian Girl," thus toying with resignifying "Australian" as Chinese. Yet she could do so because, as a famous American film star, there was no possibility of confusing her with an actual Chinese Australian. No written account of her visit did so. The *Sydney Morning Herald* review called it "a satirical tribute to Australian women," eliding the possibility that Wong could be an Australian woman. The very threat of her Chineseness made the number memorable, yet the fact of it being a performance—and one by an American cultural star—meant that the threat could be expunged and put aside once the performance ended.

What is striking is that Wong was not the only performer of Chinese descent who could have been brought to Australia to play at the Tivoli. As historian Angela Woollacott's research has demonstrated, Rose Quong, a Chinese Australian from Melbourne, had become a theatrical star in England.[16] Quong actually played a supporting role to Wong and Laurence Olivier in the play *The Circle of Chalk* in London in 1929. Quong later performed with Wong in New York City. Yet it was Wong, not Quong, who was brought to the Tivoli in 1939. Of course, Wong's film stardom made her a much bigger international star than Quong. Furthermore, Wong represented glamourous racial modernity far more than did Quong, who was older and not known for her beauty. But it was Wong's Americanness and her connections to the glamour of Hollywood that gave her the freedom to engage in cross-national performance. Quong's claims to being an "Australian girl" could not have been taken as satire so easily; they would have been too close to the truth. As a Chinese American, Wong was the perfect embodiment of glamour, which seemingly distanced her cross-national portrayals from threatening reality.

Wong's visit attracted extensive publicity beyond her theatrical appearances. Initial newspaper reports loved to portray her out and about the town. For example, one caption from Melbourne's *The Argus* read: "Miss Anna May Wong, now appearing at the Tivoli Theatre, Photographed while shopping at Fox's Fashion Corner."[17] In this photograph, Wong is depicted shopping while surrounded by a sea of interested white Australians. Another newspaper feature illustrated the immense crowds that surrounded Wong when she was in public. *The Argus* caption read: "Busy Days for Miss Anna May Wong,

---

16. Angela Woollacott, "Rose Quong Becomes Chinese: An Australian in London and New York," *Australian Historical Studies* 129 (2007): 16–31.

17. *The Argus,* June 17, 1939, 18.

screen actress, shown leaving the Capitol Theatre yesterday where she is making personal appearances before a film in which she starred is screened. Miss Wong also appears twice daily at the Tivoli Theatre."[18] Again, this photograph of Wong in the street reveals a huge crowd behind her, testifying to the interest of the Australian public.

During this era, glamour was imbued with othering mechanisms such as racial difference. Wong's particular brand of glamour is evident in a feature from the August 1939 edition of *The Home,* a publication of the *Sydney Morning Herald.* In a two-page, four-picture spread, this society women's monthly magazine portrayed Wong as an American of Chinese ancestry.[19] The accompanying article substantiated that it was Wong herself who was responsible for the dualism between Western and Chinese: "Graceful, smartly dressed and possessed of a superb sense of humor, Miss Wong is the Orient and the West in one person—one moment she will be speaking of the mystery of China's lost cities; the next moment the latest Hollywood wise crack will cross her lips. But with it all she has an arresting personality." In this narrative, Wong herself fostered the hybridity that underpinned her theatrical persona.

Alongside interest in Wong's modernity was the desire for the exotic, resulting in hybridity. Those "exotic" photographs of Wong in an elegant Chinese theatrical costume were juxtaposed against ones of Wong in Western clothing. The tale of carefully managed hybridity is elaborated in the story that accompanied the photographs, which revealed that "her real name is Wong Liu Tsong—'Frosted Yellow Willow'—and she was born in the United States. At school she was always Anna Wong. Then her acting career started. 'Anna Wong was too abrupt,' she explains, 'so I put in the name of my favorite month, May.'"[20] This account is consistent with those that Wong gave in both the United States and Europe. The process of self-naming was part of a wider process of self-fashioning. Yet, in disclosing how face, appearance, and race can trump the ears, in Australia, according to press reports, at the time of her visit, Wong was still considered to have a foreign accent. Witness the following statement: "There is the faintest trace of a foreign flavour in her accent, but it adds just a little more colour to the low-pitted voice of the exotic little star."[21] The trace of foreign flavor in all likelihood would have been the traces of her California accent. The author's use of the words "little" and "exotic" reveals

18. *The Argus,* June 15, 1939, 5.
19. "Anna May Wong," *The Home,* August 1, 1939, 50–51.
20. Ibid., 50.
21. Lon Jones, "Anna May Wong to Visit Australia," *Sydney Morning Herald,* May 1, 1939, 8.

how racialized impressions can override actual evidence. Wong's height has been listed as ranging from 5'5" to 5'7", and in some films she towers over her leading man or appears at the same height as co-stars such as German actress Marlene Dietrich, yet she was still characterized as "little."

The same newspaper reports could be of two minds in their portrayal of Wong's national origins. For example, one story stated at first, "It might be said that thousands of years of philosophy are deeply embedded beneath the penetrating personality of Anna May Wong. Just imagine the genius of this Chinese girl, one alone of her race, holding her unique position in the film world all these years."[22] One sees the operation of racial signifier blended into nation. Courtesy of her Chinese heritage, she is aligned with all of Chinese history. However, the same story also pointed out that Wong was not actually Chinese. The newspaper reported Wong as saying, "'I don't know enough of the language to read the Chinese papers.'"[23] Wong's inability to read in Chinese proclaims her American birth, and it is noteworthy that it is part of both Wong's narration of self and the newspapers' desire to report it.

The appeal to Wong of performing a diasporic Chinese diplomatic persona dovetails with Australian news accounts that stressed her disquiet with Hollywood. In an interview published in the *Sydney Morning Herald* prior to her arrival in Australia, she revealed the following dilemma around being an Asian American actress: "'You see,' she told me in her very perfect English, 'I'm a unique personality in motion pictures. I'm the only Oriental star in the world, and for that very reason I'm hampered. People insist upon looking at me as a freak—something akin to a five-legged dog or a two-headed calf.'"[24] Wong declared, "'I want to be an actress, not a freak. I want to feel that people go to see my pictures because I perform well, not just because I am an Oriental.'"[25] She continued, "'That's the main reason I want to get away from Hollywood. I want to examine myself closely and find out if I have anything really to offer the public or whether I must just go on being regarded as a freak.'"[26] At this point in her career, Wong's work options in Europe and Hollywood were drying up. Her statement "I want to be an actress" serves as another reminder that roles for her as an "oriental" actress were limited and that she was not the draw that she had been in the past. The story communicated that Wong asked, "'What is the difference between a white girl playing an Oriental and a real Oriental like myself playing them?

22. *Sydney Morning Herald Women's Supplement,* July 24, 1939, 4.
23. Ibid.
24. Jones, "Anna May Wong to Visit Australia," 8.
25. Ibid.
26. Ibid.

The only difference I can see is that in most cases I would at least look the part where the white girls definitely do not.'"[27]

Yet, despite the careful explication of her American colloquial speech, the same newspaper reportage ultimately decided that Wong's racial heritage played a greater role than her nation of birth. It stated, "[The] Daughter of an old-fashioned business man of Los Angeles who is widely respected there, one could quite easily take Miss Wong for a sophisticated New York business woman. But, rather than sophistication, there is a more sane and serene judgment in the make-up of the Chinese film star. A control of the soul which allows for rest and content. This is an inheritance of the thousands of years old tradition of her race. A frank young lady who is typically honest."[28] Race trumps nation. This narrative places China as an ancient civilization. On the one hand, it reveres the ancient Chinese civilization. On the other hand, it places China in, to use Johann Fabian's phrase, "noncoeval time," which is a common move in placing a culture in an inferior position vis-à-vis the modern West.[29]

While other newspaper accounts pointed out Wong's American birth and Chinese heritage, this particular story tried to make sense of her cultural hybridity. Quoting Wong, the story stated, "'In the beginning I used to work myself into a lather. I told one of my friends how I felt and she said that my problem wasn't physical, but mental. She told me I was in 'mental conflict' because I had inherited the Chinese attitude to life but had had an American upbringing. The Chinese are an ancient people, they have foreseen the end of personal ambition, they relax and ride along. On the other hand, America is a young, bustling country.'"[30] Hence her Chinese heritage and her American nation put her in a state of tension; notably, however, it is a tension between two equals: at no point is the value of Chinese culture portrayed as lower than the American. Further, the tension is mediated by Wong's use of the colloquial American English phrase "work myself into a lather," which would be used only by someone completely comfortable with American culture. By asserting her Americanness, and her glamour, Wong could circumvent some of the racial prejudice faced by the Chinese in Australia.

Australian understandings of Wong's hybridity stand in contradistinction to the formulations of her as chiefly Chinese in Berlin, Paris, and London in

---

27. Ibid.

28. "Hollywood Is a Gamble Says Anna May Wong," 4.

29. Johannes Fabian, *Time and the Other: How Anthropology Makes Its Object* (New York: Columbia University Press, 1983).

30. "Philosophy Is a Heritage," *Sydney Morning Herald,* July 18, 1939, 4.

the late 1920s and early 1930s.[31] Depictions of racial and national hybridity were more immediate and quotidian for the Australians than for the British or the French. Given the historical role of the Asian Australian population, the Chinese in particular formed not only an important entity against which Australia defined itself but also the basis for second- or third-class provisional incorporation as citizen-subjects. Hence the undertones of both anxiety and engagement with her Chinese heritage as revealed in the news reports.

Very Perfect English, Very Perfect Ambassador

The mutability between the poles of Chineseness and Westernness led to the demonstration of one of the most fascinating aspects of Anna May Wong's visit to Australia, what I am calling her constructed "ambassadorial persona" for China. This ambassadorial persona was demonstrated in a Fox Movietone Australia newsreel that focused on her Australian arrival. In the days before widespread television news, newsreels were played before feature films and gave audiences the news of the day. Other Fox Movietone newsreels of 1939 tended to focus on male political subjects such as Australian admirals, Pacific War scenes, and archbishops. So, as an American actress of Chinese descent, it was doubly significant that Wong was featured.

The Fox Movietone newsreel exhibited Wong as every inch the glamourous international film star. The footage begins with her disembarking from her ship, waving while walking down a steep outdoor staircase. She carries a bouquet of flowers and picks up an additional large basket of flowers on her way down the stairs. She wears a long fur coat, a dark dress, and dark high-heeled pumps. Her hair is in a wrap hat. After this, the camera cuts to Wong, having set foot on Australian soil, standing next to a man and a woman. She is wearing a dark top with a mandarin collar, a short fur cape, and a light skirt, with her hair held back in a hairnet. Wong presents an image of a powerful, modern career woman. At this point, Wong says loudly and clearly to the consul general of China and his wife, "Thank you so much, Dr. Pao and Madame Pao; you have extended me a most warm welcome and thank you very much. If the rest of my stay in Australia will be as pleasant and happy as today has been, then I know that I shall enjoy every moment of it. And to the many Chinese who are listening in, may I say ". . . [Wong delivers a Chinese greeting]."

---

31. Shirley Jennifer Lim, "'Speaking German Like Nobody's Business': Anna May Wong, Walter Benjamin, and the Possibilities of Asian American Cosmopolitanism," *Journal of Transnational American Studies* (Summer 2012): 1–17.

Anna May Wong arrives in Australia.

(Film still, Fox Movietone Australia newsreel "Anna May Wong.")

Anna May Wong with Dr. Pao.

(Film still, Fox Movietone Australia newsreel "Anna May Wong.")

Australians had been prepared for Wong's arrival through the earlier treatment of American-born Madame Pao and Madame Tsao in the press. As Mark Finnane's work explains, Chinese diplomatic spouse Madame Tsao was seen as a glamourous, modern Chinese woman and a role model to Australian women.[32] Wong followed in this trajectory. As one press report recounted, "Miss Wong has a serene manner, and a low voice. She was a charming slim figure in an ankle-length black frock, slit to the knees to display long white trousers of embroidered sheer. She also wore a smooth black turban with a gold ornament and a silver fox cape."[33] Wong's American and European modernity showed through her clothing. Remember, her ability to incorporate Chinese accents in Western high fashion won her international accolades. Using fashion to demonstrate modernity could point the way to a new model of Chineseness that worked against stereotypes of disfigured, disease-bearing, and unattractive Asians.[34]

Wong's use of the Chinese language, her reference to her Chinese Australian fans, and her mandarin collar all highlight the changing relationship of China to Australia and to Western powers in the months leading up to the Pacific War. In contrast to the Japanese, who evoked increasing anxiety, the Chinese had become Australia's ally in the Pacific, a transformation that was aided by the efforts of people such as Chinese diplomat Tsao Wenyen, who actively worked to inscribe a rich understanding of Chinese culture and society. This changed political dynamic is reflected in the newsreel. Although the Chinese in Australia were still a source of ambivalence, it was also possible to view China outside of security concerns, as embodied in the figure of Anna May Wong.

In some ways, it is remarkable that Wong acted as an ambassador and spokesperson for China, and not for the United States. At this point, her American birth is effaced both for her and for Australian audiences, and China comes to act as an imaginary homeland. She was happy to embrace this Chinese diasporic citizenship in the United States, where she worked for China Relief. Being a nonhyphenated American, which was (and still is) enmeshed in whiteness and is chiefly coded as white, was not an option for her. But, while Wong's racialized body constricted her in some ways, it simultaneously offered her the opportunity to enter an international—and

32. Mark Finnane, "In the Same Bed Dreaming Differently," in *Australia's Asia: From Yellow Peril to Asian Century,* ed. David Walker and Agnieszka Sobocinska (Perth: University of Western Australia Press, 2012), 223–244.

33. *The Argus,* June 5, 1939, 2.

34. For more on Chinese fashion and modernity, see Sean Metzger, *Chinese Looks: Fashion, Performance, Race* (Bloomington: University of Indiana Press, 2014).

cosmopolitan—sphere. It must have been highly gratifying to be received in such an official manner by the consul general and his wife—doubly so, as Wong, in fact, had neither received a warm welcome during her 1936 visit to China nor been selected to meet Madame Chiang Kai-Shek when the Wellesley College–educated Chiang visited the United States.

While she assumed the role of cultural ambassador for China, what becomes apparent in the Fox Movietone newsreel is Wong's commanding World English accent. "World English" was an invented accent, resembling some New England speech patterns as well as educated nonregional British English, which was considered ideal for educated and cultured English speakers.[35] Wong's perfect World English was particularly significant in the Australian context. The borders of white Australia were policed by a language and dictation test, administered in English or another European (but never Asian) language. This test was implemented because it authorized customs agents to continue selecting migrants based on race, while giving the appearance of being racially neutral. Australia's dictation test brings us back to the issues raised in Chapter 1, "'Speaking German Like Nobody's Business,'" and the importance of Wong's European cosmopolitanism. Australia's (white) color line disallowed Chinese migration from British colonies, thus privileging race over empire. Wong's perfect command of English, down to an accent that would have been the envy of many Australians, therefore represented a threat to the continued application of the White Australia Policy.

Wong's accent had received media attention even before her arrival. "You will like Anna May," wrote one *Sydney Morning Herald* journalist. "She is charming, friendly, and cultured. She speaks beautiful English with hardly a trace of an American accent. She told me a very interesting story of this accent she now has. When she first appeared in London on the stage the Press attacked her for her American accent. Critics said it was wrong for such a beautiful Oriental to speak with a New York twang, she should speak only pure English. The little Chinese star at once hired a first-class elocutionist and learned a pure English accent which today comes natural to her."[36] In the same interview Wong had pointed out that an English accent would hardly be more authentic for a "Chinese" actress than an American one. It is noteworthy that this self-fashioning through the acquisition of an English

---

35. Desley Deacon, "World English? How an Australian Invented 'Good American Speech,'" in *Talking and Listening in the Age of Modernity: Essays on the History of Sound*, ed. Joy Damousi and Desley Deacon (Canberra: Australian National University E-press, 2007), 76.

36. Jones, "Anna May Wong to Visit Australia," 8.

accent was part of both Wong's narration of self and the newspaper's desire to report it, ahead of her arrival.

Although on one level Wong's status as a quasi-ambassadorial figure and the widespread media attention she garnered are evidence of a greater acceptance of the Chinese in Australia, they can also be read as the act of erasing Australia's coolie past. Racial anxieties can be soothed through respectability and class. Celebrating her upper-class Chinese markers made not only Chinese heritage but also Australia's Chinese past respectable. As Fiona Paisley has argued persuasively with regard to Aborigines in the 1930s, the modern Australian nation-state has sought to make the project of settler colonization respectable.[37] Positing Wong as a Chinese ambassadorial persona assists in that project, as it places her as a respectable and nonthreatening public figure securely outside of Australia's nation-state borders.

Chinese Australians

Chinese Australian communities made claims to cultural citizenship through multiple practices that could be witnessed courtesy of their interest in Wong. In my book *A Feeling of Belonging,* I argue that Chinese Americans and other Asian American groups enacted cultural citizenship to argue for inclusion into the American polity. As anthropologist Renato Rosaldo and others have found, cultural citizenship asserts the demands of disadvantaged subjects for full citizenship in spite of cultural differences from mainstream society.[38] For those who do not bear the dominant markers of national belonging, such narratives of belonging and citizenship are frequently renegotiated through acts of modernity. Paradoxically, the need to adopt hegemonic cultural practices gives colonized and racial minority subjects the means to disrupt hegemonic power. Hence, given asymmetrical power relations, adoptions of mainstream cultural practices through cultural citizenship can create the grounds for signaling exclusion from rights and privileges. They also create a new basis for inclusion and break down the dichotomy between inclusion and exclusion. Wong's role as an outsider permitted a broader range of com-

---

37. Fiona Paisley, "'Unnecessary Crimes and Tragedies': Race, Gender and Sexuality in Australian Policies of Aboriginal Child Removal," in *Gender, Sexuality and Colonial Modernities,* ed. Antoinette Burton (London: Routledge, 1999), 134–147.

38. Shirley Jennifer Lim, *A Feeling of Belonging: Asian American Women's Public Culture* (New York: New York University Press, 2006); Renato Rosaldo, "Cultural Citizenship, Inequality, and Multiculturalism," in *Latino Cultural Citizenship: Claiming Identity, Space, and Rights,* ed. William V. Flores and Rina Benmayor (Boston: Beacon Press, 1997), 27–38.

munity responses. In particular, the construction of Chinese Australian cultural citizenship through clothing, hairstyles, and cultural activities becomes visible through Wong's visit to Australia.

The decades prior to Wong's arrival saw the harshest policies against Chinese immigration and Chinese communities in Australia. The Chinese population in Australia declined from 30,000 to 8,600, due to death, emigration, and lack of new migration, creating the material basis for whites to have a diminished fear of becoming overwhelmed by "Chinese hordes."[39] The White Australia Policy had been codified and consolidated. Chinese Australians were well situated to practice cultural citizenship, and to have it transmitted by the mainstream Australian press. During the contemporaneous immigration exclusion era in the United States, numerous Asian American populations adopted an analogous strategy of claiming belonging in America through their cultural practices.

Many Chinese Australians took a strong interest in Wong's visit. The *Sydney Morning Herald* reported that "the visiting actress is delighted by the fact that members of Australia's Chinese community have given her such a whole-hearted welcome. She has had many letters from them, and yesterday when the train arrived in Sydney deputations from the New South Wales Chinese Women's Relief fund and the Young Chinese League were there to meet her."[40] Wong had brought photographs that she could sign for China Relief, with which she was heavily involved in the United States. The Museum of Chinese Australian History in Melbourne holds an autographed photograph of Wong in their collection, presumably one of those she brought for China Relief.[41]

One of the most vivid demonstrations of Chinese Australian cultural citizenship came in the guise of the youth clubs that welcomed Wong to their respective cities. One such organization, the Young Chinese League from Melbourne, comprised debutantes and sporting young men. At the time of Wong's visit in 1939, members were extremely modern in fashion and appearance. Mainstream newspapers exhibited the community's cultural citizenship by attesting to how modern and respectable the young Chinese Australians were. The Young Chinese League appeared frequently in Melbourne's *The Argus* newspaper. For example, one story reported that the Young Chinese

---

39. Tseen Khoo and Rodney Noonan, "Wartime Fundraising in Chinese Australian Communities," *Australian Historical Studies* 42, no. 1 (2011): 94.

40. *Sydney Morning Herald,* July 18, 1939, 4.

41. Frank Chinn Collection, Museum of Chinese Australian History, Melbourne.

League organized a ball to raise money for Chinese soldiers. Fourteen "attractive young Chinese girls" were presented, debutante-style, to the Chinese consul general's wife, thus linking race, transnational diplomacy, and glamour. The story related, "They were dressed alike in white net frocks and carried red camellias, and had been trained by Miss Alma Quon."[42] Before the debutante presentation, "a special gavotte was danced by two younger Chinese girls dressed in early Victorian 'powder and patches.'" Although in an entirely different context, this performance is reminiscent of African Americans performing European social dances such as the cakewalk in front of their slave masters.

Early Victorian "powder and patches" notwithstanding, these photographs confirm that, as John Fitzgerald has found, "the Chinese were among the first Australians to embrace modern technologies and take up modishly modern lifestyles."[43] I argue that the "modishly modern" lifestyles countered orientalist stereotypes as well as prompted Chinese Australian communities to claim cultural citizenship. Historian Andrew Markus declares that the concepts of race and racial superiority were barely evident in early white settlers to Australia and that when popular hostility was expressed, it was not in the language of race but in terms of Chinese conduct and customs.[44] Thus it was doubly important for organizations such as the Young Chinese League to evince Western conduct and customs so that they could confirm their fitness for inclusion in the settler-colonial Australian nation-state. Widely circulating photographs of smiling young debutantes in white net dresses or young sporting men competing about the town stressed the respectability and acculturation of the Chinese Australian population, and symbolized their distance from traditional Chinese conduct and customs. Photographs of Young Chinese League dances from 1920s and 1930s beach outings are community-based sources that confirm the mainstream newspaper accounts of their performance of cultural citizenship.[45] These collections of photographs, as amassed from Chinese Australians' personal collections, unveil Chinese Australians adhering to modern Australian contemporary dress and recreational practices. With the outbreak of World War II in the Pacific, these

---

42. *The Argus,* September 26, 1945, 10.

43. John Fitzgerald, *Big White Lie: Chinese Australians in White Australia* (Sydney, Australia: University of New South Wales Press, 2007), 29.

44. Andrew Markus, *Fear and Hatred: Purifying Australia and California 1850–1901* (Sydney, Australia: Hale and Iremonger, 1979).

45. Chinese Australian Historical Images in Australia, Young Chinese League, Museum of Chinese Australian History, Melbourne, Australia.

markers changed to more modern Chinese dress and celebrations of Chinese culture. There was an increasingly visible role of Chinese Australian women in public campaigns, including fund-raisers for China Relief such as "Popular Girl" and "Miss China" contests.[46]

Chinese Australian cultural citizenship can be viewed in a number of ways. The Chinese Australia community soothed racial anxieties through the performance of respectability. Indeed, this had been happening in the Australian colonies since the arrival of upper-class merchants who wanted to separate themselves from working-class coolies in the 1870s. In the 1930s, the performance of cultural citizenship could also be an erasure of the coolie past and a racialized reinscription of Chineseness through the display of nonthreatening, assimilable subjects, such as those mobilized to welcome Wong as she visited Australia. At its heart, the performance of cultural citizenship was an attempt to elude the very real ongoing discrimination and marginalization experienced by Chinese Australians. Wong, as a mutable signifier of settler-colonial racial modernity, had special salience for Chinese Australians, who followed her and sought her autographed photographs at every step.

Conclusion

Following the press coverage and activities of Chinese American actress Anna May Wong allows us to trace Australia's role in the transnational reception of Asians and Asian Australians in popular culture. The mitigation of the Chinese threat through immigration exclusion and the imperatives of war culture, as well as the historical role of Chinese Australians, allowed for ambivalence and hybridity around Chineseness in press accounts of Wong's visit. The enthusiasm of popular audiences and the mainstream press for this Chinese American actress can appear surprising. The white Australians who swarm around Wong in every photograph of her out and about town were eager to catch a glimpse of this glamourous, modern actress; to them, her Chineseness did not evoke the Yellow Peril or the Chinese hordes. These changed meanings follow from the historical anxiety about the Chinese, and yet pointed to a new politics of engagement.

What is profound about this point in time is its ephemerality. It is a hint of possibility that flared up for one brief shining moment, only to disappear with the advent of World War II. The Pacific War, the "fall" of China to communism in 1949, and the changing imperatives of a Cold War world remasculinized political culture so that Wong's female ambassadorial persona

---

46. Khoo and Noonan, "Wartime Fundraising in Chinese Australian Communities."

was no longer valued; it also reinvoked old racial divisions. For a moment in 1939, a glamourous Chinese American woman could occupy a position of transnational importance. Wong's visit helped Australians engage with their relationship to Chineseness, American settler society dynamics, and imperial Europe in strikingly modern ways, but like Wong's cinematic career, this moment faded away under the increasingly harsh geopolitical and racial politics of World War II and the Cold War. However, all was not lost for Wong: as resourceful a cultural worker as ever, she used the newly ubiquitous medium of television to resuscitate her career.

Epilogue

Bold Journey, Native Land

Scene: "Native Land," an Episode of the Television Series Bold Journey

Setting: Into living rooms across the United States, television cameras transmit Anna May Wong sitting with series host John Stephenson in the ABC studio in New York City. She wears a black headscarf that evokes a nun's head covering and an unbecoming padded Chinese jacket. Her eyes flicker about back and forth, then anxiously fix on Stephenson when he speaks to her.

Wong: "I had a grand time going native. . . . Although I have been to many many places in the world, this first and only trip I made to China was the most meaningful."

On February 14, 1957, the American Broadcasting Company (ABC) nationally televised Anna May Wong's "My China Film" as an installment in the television series *Bold Journey*. Wong lobbied the television studio to air her film. The New York-based broadcast combined elements of a live television shoot with the airing of the already prepared film footage. For the majority of the televised broadcast, Wong's "My China Film" ran on the screen with her live narration. Like a theatrical production, the show had an intermission, but, unlike the theater, it featured a lengthy commercial from the sponsor Ralston Purina. This 1957 televised broadcast provides yet another framing device for understanding Wong's film, her career, and her personal history during the twilight of her life and in the new context of the contemporary Cold War cultural and political milieu.

Wong proclaimed *Bold Journey,* "Native Land," to be her own film, trumpeting her success as a cultural worker in getting the film to screen on ABC. In a letter to Carl Van Vechten and Fania Marinoff she wrote, "The next appearance will be with *my film* [italics mine] that I took in China, in a series entitled, 'Bold Journey,' over ABC on the evening of February 11th."[1] Wong emphasized her role as not only creator but also narrator: "*My picture* [italics mine] in which I do the narration is entitled, 'Native Land.'"[2] During the live broadcast, the host chimed in with commentary or questions, but for roughly 90 percent of the time, Wong's voice guided television audiences through the film. In her letter, Wong indicated that she had created the film several years before it screened on ABC: "In case you do see it in New York, I would deeply appreciate your comments on the finish[ed] product as you have seen it some years ago when we ran it in a little projection room on Broadway."[3] With those comments, Wong revealed that she longed for the feedback that would improve her craft as a filmmaker.

As an enterprising cultural worker, Wong spent years of effort trying to get the film in front of a national audience. It was not easy to get what was essentially a self-created film, with aspects of a home movie, screened on American national television, and there were many steps involved. As she explained to Van Vechten and Marinoff in a subsequent letter, "This is to let you and Carlo know I expect to be in New York on or about February 7th. It all depends on how a TV deal here pans out prior to my departure to New York. The reason for the trip there is to appear personally on the program that I have written you about in connection with my first visit to China film."[4] A Los Angeles broadcast of *Bold Journey,* "Native Land," went so well that Wong worked to reprise it in New York. As she further explained to Van Vechten and Marinoff, "It seems the response was so good apropos of the local showing of the above film when I personally appeared and did the narration that they would like to repeat the same setup in New York as I being the only well-known name and my film on China having been so enthusiastically received, they are planning a big publicity campaign and

---

1. Anna May Wong to Carl Van Vechten and Fania Marinoff, January 2, 1957, Carl Van Vechten Manuscript Collection, Beinecke Library, Yale University (hereafter, CVVMC).

2. Ibid.

3. Ibid.

4. Anna May Wong to Carl Van Vechten and Fania Marinoff, January 23, 1957, CVVMC.

using my appearance with the film as the springboard for the beginning of their new season's series."[5] Long after Wong's heyday, she still projected the star power necessary to command television executives' attention, draw in a national audience, and launch the new season of a television series.

As one of Wong's most important visual performances of her career, this televised broadcast of "My China Film" necessitated crucial choices in self-fashioning. Wong gained the national attention that she deserved by exhibiting her own film to a broad American viewership. At long last she enjoyed a nationwide forum for displaying her creative work. How would she, who had spent a lifetime dressing for her roles and public appearances, decide to self-present in front of the camera? In the live television transmission, Wong displays her persona as the transnational Chinese ambassadorial figure that she developed during her 1936 visit to China and realized more fully during her 1939 sojourn in Australia. She reinforces her ambassadorial character with her World English accent and her staid outfit. Wong delivers a Chinese greeting on television in order to authenticate her Chinese ancestry, but then speaks in her World English accent from then on. Wong's ugly costume, consisting of a peculiar headscarf and a torso-thickening jacket more suited to an older and more modest woman, evoked Chinese "folk" (quaint) culture.

John Stephenson, the host of *Bold Journey,* introduced both the film and Wong to the audience. Stephenson established Wong's fame in his opening narration, stating: "Possibly no Chinese woman in the world today is as well-known as our guest this evening. I am sure you are familiar with the international motion picture favorite, Anna May Wong." As Wong had not had a starring role in a major film in decades, Stephenson enunciated a bold claim. Still, she was one of the best-known women of Chinese descent in the world. Note that he refers to her as Chinese, not American, which would have been in keeping with the language at the time. The category "Chinese American" did not exist in popular discourse before the civil rights movement.

In 1957, a television program featuring China was politically fraught. After the "fall" of China to communism in 1949, not only was the country a U.S. political antagonist; many Americans regarded it as a threat to world peace and feared the so-called "domino" effect of one country's fall to communism causing nearby countries to follow. Asia was considered an especially vulnerable locale. After the Korean War ended in a stalemate in 1954 and as the United States began paying for 75 percent of the French military operations in Vietnam, regional tensions were high. China emerged as one of the United States' enemies and as the chief adversarial force behind these con-

---

5. Ibid.

flicts.[6] Given these political circumstances, it became all important that the televised broadcast differentiated between contemporary Cold War China and the U.S.-allied China revealed in Wong's film.

American Cold War agendas regarding China not only prompted ABC to revive and promote Wong's movie; they were made overt through the critique of Communist China and the celebration of a vanished non-Communist past that Wong had captured in her film. As Stephenson explained, "I think we should make clear at the outset ladies and gentlemen that this is not a new film and therefore it's not related in any way to the political upheavals which have taken place in China in recent years." The film invokes a pre–Cold War, pre–Communist China nostalgia. He continues: "And from our point of view this is the beauty of Miss Wong's film. It rekindles the memory of a China that was and possibly will never be again." The ability to show pre–Communist China in the midst of the Cold War made it attractive for both the network and the sponsors. A print advertisement for the series *Bold Journey* sought to pique viewers' curiosity, proclaiming: "Anna May Wong narrates a true-life adventure with films taken in China before Communist domination."[7] The program begins with a male voice-over (presumably Stephenson) stating, "She saw the China she'd read about in school books, the China of rickshaws and straw-headed coolies." Then the visuals begin, quickly cutting to the scene with Wong peering through the lens of her film camera. She wears a pale cheongsam while filming a procession. The male voice-over continues, "and the aromatic shops on the narrow winding streets and finally on the farm where her father was born and his fathers before him, Wong found the China of old, the slumbering giant in peaceful tranquility."

Television producer Julian Lesser corroborated the Cold War political appeal of Wong's film. As he stated in an oral history interview, "Anna had a 35mm film and she had a knack. She had the colorful stuff. It was in China, and at that time China was anti-United States. It was Red and was in effect our enemy. . . . So this was of a peaceful China, and it made a wonderful episode."[8] Lesser's words confirmed Wong's talent ("knack") in creating an effective cinematic visual narrative.

ABC heightened the heartwarming patriotic allure of Wong's film by framing it as an American citizen's travelogue of family reunification and

---

6. Mae Ngai, *Impossible Subjects: Illegal Aliens and the Making of Modern America* (Princeton, NJ: Princeton University Press, 2004), 208.

7. Anna May Wong Clipping File, Lester Sweyd Collection, Billy Rose Theatre Division, New York Public Library.

8. Julian "Bud" Lesser, Oral History Interview, 1992 Margaret Herrick Library, Academy of Motion Pictures, Arts and Sciences, Los Angeles, 74.

return to the ancestral village. As historian Elaine Tyler May has substantiated so persuasively in her classic work, *Homeward Bound,* the nuclear family was an integral part of Cold War culture.[9] Wong's heteronormative family reunion with her father would be reassuringly patriotic, viewed around the new family hearth—the television—within the domestic space of the family home, reaffirming the wholesomeness of all of those things. Wong's film brought the China of old into American living rooms with a supposedly nonthreatening Chinese American woman serving as a palatable guide through time and space to a bygone China friendly to the West. Although not surprising, it is nonetheless noteworthy that the television broadcast made no mention of the *Good Earth* casting debacle or of Wong's critique of Hollywood racism that were her real motives for traveling to China.

During the broadcast, Stephenson immediately asserted Wong's patriotism by telling the audience that "Miss Wong was born not in China, but in the United States. But in the thirties Miss Wong's father returned to his native land to regain possession of his ancestral farm. Later, when Miss Wong was firmly established as a Hollywood leading actress, she realized her childhood ambition to visit the native land of her parents." Stephenson carefully frames the narrative so that the United States is Wong's "Native Land," China is the "Native Land" of her parents. After the family reunion scene that ends the film, Stephenson asks Wong if her father is still alive, and Wong replies in the negative, underscoring the importance of her film as a reliquary of precious memories of nation and family.

Displays of wholesome patriotic Americanness made Wong and her film appealing, an image that other Chinese Americans sought to cultivate during the Cold War era. In 1957, the same year as the televised broadcast of "My China Film," the Chinese Consolidated Benevolent Association conference "promoted an image of the Chinese as solid American citizens, not overseas Chinese."[10] At the same time, the U.S. government, while demonizing Communist China, actively disseminated "a positive image of Chinese Americans who were aligned with the Chinese nationalist government."[11] Just as women such as Madame Chiang-Kai Shek had worked as an ambassadorial figure for nationalist China in the 1930s, soothing racial and political anxieties through femininity, so did Wong's presence on ABC in 1957.[12]

9. Elaine Tyler May, *Homeward Bound: American Families in the Cold War Era* (New York: Basic Books, 1988).

10. Ngai, *Impossible Subjects,* 218.

11. Ibid., 15.

12. Karen Leong, *China Mystique: Pearl S. Buck, Anna May Wong, Mayling Soong, and the Transformation of American Orientalism* (Berkeley: University of California Press, 2005).

When Wong's China film aired on ABC in 1957, television had become an enormous cultural force in American life. Between 1948 and 1955, nearly two-thirds of all American families had bought a television set, making the majority of the American population Wong's potential audience. As scholar Lynn Spiegel argues in her classic work on television, the American public was fascinated with television as part of a "long-standing obsession with communication technologies."[13] In addition, television functioned as a new "window on the world," which apparently included Wong's China film.[14] As television underrepresented the increasing numbers of women in the workforce, it was striking that Wong as a career woman in the public sphere of television was brought into American living rooms across the country.

Although Wong had spent her entire career in front of the film camera, she appears shockingly nervous when performing in this new medium. As the cameras first settle on her in the television studio, her eyes flicker about back and forth, then anxiously fix on Stephenson when he speaks to her. Counter to her usual poise on the film set, Wong stumbles over her words. Wong previously had acknowledged her discomfort with live television when she confided, "Whether we like it or not, television is here to stay. . . . In a way it is much better that the television is filmed as it gives an artist an opportunity to correct any fluff and the lighting will be more effective than the crude lighting that live shows permit."[15] Wong clearly preferred television produced more like film rather than live programming. This would explain the unease she projected during the live television broadcast of "My China Film," especially when she first appears on camera looking visibly agitated. The enhanced lighting of a movie production would presumably make her look better (and less old) than the "crude lighting" of the live ABC broadcast.

One of the most poignant revelations from the 1957 broadcast of "My China Film" is the unkind passage of time. Wong looks old, and we can see the ravages of Laennec's cirrhosis, a disease of the liver that would eventually kill her in 1961, on her face. Television viewers witness her crooked teeth, whereas in the film from two decades earlier, she flashes her straight teeth as she speaks and smiles. Wong's Chinese robe and headdress, the most unbecoming outfit that she had ever worn in public, did not enhance her appeal. This contrasts starkly with her glamourous image in "My China Film," where her beauty dazzled. The coolie-chic ensemble that she sported to the

13. Lynn Spiegel, *Make Room for TV: Television and the Family Ideal in Postwar America* (Chicago: University of Chicago Press, 1992), 7.

14. Ibid., 9.

15. Anna May Wong to Carl Van Vechten and Fania Marinoff, December 31, 1951, CVVMC.

temple in the Western Hills and the devastatingly simple yet perfect suit that she modeled at the Chinese tailor shop prove visually why she had won the 1934 Mayfair Mannequin award for best-dressed woman in the world. Her thick speech (had she been drinking alcohol?) and nervousness in front of the live television camera serve as a dismaying contrast to the poise and warm engagement that she exuded throughout "My China Film."

Despite the nerves and unbecoming costuming on display, the airing of "My China Film" marked an upswing in the final stage of Wong's career. Like other actresses of her era, Wong exploited the medium of television to reinvigorate her faltering career.[16] Just as Wong pioneered and successfully navigated the transition from silent film to talking film, she had to adjust her film skills to the demands of the newly ubiquitous television programming because traditional film work was vanishing. Fully cognizant of the decline of film, Wong wrote, "We have had a very quiet summer so far, I haven't done anything professionally speaking." She explained the reason for the lack of work was that "CBS has built an enormous structure for their television shows and several of the major studios have converted their studios to make films for television exclusively, so looks like film business for theatre consumption is rapidly vanishing from the scene, as theatres have been closing and with few exceptions they are usually half-empty." Wong's film work had essentially dried up. Note Wong's rueful word choice: "We [Wong and brother Richard] finally broke down and acquired a little television set which is nice to have but can give one televisionitis."[17] Despite the lack of work, her playful sense of humor, reminiscent of her Berlin days, was still intact. "Televisionitis," Wong's way of turning television into a disease like tonsillitis, discloses her misgivings about it as a form of entertainment.

Even though she found television work to be difficult and very different from acting in film, she met the challenge with her trademark perseverance and optimism. This was the case for not only "My China Film" airing on *Bold Journey,* "Native Land," but other productions as well. In 1951, she starred in her own television series, *The Gallery of Madame Liu-Tsong,* produced by the defunct DuMont Television Network. In the first television series to feature an Asian American lead, Wong played a gallery owner–detective in what appears to be a reprise of her *Daughter of Shanghai* (1937) role. In her letters, Wong reveals that television acting did not come easily to her but she had to work to make it successful. "I hope you honestly enjoyed our sessions in

---

16. Mary R. Desjardins, *Recycled Stars: Female Film Stardom in the Age of Television and Video* (Durham, NC: Duke University Press, 2015).

17. Anna May Wong to Carl Van Vechten and Fania Marinoff, July 28, 1953, CVVMC.

knocking out Madam Liu Tsong every week as much as I have. I feel it has been a very interesting experience to learn TV the hard way, but as I said to you before, the hours spent with you have proved the most stimulating of all. Thanks and thanks again."[18] Presumably Van Vechten worked with her on the part. One wonders what exactly Wong meant by the "hard way"—is she referring to the hard work of the rehearsal sessions, or mistakes she made while filming live television, or something else? Unhappily, after just one season, DuMont cancelled the ten-episode half-hour show. Even worse for posterity, no scripts or episodes of the show are known to have survived: DuMont infamously loaded its archive onto a barge and dumped it into the "upper New York bay."[19]

Yet, despite her success starring in *The Gallery of Madame Liu-Tsong,* Wong struggled throughout the first half of the 1950s. The background story behind the unkind passage of time revealed by "My China Film" is exhibited in her letters to Van Vechten and Marinoff in which Wong discloses that she found aging to be a difficult process. On October 3, 1952, Wong, age forty-seven, wrote to Marinoff about menopause. She confessed "what kind of queer deal I'm going through now physically during menopause and for him to tell you but not to spread the news abroad. It is certainly a very strange experience and I don't know from day to day how I am going to feel from day to day as the physical aspects seem to affect one mentally in a very depressing way on occasions. I hate to write all this, but then I wanted you to know that I think of you and Carlo constantly when I am in good spirits."[20] Although Wong felt comfortable revealing how menopause affected her in "a very depressing way," she stressed confidentiality to ensure that the news would not spread.

Other stressors that led to her ravaged visage on display during the airing of "My China Film" included money and health problems. The sequence of events that Wong disclosed in her letters from roughly Christmas 1953 to the beginning of March 1954 divulged that she suffered from a major illness, was unable to find work, and, with the utmost reluctance, put her personal jewelry up for sale. In December 1953, Wong had suffered an internal hemorrhage due to Laennec's cirrhosis, the disease that would later claim her life. Writ-

---

18. Anna May Wong to Carl Van Vechten and Fania Marinoff, December 31, 1951, CVVMC.

19. "Edie Adams's Testimony RE: Saving of TV's Golden Years," Library of Congress, March 6, 1996, 46, https://www.loc.gov/programs/static/national-film-preservation-board/documents/tvadams.pdf (accessed May 17, 2018).

20. Anna May Wong to Carl Van Vechten and Fania Marinoff, October 3, 1952, CVVMC.

ing from the Sierra Madre Lodge in Pasadena just after Christmas in 1953, Wong apologized, "I am so deeply sorry to have given you my good friends so much concern and worry with my recent siege at the Santa Monica Hospital." Writing that the lodge was a very pleasant convalescent home, Wong sprightly reported that the "food is excellent and appetizingly prepared, which whets one's appetite and it is not difficult to obey the doctor[']s orders to eat like a pig, as that is exactly what I'm doing."[21] A supremely slender woman throughout her youth, it was doubtlessly a relief, under doctor's orders, to eat whatever she wanted. Wong's sense of humor in light of her near-death experience proclaims her resolve.

At the end of the next month (January 1954), Wong's mood was optimistic as she recuperated and sought work that would pay her medical bills. Wong wrote about her "recuperation" and "restful weekend in Palm Springs." In addition, she was well enough to seek work. "Had lunch with Charlie Farrell at the Hal Roach Studio where he and Gale Storm are filming an episode from 'My Little Margie.' Charlie introduced me to all the people on the set with glowing remarks about wanting to see us busy again, which was nice of him. As I am one, who definitely thinks work is the best Therapy of all. Had a good talk with Gale Storm's agent and he is going to check on some possibilities. On Wednesday I lunched at Paramount."[22] Wong used her connections to the best of her ability to find work.

However, by the beginning of March, work had not materialized, and Wong urgently needed funds to pay her medical bills, so she arranged for a quick sale of her personal jewelry. On March 6, 1954, Wong revealed her anguish about her jewelry sale. "One of the reasons for the delay was due to trying to set in my mind the lowest price possible for their quick disposal. As you say one cannot expect to get anywhere near what one pays for things originally. It isn't an easy thing for me to ask a good friend like you help me on such a matter but it so happens I do need the money, otherwise I wouldn't part with them."[23] Wong articulated her disappointment at having to make such a sale, but clearly she was desperate. In addition, she disclosed that her real estate property was for sale. "Richard and I have talked it over and considered every angle and think it wisest to sell my Santa Monica property as it is too much for us to cope with the financial upkeep and the work entailed."[24]

---

21. Anna May Wong to Carl Van Vechten and Fania Marinoff, December 28, 1953, CVVMC.

22. Anna May Wong to Carl Van Vechten and Fania Marinoff, January 31, 1954, CVVMC.

23. Anna May Wong to Carl Van Vechten and Fania Marinoff, March 6, 1954, CVVMC.

24. Ibid.

The upswing in Wong's career began the next year, in 1955, with her trip to London.[25] An avid theatergoer her whole life, Wong saw two plays in London, one a musical, the other an Agatha Christie play, though she was "not too enraptured with either one of them." Continuing her interest in consorting with fellow artists, she reported that she was going to have "lunch with Somerset Maugham at the Dorchester and look forward to that very much."[26] This lunch would prove to be auspicious.

The networking courtesy of the London lunch paid off when the famous and critically acclaimed director William Wyler hired Wong in 1956 to take a role in his NBC *Producer's Showcase* dramatization of Maugham's *The Letter*. She played the biracial character Mrs. Hammond. From a commercial standpoint, what was showcased was the new innovation of color television in the hopes of generating television set sales. This harkens back to Wong's previous pioneering role in the use of color in another medium, the two-tone color process as one of the first experiments in cinematic color in the film *The Toll of the Sea* (1922).

Wong's work in television entitled her to mingle with Hollywood glitterati. Upon returning home from New York, Wong triumphantly reported that "the phone was ringing frantically and it appears that William Wyler's public relations man had been trying to contact me both here and New York to invite me to attend a tribute being given for William Wyler."[27] The caller proffered an invitation to the film *Friendly Persuasion* (1956) as well as the reception at the Crystal Room at the Beverly Hills Hotel. *Friendly Persuasion*, based on the novel by Jessamyn West, features a Quaker family in the early days of the U.S. Civil War and starred the A-list actors Gary Cooper, Dorothy McGuire, and Anthony Perkins. Wyler had taken over the project after Michael Wilson and later director Frank Capra were placed on the Hollywood blacklist. This was another, albeit indirect way, that anticommunism bolstered Wong's career.

Despite all of the misgivings she articulated around television and despite the fact that performing for television did not come naturally to her as a film actress, Wong did her best to learn TV "the hard way." Wong made a number of guest appearances on serials such as *Wyatt Earp*, CBS's *Climax Mystery Theater*, ABC's *Adventures in Paradise*, and *The Barbara Stanwyck Show*. She still devoted herself to improving her craft. She wrote, "I'm trying a new approach

25. Anna May Wong to Carl Van Vechten and Fania Marinoff, October 6, 1955, CVVMC.

26. Ibid.

27. Anna May Wong to Carl Van Vechten and Fania Marinoff, November 5, 1956, CVVMC.

to acting and that is to be as relaxed as possible myself but when necessary, to be intense in the character."[28] Wong proudly reported that the local paper the *Herald Express* "consider it [the *Climax Mystery Theater* show in which her episode was titled "Chinese Game"] as the best dramatic show they've seen over a period of two years."[29] Wong's new acting approach worked.

Wong's hard work and increased national and international recognition paid off in 1957. First, she was featured in a corporate advertisement for Qantas Airlines. Wong was photographed as one of the judges for a Qantas Airlines geography contest. Doubtlessly this speaks to Wong's reputation as a world traveler and cosmopolitan figure. It may have been the case that Wong's 1939 trip to Australia was still fondly remembered by Australians. Second, Wong's full name was used as a line in the song "Drop that Name" from the Broadway musical *Bells are Ringing*.[30] In this critically acclaimed production, Judy Holliday received a Tony Award for Best Actress in a Musical for singing that song, among others.

As for film, Wong spent her post–World War II career playing minor roles such as the maid Su Lin in *Impact* (1949) and Lana Turner's maid in *Portrait in Black* (1960). This is in marked contrast to the long-lived and successful performing careers of Josephine Baker, who died in 1975 in Paris four days after a gala performance, and Dolores del Río, who made nineteen films between 1944 and 1960, mainly in Mexico. Tragically, Lupe Vélez committed suicide through an overdose of seconal in 1944. Wong's film career flagged in the postwar period because the United States enjoyed substantially changed relations with Asia. Interest in Asia shifted from China to Japan because of the American occupation of that country. In Hollywood, the cinematic portrayal of the female oriental in the 1940s and 1950s shifted to ingénue beauties represented by Japanese actress Miyoshi Umeki and Japanese American actress Miiko Taka in *Sayonara*. Yet there were signs that Wong's film career was finally on the upswing, for she was cast to play a leading role in a major Hollywood film production, Madam Liang in the Rogers and Hammerstein epic Asian American musical, *Flower Drum Song* (1961). But it was not to be. From December 1960 until February 1961, Wong's doctors placed her under intensive care at her home in Santa Monica, where she finally succumbed, on February 3, 1961, to a heart attack, most likely as a result of her Laennec's cirrhosis.

---

28. Anna May Wong to Carl Van Vechten and Fania Marinoff, January 2, 1957, CVVMC.

29. Ibid.

30. I thank Megan Marcus for telling me about this song.

J. DUNLAP McNAIR EMERGES VICTORIOUS

Our Judges: Mr. Stan Freberg; The Rev. Bob Richards; Parky the Tidy Kangaroo*; Miss Anna May Wong; Mr. Stanley Slotkin, Pres., Abbey Rents

The latest, and very likely the last, Qantas contest is history. Its purpose, you may recall, was to secure new and fitting names for the 5 continents served by Qantas Super-G Constellations; new names as appropriate as Qantasylvania is to the Pacific area.

After much soul searching, the judges awarded First Prize to Mr. J. Dunlap McNair of 512 South Talley Avenue, Muncie, Indiana for his entry: Natasq (North America); Antsaq (Australia); Sqanta (Africa); Asqant (Asia); and Tanqas (Europe). The panel felt that these names, while a trifle odd, had each the virtue of containing the same letters as the name of a prominent global airline. The next move is up to Rand McNally.

Many promising entries were discarded because of certain confusion factors; i.e., naming all the continents Texas, or Boston, or Zimmerman.

Thus Mr. McNair becomes Vernon VI, Hereditary Archduke of Qantasylvania and, in addition, wins permanent custody of a 5-foot stuffed koala bear, a lovable but bulky creature weighing 7 stone 5 (103 lbs.). Chief Judge Freberg has volunteered to deliver it in person. Good on him, we say.

In his coronation statement Vernon VI, a metallurgist for the Indiana Steel & Wire Co., Inc. and a family man, said "There are indeed few Archdukes in Muncie."

The other 99 winners will be notified by mail. Congratulations, all!

*Parky hops around Griffith Park Zoo, Los Angeles, picking up paper and stuffing it in her pouch. An example for us all. While not actually a judge, Parky performed yeoman duty collecting the ballots.

QANTAS — *Australia's Overseas Airline*

Anna May Wong in Qantas advertisement.

(Author's collection.)

Contemporary interest in Wong has been escalating, and, in recent years, she has been steadily re-infiltrating popular culture. But, Wong's legacy is still under construction. Peter Ho Davies's 2016 novel, *The Fortunes,* devotes its second chapter, "Silver: Your Name in Chinese," to Wong.[31] Davies's fictionalized account, however, recycles the tired mythology of Wong as an abject, almost-famous Hollywood film star. Not surprisingly, homages to Wong reveal traces of historical racial and gendered mores. The Metropolitan Museum of Art's 2015 blockbuster exhibit, *China: Through the Looking Glass,* dedicated a whole gallery, strategically situated in a position of honor at the front of the second-floor entrance, to Wong.[32] As stated on the wall of the exhibit, "In terms of shaping Western fantasies of China, no figure has had a greater impact on fashion than the Chinese-American actress Anna May Wong."[33] Although, in terms of fashion, Wong did create "Western fantasies of China," what the text misses is the hybrid modernity of Wong's American style. In addition, the exhibit brought to the fore Wong as an epitome of the gendered dimensions of power. As the *New York Times* reported regarding *The First Monday in May,* the documentary about *China: Through the Looking Glass,* "Ms. [Anna] Wintour's fabled steeliness is a major feature of the film (she is juxtaposed, as a paradigm of "dragon lady" grit, with Anna May Wong, the Chinese-American film star, in a way that both questions and reinforces the stereotype)."[34] Wong is cast, albeit in questionable terms, as a career touchstone for the famed *Vogue* magazine editor.

Other currents in popular culture evince Wong's relevance to modernity, cosmopolitanism, and glamour. Noteworthy figures have expressed appreciation for Wong as an iconic figure. As Broadway legend Tommy Tune enthused, "I was 17 years old and got on the elevator at the Algonquin Hotel and there was the famous actress Anna May Wong. I went into my room starstruck."[35] What could be more exciting for the young Texan than being in

31. Peter Ho Davies, *The Fortunes* (New York: Houghton Mifflin Harcourt, 2016).

32. *China: Through the Looking Glass* exhibit, Gallery 209, Metropolitan Museum of Art, New York City, 2015; Rosemary Feitelberg, "'China: Through the Looking Glass' Exceeds 500,000 Visitors," *Women's Wear Daily,* July 22, 2015. This exhibit was so popular that tennis star Roger Federer, when asked in a U.S. Open tennis tournament courtside postmatch interview what fun things he had been doing in New York City, he said that he had gone to see the China costume exhibit at the Metropolitan Museum.

33. *China: Through the Looking Glass* exhibit.

34. Matthew Schneier, "A Party to Mark the Party of the Year," *New York Times,* April 15, 2016, https://www.nytimes.com/2016/04/17/fashion/moma-anna-wintour-met-gala.html (accessed May 18, 2018).

35. "Waking Up to New York," *New York* magazine, April 12, 2009, nymag.com/news/features/56014/index9.html (accessed May 18, 2018).

such close proximity to Wong, who signified all of the promise and glamour of being a thespian in New York?[36] What is fascinating is this anecdote's repeated invocation, first, in a 2009 *New York* magazine segment, and then in 2017 as the "hook" in a *New York Post* profile on Tune. In a 2014 *New Yorker* article on luxury airline seats, reporter David Owen recounts a passenger's anecdote from 1937: "the actress Anna May Wong ". . . was in the berth across the aisle, and that he knew she was asleep, on the other side of the curtain, because he could hear 'a kind of soft snore.'"[37] Owen's evocation of Wong as a historical exemplar of glamourous international travel shows her abiding salience as a cosmopolitan figure as well as a symbol of mobility and modernity. All of these moments demonstrate the contemporary desire to understand American and global pasts and presents through the figure of a stylish Chinese American woman. As long as we cherish films, magazines, and other forms of replicable media, there will continue to be interest in reevaluating the meaning of Anna May Wong.

I end with some words from Wong. Written a few months before the ABC *Bold Journey,* "Native Land," broadcast, her thoughts, ostensibly about travel, sum up her philosophy of life. These sentiments can be read as Wong imparting to her audiences and her public a philosophy that, despite all the strictures placed on her as an Asian American woman, would allow her to continue to struggle for a career commensurate with her worth:

However, being up in mid-air and detached from earth if only temporary, gives one a chance to sort out one's thoughts and keep the lovely ones and toss out the worthless ones.[38]

---

36. Barbara Hoffman, "6-Foot-6 Crooner Tommy Tune Paints, Too—but Only Tall Things," *New York Post,* August 18, 2017, https://nypost.com/2017/08/18/6-foot-6-crooner-tommy-tune-paints-too-but-only-tall-things/ (accessed May 17, 2018).

37. David Owen, "Game of Thrones: How the Airlines Woo the One Per Cent," *New Yorker,* April 21, 2014, 45.

38. Anna May Wong to Carl Van Vechten and Fania Marinoff, November 5, 1956, CVVMC.

Acknowledgments

If it takes a village to raise a child, then it took a world to write this book.

First and foremost, I thank Anna May Wong. I have been studying the extraordinary complexities of her life and cultural labors since my very first research paper in graduate school at the University of California, Los Angeles, in 1992. Recently, when asked whether I am tired of researching her, I answered with a resounding "no." Many of the difficult issues that she faced in her career are familiar to me as an Asian American feminist academic, and Wong's determination and unflappable good cheer have brightened my days and encouraged me to continue. She has been an inspiration to me, and it is my fervent wish that this book, in turn, inspires readers for generations to come.

I am in cheerful awe that Temple University Press, the leading press in Asian American studies, agreed to publish this work. Invoking the names of the editors of the *Asian American History and Culture* series yields a veritable academic who's who: founding editor Sucheng Chan; editors emeriti David Palumbo-Liu, Michael Omi, K. Scott Wong, and Linda Trinh Võ; current editors Cathy Schlund-Vials, Shelley Sang-Hee Lee, and Rick Bonus. Equally intimidating, many giants in the field have published in this august series. To paraphrase *Saturday Night Live*'s Wayne and Garth, I'm not worthy! Cheers to series editor extraordinaire Cathy Schlund-Vials; to my editor Sara Cohen; to rights and permissions coordinator Nikki Miller; to art director Kate Nichols; to production editor Joan Vidal; and to the publicity and marketing staffs. I thank Virginia Perrin for her meticulous copyediting and David Martinez for the stellar index.

A historian's work is made possible only through the good graces of archives, archivists, and libraries around the world. Research for this book was conducted at the following institutions: Arts Centre, Performing Arts Collection and Research Library, Melbourne; Australian National Library, Canberra; Beinecke Rare Book and Manuscript Library, Yale University; Bibliothèque Nationale de France; University of California, Los Angeles Special Collections and Archives; British Film Institute; British Library; Deutsche Kinemathek (Film Museum, Berlin); Film and Television Archive, University of California, Los Angeles; Margaret Herrick Library of the Academy of Motion Pictures Arts and Sciences; Museum of Modern Art, New York; Library of Congress, Prints and Photographs Division; National Archive of Film and Sound, Canberra; Museum of Chinese Australian History, Melbourne; National Museum of American History, Smithsonian Institution; National Portrait Gallery, Smithsonian Institution; New York Public Library, Performing Arts Branch, Billy Rose Theatre Collection; Theatre Museum, London; University of the Witwatersrand Libraries, Johannesburg; and Donna Sammis and the Interlibrary Loan staff at the State University of New York (SUNY), Stony Book. They have all been phenomenal.

The Australian National University Humanities Research Fellowship and SUNY's Nuala McGann Drescher Faculty Leave Program generously supported the research and writing. SUNY Stony Brook provided crucial funding through the Faculty in the Arts, Humanities, and Lettered Social Sciences Grant; the United University Professions Individual Development Award; the Arts, Humanities, and Lettered Social Sciences Faculty Research Program Fellowship; and sabbatical leaves. I am indebted to my numerous chairs and deans for securing these leaves.

Portions of this book have been presented at various venues. I thank the audiences for their questions and feedback and the following organizers for their support: Australian National University in Canberra, Australia; City University of New York; David Walker and Agnieszka Sobocinska at Deakin University in Melbourne, Australia; Museum of the Moving Image, New York City; New School for Social Research; Ohio State University; Valerie Smith at Princeton University's African American Studies Center; Mary Dillard for the Gerda Lerner Lecture in Women's History at Sarah Lawrence College; Amanda Frisken at SUNY Old Westbury; Kristin Nytray at the University Library Series at SUNY Stony Brook; Ann Kaplan for the SUNY

Stony Brook Humanities Institute Cosmopolitanism Conference; Università di Padova; Linda Trinh Võ at the University of California, Irvine; Vernadette Gonzalez at the University of Hawaii at Manoa; Mia Carter at the University of Texas, Austin; and Colleen McDannell and Noël Voltz for the O. Meredith Wilson Symposium in History at the University of Utah.

Mentors par excellence have provided intellectual and spiritual sustenance throughout. Valerie Matsumoto continues to dispense sage counsel; Lisa Lowe talked me through the finer points of cosmopolitanism; Vicki Ruiz has been incredibly smart and kind, not to mention an amusing conference companion; Val Smith bestowed serene wisdom, as did Sharon Traweek, who, when I turned ABD, cautioned me about the stalled female associate professor phenomenon. At SUNY Stony Brook, Kathleen Wilson imparted shrewd editing and hilarious commentary, Ann Kaplan supported me from the beginning, Nancy Tomes and Michael Barnhart hired me and chaperoned me through the tenure process, and Marci Lobel personified an ideal outside department mentor.

Colleagues and friends have been central to the process. I am grateful to the following for commenting on my unformed ideas and prose: Nerissa Balce-Cortes, Mary Dillard, Daniela Flesler, Victoria Hesford, Grace Hong, Sanda Lwin, April Masten, Janis Mimura, Susette Min, Adrián Pérez-Melgosa, Patrice Petro, Martha Chew Sanchez, Jeffrey Santa Ana, Cynthia Tolentino, and the Asian American Women's Writing Group of the Greater New York area. Matthew James Christensen read the entire manuscript and offered stellar advice. For sharing primary sources with me, I salute Lloys Frates, William Glenn, Celia Marshik, and Alicia Rodríquez-Estrada. Jenny Anderson suggested the addition of the historical re-creations, and Kerwin Klein advised me to look closely at Wong's associates. I am grateful to Jeff Fort for translating Walter Benjamin's words with such care and skill.

I thank the following people for providing shelter during research trips, meals, conversation, and overall support: Kai-Uwe Bergman, Daphne Brooks, Connie Chen, Edith Chen, Janet Clarke, Lisa Diedrich, Roxanne Fernandez, Cymone Fourshey, Timur Friedman, Mandy Frisken, Sarah Mikels Harrington, Tamara Ho, Tiffany Joseph, Katherine King, Laura Kreutzer, Muriel McClendon, Ryan Minor, Elizabeth Terese Newman, Jasmin Rostam-Kolayi, Victoria Sams, Ana Silva, Michael Solo, Susan Solo, Katherine Sugg, Alan Tener, Adrienne Unger, Judy Wu, and everyone acknowledged above. Ginger snaps to Karen J. Leong for her solidarity throughout the continuing Anna May Wong madness.

Students, undergraduate and graduate, have sharpened my focus and my ideas. All of my students, past and present, have been instrumental in my work. I extend special recognition to Alessandro Buffa, Arieh Sclar, Chanhaeng Lee, Kim Donaldson, Leah Savage, Caroline Propersi, Anna Obermeyer, Rebecca Kim, Kelly Jones, Aishah Scott, and Yallile Suriel.

In Australia, I benefited from the wisdom of Kate Bagnall, Desley Deacon, Debjani Ganjuly, Jacqueline Lo, Agnieszka Sobocinska, David Walker, Angela Woollacott, and scholars at the Humanities Research Centre at Australian National University.

An earlier version of part of Chapter 1 appeared as "'Speaking German Like Nobody's Business': Anna May Wong, Walter Benjamin, and the Possibilities of Asian American Cosmopolitanism," *Journal of Transnational American Studies* 4, no. 1 (Summer 2012): 1–17. I thank special issue editors Tanfer Emin Tunc, Elisabetta Marino, and Daniel Y. Kim and the anonymous readers.

An earlier version of Chapter 2 appeared as "'The Most Beautiful Chinese Girl in the World': Anna May Wong's Transnational Racial Modernity," in *Body and Nation: The Global Realm of U.S. Body Politics in the Twentieth Century,* ed. Emily Rosenberg and Shanon Fitzpatrick (Durham, NC: Duke University Press, 2013). Republished by permission of the copyright holder, Duke University Press. I thank Emily and Shanon for their many insightful comments.

The Advertising Education Foundation's project on Race and Ethnicity shaped my thinking on Chapter 4. For that, I acknowledge Fath Davis Ruffins, Paula Alex, Janice Spector, and all of the advisory board co-members.

An earlier version of Chapter 6 appeared as "Glamorising Racial Modernity," in *Australia's Asia: From Yellow Peril to Asian Century,* ed. David Walker and Agnieszka Sobocinska (Perth: University of Western Australia Press, 2012). It is republished by permission of David Walker and Agnieszka Sobocinska. I owe special thanks to David and Agnieszka.

I appreciate the support and tolerance of the Lim, Christensen, and Adams families over the decades. During the research and writing of this book, Joy Adams Slingerland died of Amyotrophic Lateral Sclerosis (ALS), Phyllis Adams of cancer, and Soei Nio Lim, though still alive, in her sixties became completely mentally and physically incapacitated by Alzheimer's. This work is dedicated to them in appreciation of their under-recognized labor.

Most of all, I am grateful to Matthew James Christensen, who is the most beautiful human being in the world.

Scholarship on Anna May Wong

Anna May Wong's life, career, and legacy reflect complex issues of race, gender, and representation, many of which persist decades after her death. As the first Asian American female star, her place in American and global cinematic history is vital. Given the importance of Wong to the global construction of race and gender, there are surprisingly few works on Wong compared to other well-researched topics in Asian American history, such as studies of laboring male Chinese coolies, the 1882 Chinese Exclusion Act, or the Japanese American internment during World War II. This can be attributed to the prioritization of working-class males as a subject within the field and the scattered primary source materials on Wong, as well as the difficulty of interpreting her work. In the 1970s, the growing importance of racial and ethnic studies such as Asian American studies increased scholarship that corrected the historical neglect of nonwhite performers in the American entertainment industry. Through looking at popular magazines, Judy Chu's "Anna May Wong," published in the Asian American anthology *Counterpoint,* pioneered the Asian American studies re-examination of Wong's career.[1] However, Asian American scholars and activists from the civil rights

---

1. Judy Chu, "Anna May Wong," in *Counterpoint: Perspectives on Asian America,* ed. Emma Gee (Los Angeles: Asian American Studies Center of the University of California, 1976), 284–289.

generation such as theater and visual arts scholar James S. Moy argued that Wong's Hollywood screen characters "died, or at best survived to live out clearly defined marginal roles," which was part of the larger trend of Asians "find[ing] death on the American field of representation."[2] Although I would argue for a more complex analysis of Wong's Hollywood career, this dismissal of Wong has haunted the field and doubtlessly prompted my own urge to examine Wong's work chiefly outside of mainstream Hollywood A-list productions. Later on, film scholar Tim Bergfelder's "Negotiating Exoticism: Hollywood, Film Europe and the Cultural Reception of Anna May Wong," opened up scholarly inquiry about Wong's transnational career in Europe.[3]

Around the centennial of Wong's birth (2005), a re-examination of her life and career took shape: three major works appeared, and comprehensive retrospectives of her films were held at both the Museum of Modern Art and the Museum of the Moving Image in New York City. Anthony Chan's 2003 biography, *Perpetually Cool: The Many Lives of Anna May Wong (1905–1961)*, was written "from a uniquely Asian-American perspective and sensibility." In the same year, Philip Leibfried and Chei Mi Lane published *Anna May Wong: A Complete Guide to Her Film, Stage, Radio and Television Work*, and in 2004, another full-length biography, *Anna May Wong: From Laundryman's Daughter to Hollywood Legend*, was authored by Graham Russell Hodges.[4] In addition, psychoanalytic cinema studies articles by Anne Anlin Cheng and Laura Mulvey focused on Wong's British film *Piccadilly* (1929).[5] There have been two major documentary film biographies of Wong's life: Elaine May Woo's *Anna*

2. James S. Moy, *Marginal Sights: Staging the Chinese in America* (Iowa City: University of Iowa Press, 1993), 90, 82. For similar approaches, see Jun Xing, "Cinematic Asian Representation in Hollywood," in *Performing Difference: Representations of the "Other" in Film and Theatre*, ed. Jonathan C. Friedman (Lanham, MD: Rowman and Littlefield, 2008), chap. 7; Eugene M. Wong, *On Visual Media Racism: Asians in the American Motion Pictures* (North Stratford, NH: Ayer, 1979).

3. Tim Bergfelder, "Negotiating Exoticism: Hollywood, Film Europe and the Cultural Reception of Anna May Wong," in *"Film Europe" and "Film America": Cinema, Commerce and Cultural Exchange, 1920–1939*, ed. Andrew Higson and Richard Maltby (Exeter, UK: University of Exeter Press, 1999), 302–384.

4. Graham Hodges, *Anna May Wong* (New York: Palgrave, 2004); Philip Leibfried and Chei Mi Lane, *Anna May Wong: A Complete Guide to Her Film, Stage, Radio, and Television Work* (New York: McFarland, 2003); Anthony C. Chan, *Perpetually Cool: The Many Lives of Anna May Wong, 1905–1961* (Lanham, MD: Rowman and Littlefield, 2003).

5. Anne Anlin Cheng, "Shine: On Race, Glamour, and the Modern," *PMLA* 126, no. 4 (2011): 1022–1041; Laura Mulvey, "Love in Two British Films of the Late Silent Period: *Hindle Wakes* (Maurice Elvey, 1927) and *Piccadilly* (E. A. Dupont, 1929)," in *Europe in Love and Cinema*, ed. Luisa Passerini, Jo Labanyi, and Karen Diehl (Bristol, UK: Intellect Books distributed by University of Chicago Press, 2012), chap. 4.

May Wong: Frosted Yellow Willows (2007) and Yunah Hong's *Anna May Wong: In Her Own Words* (2011).

As mentioned in the Introduction, of the existing recent scholarship, the writings of film scholar Yiman Wang, theater scholar Sean Metzger, and historian Karen Leong have informed this work. Leong's *China Mystique* elucidates the "gendered embodiment of orientalism."[6] Metzger interrogates "the discursive production of a wardrobe—to get readers to think differently about existing categories such as race and Asian American."[7] In her important article on screen passing, Wang insists that Wong is not a performer who naturally plays Asian American roles but one who employs tactics such as screen passing or ironic ethnic masquerade in ways that can be understood as subversive of dominant racial stereotypes.[8] All of their interpretations have enhanced our understanding of Wong.

---

6. Karen Leong, *China Mystique: Pearl S. Buck, Anna May Wong, Mayling Soong, and the Transformation of American Orientalism* (Berkeley: University of California Press, 2005).

7. Sean Metzger, *Chinese Looks: Fashion, Performance, Race* (Bloomington: University of Indiana Press, 2014), 20.

8. Yiman Wang, "The Art of Screen Passing: Anna May Wong's Yellow Yellowface Performance in the Art Deco Era," *Camera Obscura* 60 (2005): 159–191.

Selected Bibliography

This bibliography includes the books, chapters from edited collections, and journal articles consulted for this book.

Anderson, Benedict. *Imagined Communities: Reflections on the Origin and Spread of Nationalism.* New York: Verso, 1991.

Ang, Ien. *On Not Speaking Chinese: Living between Asia and the West.* New York: Routledge, 2001.

Appadurai, Arjun. *Modernity at Large: Cultural Dimensions of Globalization.* Minneapolis: University of Minnesota Press, 1996.

Baker, Jean-Claude, and Chris Chase. *Josephine.* Holbrook, MA: Adams Media, 1993.

Balce, Nerissa. *Body Parts of Empire: Visual Abjection, Filipino Images, and the American Archive.* Ann Arbor: University of Michigan Press, 2016.

Beauchamp, Cari. *Without Lying Down: Frances Marion and the Powerful Women of Early Hollywood.* New York: Scribner, 1997.

Benjamin, Walter. "Gespräch mit Anne May Wong." *Die Literarische Welt,* July 6, 1928.

———. "The Task of the Translator." In *Illuminations,* 69–82. New York: Schocken, 1969.

Bergfelder, Tim. "Negotiating Exoticism: Hollywood, Film Europe and the Cultural Reception of Anna May Wong." In *"Film Europe" and "Film America": Cinema, Commerce and Cultural Exchange, 1920–1939,* ed. Andrew Higson and Richard Maltby, 302–384. Exeter, UK: University of Exeter Press, 1999.

Bernard, Emily. *Carl Van Vechten and Harlem Renaissance.* New Haven, CT: Yale University Press, 2012.

Bernardi, Daniel, ed., *The Birth of Whiteness: Race and the Emergence of U.S. Cinema.* New Brunswick, NJ: Rutgers University Press, 1996.

Blakely, Allison. *Blacks in the Dutch World: The Evolution of Racial Imagery in a Modern Society.* Bloomington: Indiana University Press, 1993.

Bloch, Ernest. "Erinnerungen." In *Uber Walter Benjamin,* ed. Theodor W. Adorno and Rolf Tiedemann, 16–23. Frankfurt am Main, Germany: Suhrkamp Verlag, 1968.

Boittin, Jennifer. *Colonial Metropolis: The Urban Grounds of Feminism and Anti-imperialism in Interwar Paris.* Lincoln: University of Nebraska Press, 2010.

Borshuk, Michael. "An Intelligence of the Body: Disruptive Parody through Dance in the Early Performances of Josephine Baker." In *Embodying Liberation: The Black Body in American Dance,* ed. Dorothea Fischer-Hornung and Allison Goeller, 41–58. Piscataway, NJ: Transaction, 2001.

———. "'Queen of the Colonial Exposition': Josephine Baker's Strategic Performance." In *Critical Voicings of Black Liberation: Resistance and Representation in the Americas,* ed. Hermine D. Pinson, Kimberly Phillips, Lorenzo Thomas, and Hanna Wallinger, 47–65. Piscataway, NJ: Transaction, 2003.

Bourne, Randolph. "Trans-National America." In *The History of a Literary Radical and Other Papers.* New York: S. A. Russell, 1956. Originally published in *The Atlantic,* July 1916.

Bowser, Pearl, and Louise Spence. *Writing Himself into History: Oscar Micheaux, His Silent Films, and His Audiences.* New Brunswick, NJ: Rutgers University Press, 2000.

Breckenridge, Carol A., Sheldon Pollack, Homi L. Bhabha, and Dipesh Chakrabarty, eds. *Cosmopolitanism.* Durham, NC: Duke University Press, 2002.

Brooks, Daphne. *Bodies in Dissent: Spectacular Performances of Race and Freedom, 1850–1910.* Durham, NC: Duke University Press, 2006.

Brown, Jayna. *Babylon Girls: Black Women Performers and the Shaping of the Modern.* Durham, NC: Duke University Press, 2008.

Brown, Judith. *Glamour in Six Dimensions: Modernism and the Radiance of Form.* Ithaca, NY: Cornell University Press, 2009.

Browne, Nick. "The Undoing of the Other Woman: Madame Butterfly in the Discourse of American Orientalism." In *The Birth of Whiteness: Race and the Emergence of U.S. Cinema,* ed. Daniel Bernardi, 227–256. New Brunswick, NJ: Rutgers University Press, 1996.

Buck-Morss, Susan. *The Dialectics of Seeing: Walter Benjamin and the Arcades Project.* Cambridge, MA: MIT Press, 1991.

Burke, Timothy. *Lifebuoy Men, Lux Women: Commodification, Consumption, and Cleanliness in Modern Zimbabwe.* Durham, NC: Duke University Press, 1996.

Burt, Ramsay. "'Savage' Dancer: Tout Paris Goes to See Josephine Baker." In *Alien Bodies: Representations of Modernity, "Race" and Nation in Early Modern Dance,* 57–83. London: Routledge, 1998.

Butler, Judith. *Gender Trouble: Feminism and the Subversion of Identity.* New York: Routledge, 1990.

Chakrabarty, Dipesh. *Provincializing Europe: Postcolonial Thought and Historical Difference.* Princeton, NJ: Princeton University Press, 2000.

Chan, Anthony C. *Perpetually Cool: The Many Lives of Anna May Wong, 1905–1961.* Lanham, MD: Rowman and Littlefield, 2003.

Chan, Sucheng. *Asian Americans: An Interpretive History.* Boston: Twayne, 1991.

———, ed. *Entry Denied: Exclusion and the Chinese Community in America, 1882–1943.* Philadelphia: Temple University Press, 1991.

———. "The Exclusion of Chinese Women, 1870–1943." In *Entry Denied: Exclusion and the Chinese Community in America,* ed. Sucheng Chan, 94–146. Philadelphia: Temple University Press, 1991.

Chávez, Ernesto. "'Ramón Is Not One of These': Race and Sexuality in the Construction of Silent Film Actor Ramón Novarro's Star Image." *Journal of the History of Sexuality* 20, no. 3 (September 2011): 520–544.

Cheah, Pheng, and Bruce Robbins, eds. *Cosmopolitics: Thinking and Feeling beyond the Nation.* Minneapolis: University of Minnesota Press, 1998.

Cheng, Anne Anlin. *Second Skin: Josephine Baker and the Modern Surface.* New York: Oxford University Press, 2010.

———. "Shine: On Race, Glamour, and the Modern." *PMLA* 126, no. 4 (2011): 1022–1041.

Chow, Rey. *Primitive Passions: Visuality, Sexuality, Ethnography and Contemporary Chinese Cinema.* New York: Columbia University Press, 1995.

Chu, Judy. "Anna May Wong." In *Counterpoint: Perspectives on Asian America,* ed. Emma Gee, 284–289. Los Angeles: Asian American Student Center of the University of California, 1976.

Chuh, Kandace. *Imagine Otherwise: On Asian Americanist Critique.* Durham, NC: Duke University Press, 2003.

Chun, Gloria. "Go West ". . . to China." In *Claiming America: Constructing Chinese American Identities during the Exclusion Era,* ed. K. Scott Wong and Sucheng Chan, 165–190. Philadelphia: Temple University Press, 1998.

Chung, Hye Seung. *Hollywood Asian: Philip Ahn and the Politics of Cross-Ethnic Performance.* Philadelphia: Temple University Press, 2006.

Clancy-Smith, Julia Ann, and Frances Gouda. *Domesticating the Empire: Race, Gender, and Family Life in French and Dutch Colonialism.* Charlottesville: University of Virginia Press, 1998.

Cohen, Julia Phillips. "Oriental by Design: Ottoman Jews, Imperial Style, and the Performance of Heritage." *American Historical Review* (April 2014): 364–398.

Cohen, Lizbeth. *A Consumer's Republic: The Politics of Mass Consumption in Postwar America.* New York: Borzoi Books (Knopf), 2003.

Coulthard, Glen. *Red Skin, White Masks: Rejecting the Colonial Politics of Recognition.* Minneapolis: University of Minnesota Press, 2014.

Courtney, Nancy. *Hollywood Fantasies of Miscegenation: Spectacular Narratives of Gender and Race, 1903–1967.* Princeton, NJ: Princeton University Press, 2005.

Cripps, Thomas. *Slow Fade to Black: The Negro in American Film, 1900–1942.* New York: Oxford University Press, 1993.

Dalton, Karen C. C., and Henry Louis Gates Jr. "Josephine Baker and Paul Colin: African American Dance Seen through Parisian Eyes." *Critical Inquiry* 24, no. 4 (1998): 903–934.

Davies, Peter Ho. *The Fortunes.* New York: Houghton Mifflin Harcourt, 2016.

Davis, Angela Y. *Blues Legacies and Black Feminism: Gertrude "Ma" Rainey, Bessie Smith, and Billie Holiday.* New York: Vintage, 1998.

Davis, Keith. *The Passionate Observer: Photographs by Carl Van Vechten.* Kansas City: Hallmark Cards, 1993.

Day, Iyko. *Alien Capital: Asian Racialization and the Logic of Settler Colonial Capitalism.* Durham, NC: Duke University Press, 2016.

Deacon, Desley. "World English? How an Australian Invented 'Good American Speech.'" In *Talking and Listening in the Age of Modernity: Essays on the History of Sound,* ed. Joy Damousi and Desley Deacon, 73–82. Canberra: Australian National University E-press, 2007.

deCordova, Richard. *Picture Personalities: The Emergence of the Star System in America.* Urbana-Champaign: University of Illinois Press, 2001.

Desjardins, Mary. *Recycled Stars: Female Film Stardom in the Age of Television and Video.* Durham, NC: Duke University Press, 2015.

Doane, Mary Ann. "Dark Continent: Epistemologies of Racial and Sexual Difference in Psychoanalysis and the Cinema." In *Femmes Fatales: Feminism, Film Theory, and Psychoanalysis.* London: Routledge, 1991.

Dong, Madeline. "Who Is Afraid of the Chinese Modern Girl?" In *The Modern Girl around the World: Consumption, Modernity, and Globalization,* ed. Modern Girl around the World Research Group. Durham, NC: Duke University Press, 2008.

Dudziak, Mary L. "Josephine Baker, Racial Protest, and the Cold War." *Journal of American History,* September 1994, 543–570.

Dwyer, Tessa. "Universally Speaking: Lost in Translation and Polyglot Cinema." *Linguistica Antverpiensia* 4 (2005): 295–310.

Dyer, Richard. *Stars.* London: British Film Institute, 1998.

Echenberg, Myron. *Colonial Conscripts: The Tirailleurs Sénégalais in French West Africa, 1857–1960.* Portsmouth, NH: Heinemann, 1991.

Edwards, Brent Hayes. *The Practice of Diaspora: Literature, Translation, and the Rise of Black Internationalism.* Cambridge, MA: Harvard University Press, 2003.

Ellison, Ralph. "Change the Joke and Slip the Yoke." In *Shadow and Act.* New York: Random House, 1953.

Emery, Lynne Fauley. *Black Dance: From 1619 to Today.* Princeton, NJ: Princeton Book, 1988.

Everett, Anna. *Returning the Gaze: A Genealogy of Black Film Criticism, 1909–1949.* Durham, NC: Duke University Press, 2001.

Ezra, Elizabeth. *The Colonial Unconscious: Race and Culture in Interwar France.* Ithaca, NY: Cornell University Press, 2000.

Fabian, Johannes. *Time and the Other: How Anthropology Makes Its Object.* New York: Columbia University Press, 1983.

Feng, Peter. *Identities in Motion: Asian American Film and Video.* Durham, NC: Duke University Press, 2002.

Ferris, David S., ed. *The Cambridge Companion to Walter Benjamin.* Cambridge: Cambridge University Press, 2004.

Finnane, Mark. "In the Same Bed Dreaming Differently." In *Australia's Asia: From Yellow Peril to Asian Century,* ed. David Walker and Agnieszka Sobocinska, 223–244. Perth: University of Western Australia Press, 2012.

Fischer, Lucy. *Designing Women: Cinema, Art Deco, and the Female Form.* New York: Columbia University Press, 2003.

Fischer, Marilyn. "A Pragmatist Cosmopolitan Moment: Reconfiguring Nussbaum's Cosmopolitan Concentric Circles." *Journal of Speculative Philosophy* 21, no. 3 (2007): 151–165.

Fitzgerald, John. *Big White Lie: Chinese Australians in White Australia.* Sydney, Australia: University of New South Wales Press, 2007.

Flanner, Janet. *"Paris Journal," 1965–1971.* New York: Harcourt Brace Jovanovich, 1977.

———. *Paris Was Yesterday: 1925–1939.* New York: Viking, 1972.

Fleming, Crystal. *Resurrecting Slavery: Racial Legacies and White Supremacy in France.* Philadelphia: Temple University Press, 2017.

Fregoso, Rosa Linda. "Lupe Vélez: Queen of the Bs." In *From Bananas to Buttocks: The Latina Body in Popular Film and Culture,* ed. Myra Mendible, 51–68. Austin: University of Texas Press, 2009.

Fuller, Karla Rae. *Hollywood Goes Oriental: CaucAsian Performance in American Film.* Detroit, MI: Wayne State University Press, 2010.

Gabbard, Krin, ed. *Jazz among the Discourses.* Durham, NC: Duke University Press, 1995.

———, ed. *Representing Jazz.* Durham, NC: Duke University Press, 1995.

Gabler, Neil. *An Empire of Their Own: How the Jews Invented Hollywood.* New York: Anchor, 1989.

Garber, Marjorie. *Vested Interests: Cross-Dressing and Cultural Anxiety.* New York: Routledge, 1991.

Gates, Henry Louis, Jr. *Signifying Monkey: A Theory of African American Literary Criticism.* New York: Oxford University Press, 1988.

Genova, James. *Colonial Ambivalence, Cultural Authenticity, and the Limitations of Mimicry in French-Ruled West Africa, 1914–1956.* New York: Peter Lang, 2004.

Gikandi, Simon. "Picasso, Africa, and the Schemata of Difference." *Modernism/Modernity* 10, no. 3 (2003): 455–480.

Gilman, Sander. *Difference and Pathology: Stereotypes of Sexuality, Race, and Madness.* Ithaca, NY: Cornell University Press, 1985.

Gilroy, Paul. *The Black Atlantic: Modernity and Double-Consciousness.* Cambridge, MA: Harvard University Press, 1995.

Goldberg, D. T. "Modernity, Race, and Morality." *Cultural Critique,* no. 24 (Spring 1993): 193–227.

Goldsmith, Meredith. "Shopping to Pass, Passing to Shop: Consumer Self-Fashioning in the Fiction of Nella Larsen." In *Middlebrow Moderns: Popular American Women Writers of the 1920s,* ed. Lisa Botshon and Meredith Goldsmith, 263–290. Boston: Northeastern University Press, 2003.

Gomez, Michael. *Exchanging Our Country Marks: The Transformation of African Identities in the Colonial and Antebellum South.* Chapel Hill: University of North Carolina Press, 1998.

Gonzalez, Vernadette Vicuña. *Securing Paradise: Tourism and Militarism in Hawai'i and the Philippines.* Durham, NC: Duke University Press, 2013.

Gottschild, Brenda Dixon. *Digging the Africanist Presence in American Performance Dance and Other Contexts.* Westport, CT: Greenwood Press, 1996.

Greenblatt, Stephen. *Renaissance Self-Fashioning.* Chicago: University of Chicago Press, 1980.

Groves, Derham. *Anna May Wong's Lucky Shoes: 1939 Australia through the Eyes of an Art Deco Diva.* Ames, IA: Culicidae Architectural Press, 2013.

Guerrero, Ed. *Framing Blackness: The African American Image in Film.* Philadelphia: Temple University Press, 1993.

Gundle, Stephen. *Glamour: A History.* New York: Oxford University Press, 2009.

Guterl, Matthew. *Josephine Baker and the Rainbow Tribe.* Cambridge, MA: Harvard University Press, 2014.

Gutinger, Erich. "A Sketch of the Chinese Community in Germany: Past and Present." In *The Chinese in Europe,* ed. Gregor Benton and Frank Pieke, 42–67. New York: St. Martin's Press, 1998.

Gyory, Andrew. *Closing the Gate: Race, Politics, and the Chinese Exclusion Act.* Chapel Hill: University of North Carolina Press, 1998.

Hake, Sabine. *German National Cinema.* New York: Routledge, 2007.

Halberstam, Judith. *Female Masculinities.* Durham, NC: Duke University Press, 1998.

Hale, Dana. *Races on Display: French Representations of Colonized Peoples, 1886–1940.* Bloomington: Indiana University Press, 2008.

Hall, Linda. *Dolores del Río: Beauty in Light and Shadow.* Palo Alto, CA: Stanford University Press, 2013.

Harvey, David. *Paris, Capital of Modernity.* New York: Routledge, 2003.

Hershfield, Joanne. *The Invention of Dolores del Río.* Minneapolis: University of Minnesota Press, 2000.

Higashi, Sumiko. "DeMille's *The Cheat.*" In *Unspeakable Images: Ethnicity and the American Cinema,* ed. Lester Friedman, 112–139. Urbana: University of Illinois Press, 1991.

Hirata, Lucie Cheng. "Free, Indentured, Enslaved: Chinese Prostitutes in Nineteenth-Century America." *Signs: Journal of Women in Culture and Society* 5, no. 1 (Autumn 1979): 3–29.

Hodges, Graham Russell. *Anna May Wong: From Laundryman's Daughter to Hollywood Legend.* New York: Palgrave, 2004.

Hsu, Madeline. *Dreaming of Gold, Dreaming of Home: Transnationalism and Migration between the United States and South China, 1882–1943.* Stanford, CA: Stanford University Press, 2000.

Hughes, Langston. *Remember Me to Harlem: The Letters of Langston Hughes and Carl Van Vechten,* ed. Emily Bernard. New York: Vintage, 2002.

Hugill, Peter J. "German Great-Power Relations in the Pages of 'Simplicissimus,' 1896–1914." *Geographical Review* 98, no. 1 (2008): 1–23.

Imada, Adria. *Aloha America: Hula Circuits through the US Empire.* Durham, NC: Duke University Press, 2012.

Irving, Helen. *To Constitute a Nation: A Cultural History of Australia's Constitution.* Melbourne, Australia: Cambridge University Press, 1977.

Isaacs, Harold. *Scratches on Our Minds: American Views of China and India.* New York: Routledge, 1980.

Jacobson, Matthew Frye. *Whiteness of a Different Color: European Immigrants and the Alchemy of Race.* Cambridge, MA: Harvard University Press, 1998.

Jelavich, Peter. *Berlin Cabaret.* Cambridge, MA: Harvard University Press, 1996.

Jenkins, Jennifer. "German Orientalism: Introduction." *Comparative Studies of South Asia, Africa and the Middle East* 24, no. 2 (2004): 97–100.

Johnston, Patricia A. *Real Fantasies: Edward Steichen's Advertising Photography.* Collingdale, PA: Diane Publishing, 1997.

Jules-Rosette, Bennetta. *Josephine Baker in Art and Life: The Icon and the Image.* Urbana: University of Illinois Press, 2007.

Kalinak, Kathryn M. "Disciplining Josephine Baker: Gender, Race, and the Limits of Disciplinarity." In *Music and Cinema,* ed. James Buhler, Caryl Flinn, and David Neumeyer, 316–336. Hanover, NH: Wesleyan University Press, 2000.

Kaplan, Amy, and Donald E. Pease. *Cultures of United States Imperialism.* Durham, NC: Duke University Press, 1993.

Kaplan, Caren, Norma Alarcon, and Minoo Moallem, eds. *Between Woman and Nation: Nationalisms, Transnational Feminisms, and the State.* Durham, NC: Duke University Press, 1999.

Kaplan, E. Ann. *Looking for the Other: Feminism, Film, and the Imperial Gaze.* New York: Routledge, 1997.

Kasson, Joy S. *Buffalo Bill's Wild West: Celebrity, Memory, and Popular History.* New York: Hill and Wang, 2000.

Keaton, Tricia Danielle, T. Denean Sharpley-Whiting, and Tyler Stovall, eds. *Black France/France Noire: The History and Politics of Blackness.* Durham, NC: Duke University Press, 2012.

Khoo, Tseen, and Rodney Noonan. "Wartime Fundraising in Chinese Australian Communities." *Australian Historical Studies* 42, no. 1 (2011): 92–110.

Kim, Ju Yon. *The Racial Mundane: Asian American Performance and the Embodied Everyday.* New York: New York University Press, 2015.

Kirihara, Donald. "The Accepted Idea Displaced: Stereotype and Sessue Hayakawa." In *The Birth of Whiteness: Race and the Emergence of U.S. Cinema,* ed. Daniel Bernardi, 81–99. New Brunswick, NJ: Rutgers University Press, 1996.

Klein, Christina. *Cold War Orientalism: Asia in the Middlebrow Imagination, 1945–1961.* Berkeley: University of California Press, 2003.

Klein, Kerwin. *Frontiers of Historical Imagination.* Berkeley: University of California Press, 1997.

Knight, Arthur. *Disintegrating the Musical: Black Performance and American Musical Film.* Durham, NC: Duke University Press, 2002.

Kuo, Karen. *East Is East and West Is East: Gender, Culture, and Interwar Encounters between Asia and America.* Philadelphia: Temple University Press, 2012.

Lai, Him Mark. "The Chinese Vernacular Press in North America, 1900–1950: Their Role in Social Cohesion." *Annals of the Chinese Historical Society of the Pacific Northwest* (1984): 170–178.

Lai, Him Mark, Genny Lim, and Judy Yung. *Island: Poetry and History of Chinese Immigration on Angel Island, 1910–1940.* Seattle: University of Washington Press, 1999.

Lake, Marilyn, and Henry Reynolds. *Drawing the Global Colour Line: White Men's Countries and the International Challenge of Racial Equality.* London: Cambridge University Press, 2008.

Laplanche, Jean. "The Wall and the Arcade." In *Seduction, Translation, Drives,* a dossier compiled by John Fletcher and Martin Stanton, with translation by Martin Stanton, 201. London: Institute of Contemporary Arts, 1992.

Lears, Jackson. *Fables of Abundance: A Cultural History of Advertising in America.* New York: Basic Books, 1995.

Lee, Anthony. *Picturing Chinatown: Art and Orientalism in San Francisco.* Berkeley: University of California Press, 2001.

Lee, Erika. *At America's Gates: Chinese Immigration during the Exclusion Era, 1882–1943.* Chapel Hill: University of North Carolina Press, 2003.

Lee, Josephine. *The Japan of Pure Invention: Gilbert and Sullivan's "The Mikado."* Minneapolis: University of Minnesota Press, 2010.

———. *Performing Asian America: Race and Ethnicity on the Contemporary Stage.* Philadelphia: Temple University Press, 1997.

Lee, Leo Ou-fan. *Shanghai Modern: The Flowering of a New Urban Culture in China, 1930–1945.* Cambridge, MA: Harvard University Press, 1999.

Lee, Robert. *Orientals: Asian Americans in Popular Culture.* Philadelphia: Temple University Press, 1999.

Leibfried, Philip, and Chei Mi Lane. *Anna May Wong: A Complete Guide to Her Film, Stage, Radio, and Television Work.* New York: McFarland, 2003.

Lemke, Sieglinde. *Primitivist Modernism: Black Culture and the Origins of Transatlantic Modernism.* New York: Oxford University Press, 1998.

Leong, Karen J. "Anna May Wong and the British Film Industry." *Quarterly Review of Film and Video* 21 (2006): 13–22.

———. *China Mystique: Pearl S. Buck, Anna May Wong, Mayling Soong, and the Transformation of American Orientalism.* Berkeley: University of California Press, 2005.

Leong, Karen J., and Myla Vicenti Carpio. "Carceral Subjugations: Gila River Indian Community and Incarceration of Japanese Americans on Its Lands." *Amerasia Journal* 42, no. 1 (2016): 103–120.

Leung, Maggi W. H. "Notions of Home among Diaspora Chinese in Germany." In *The Chinese Diaspora: Space, Place, Mobility and Identity,* ed. Laurence J. C. Ma and Carolyn Cartier, 237–260. Lanham, MD: Rowman and Littlefield, 2003.

Levinson, Andre. "The Negro Dance under European Eyes." *Theater Arts,* April 1927, 282–293.

Lim, Shirley Jennifer. *A Feeling of Belonging: Asian American Women's Public Culture.* New York: New York University Press, 2006.

———. "Glamorising Racial Modernity." In *Australia's Asia: From Yellow Peril to Asian Century,* ed. David Walker and Agnieszka Sobocinska, 145–169. Perth: University of Western Australia Press, 2012.

———. "'The Most Beautiful Chinese Girl in the World': Anna May Wong's Global Cinematic Modernity." In *Body and Nation: The Global Realms of U.S. Body Politics in the Twentieth Century,* ed. Emily Rosenberg and Shanon Fitzpatrick, 109–124. Durham, NC: Duke University Press, 2014.

———. "'Speaking German Like Nobody's Business': Anna May Wong, Walter Benjamin, and the Possibilities of Asian American Cosmopolitanism." *Journal of Transnational American Studies* (Summer 2012): 1–17.

Liu, Cynthia. "When Dragon Ladies Die, Do They Come Back as Butterflies? Re-Imagining Anna May Wong." In *Countervisions: Asian American Film Criticism,* ed. Darrell Hamamoto and Sandra Liu, 23–39. Philadelphia: Temple University Press, 2000.

Lo, Karl, and Him Mark Lai. *Chinese Newspapers Published in North America, 1854–1975.* Washington, DC: Center for Chinese Research Materials, Association for Research Libraries, 1975.

López, Ana. "Are All Latins from Manhattan? Hollywood, Ethnography and Cultural Colonialism." In *Unspeakable Images: Ethnicity and American Cinema,* ed. Lester Friedman, 404–424. Urbana-Champaign: University of Illinois Press, 1991.

Lott, Eric. *Love and Theft: Blackface Minstrelsy and the American Working Class.* New York: Oxford University Press, 1993.

Lowe, Lisa. *Critical Terrains: French and British Orientalisms.* Ithaca, NY: Cornell University Press, 1991.

———. *Immigrant Acts: On Asian American Cultural Politics.* Durham, NC: Duke University Press, 1996.

Malone, Jacqui. *Steppin' on the Blues: The Visible Rhythms of African American Dance.* Chicago: University of Illinois Press, 1996.

Mann, Gregory. *Native Sons: West African Veterans and France in the 20th Century.* Durham, NC: Duke University Press, 2006.

Marchand, Roland. *Advertising the American Dream: Making Way for Modernity, 1920–1940.* Berkeley: University of California Press, 1985.

Marchetti, Gina. *Romance and the "Yellow Peril": Race, Sex, and Discursive Strategies in Hollywood Fiction.* Berkeley: University of California Press, 1993.

Markus, Andrew. *Fear and Hatred: Purifying Australia and California 1850–1901.* Sydney, Australia: Hale and Iremonger, 1979.

Masten, April. "Challenge Dancing in Antebellum America: Sporting Men, Vulgar Women, and Blacked-Up Boys." *Journal of Social History* 48, no. 3 (Spring 2015): 605–634.

Matsumoto, Valerie. *City Girls: The Nisei Social World in Los Angeles, 1920–1950.* New York: Oxford University Press, 2014.

Matthews, Jill. *Dance Hall and Picture Palace: Sydney's Romance with Modernity.* Sydney, Australia: Currency Press, 2005.

May, Elaine Tyler. *Homeward Bound: American Families in the Cold War Era.* New York: Basic Books, 1988.

May, Lary. *Screening Out the Past: The Birth of Mass Culture and the Motion Picture Industry.* Chicago: University of Chicago Press, 1980.

McBride, Bunny. *Molly Spotted Elk: A Penobscot in Paris.* Norman: University of Oklahoma Press, 1995.

Mendible, Myra. "Introduction." In *From Bananas to Buttocks*: *The Latina Body in Popular Film and Culture.* Austin: University of Texas Press, 2007.

Metzger, Sean. *Chinese Looks: Fashion, Performance, Race.* Bloomington: University of Indiana Press, 2014.

———. "Patterns of Resistance? Anna May Wong and the Fabrication of China in American Cinema of the Late 30s." *Quarterly Review of Film and Video* 23 (2006): 1–11.

Mirzoeff, Nicholas. *An Introduction to Visual Culture.* New York: Routledge, 2009.

Miyao, Daisuke. *Sessue Hayakawa: Silent Cinema and Transnational Stardom.* Durham, NC: Duke University Press, 2007.

Modern Girl around the World Research Group, ed. *Modern Girl around the World: Consumption, Modernity, and Globalization.* Durham, NC: Duke University Press, 2008.

Moon, Krystyn. *Yellowface: Creating the Chinese in American Popular Music and Performance: 1850s–1920s.* New Brunswick, NJ: Rutgers University Press, 2005.

Morlat, Patrice. *La repression coloniale au Vietnam (1908–1940).* Paris: L'Harmattan, 1990.

———. *Les affaires politiques de l'Indochine, 1895–1923: Les grands commis, du savoir au pouvoir.* Paris: L'Harmattan, 1995.

Moy, James. *Marginal Sights: Staging the Chinese in America.* Iowa City: University of Iowa Press, 1993.

Mulvey, Laura. "Love in Two British Films of the Late Silent Period: *Hindle Wakes* (Maurice Elyey, 1927) and *Piccadilly* (E.A. Dupont, 1929)." In *Europe in Love and Cinema,* ed. Luisa Passerini, Jo Labanyi, and Karen Diehl, chap. 4. Bristol, UK: Intellect Books, 2012.

Muñoz, José Esteban. *Disidentifications: Queers of Color and the Performance of Politics.* Minneapolis: University of Minnesota Press, 1999.

Nenno, Nancy. "Femininity, the Primitive, and Modern Urban Space: Josephine Baker in Berlin." In *Women in the Metropolis: Gender and Modernity in Weimar Culture,* ed. Katharina von Ankum, 145–161. Berkeley: University of California Press, 1997.

Ngai, Mae. *Impossible Subjects: Illegal Aliens and the Making of Modern America.* Princeton, NJ: Princeton University Press, 2004.

———. *The Lucky Ones: One Family and the Extraordinary Invention of Chinese America.* New York: Houghton Mifflin Harcourt, 2010.

Nussbaum, Martha C. "Kant and Stoic Cosmopolitanism." *Journal of Political Philosophy* 5, no. 1 (1997): 1–25.

Ovalle, Priscilla Peña. *Dance and the Hollywood Latina: Race, Sex, and Stardom.* New Brunswick, NJ: Rutgers University Press, 2011.

Paisley, Fiona. "'Unnecessary Crimes and Tragedies': Race, Gender and Sexuality in Australian Policies of Aboriginal Child Removal." In *Gender, Sexuality and Colonial Modernities,* ed. Antoinette Burton, 134–147. London: Routledge, 1999.

Palumbo-Liu, David. *Asian/American: Historical Crossings of a Racial Frontier.* Palo Alto, CA: Stanford University Press, 1999.

Paris, Barry. *Louise Brooks.* 1990. Reprint, London: Mandarin Paperbacks, 1991.

Pascoe, Peggy. "Miscegenation Law, Court Cases, and Ideologies of 'Race' in Twentieth-Century America." In *Unequal Sisters: An Inclusive Reader in U.S. Women's History,* 4th ed., ed. Vicki Ruiz and Ellen Dubois, 303–324. New York: Routledge, 2008.

———. *What Comes Naturally: Miscegenation Law and the Making of Race in America.* New York: Oxford University Press, 2009.

Peabody, Sue, and Tyler Stovall, eds. *The Color of Liberty: Histories of Race in France.* Durham, NC: Duke University Press, 2003.

Peffer, George A. *If They Don't Bring Their Women Here: Chinese Female Immigration before Exclusion.* Urbana: University of Illinois Press, 1999.

Pegler-Gordon, Anna. *In Sight of America: Photography and the Development of U.S. Immigration Policy.* Berkeley: University of California Press, 2009.

Peiss, Kathy. *Hope in a Jar: The Making of America's Beauty Culture.* 1998. Reprint, Philadelphia: University of Pennsylvania Press, 2011.

Pérez-Melgosa, Adrián. *Cinema and Inter-American Relations: Tracking Transnational Affect.* London: Routledge, 2012.

Petro, Patrice. "Cosmopolitan Women: Marlene Dietrich, Anna May Wong, and Leni Riefenstahl." In *Border Crossings: Silent Cinema and the Politics of Space,* ed. Jennifer M. Bean, Anupama Kapse, and Laura Horak, 295–312. Bloomington: Indiana University Press, 2014.

———. *Idols of Modernity.* New Brunswick, NJ: Rutgers University Press, 2010.

Phu, Thy. *Picturing Model Citizens: Civility in Asian American Visual Culture.* Philadelphia: Temple University Press, 2012.

Poinger, Uta. "Imperialism and Empire in Twentieth-Century Germany." *History and Memory* 17, nos. 1–2 (2005): 117–143.

Raeburn, John. *A Staggering Revolution: A Cultural History of Thirties Photography.* Urbana-Champaign: University of Illinois Press, 2006.

Raphael-Hernandez, Heike. *Blackening Europe: The African American Presence.* New York: Routledge, 2003.

Rodriguez, Clara. *Heroes, Lovers, and Others: The Story of Latinos in Hollywood.* Washington, DC: Smithsonian Books, 2004.

Rodríquez-Estrada, Alicia. "Dolores del Río and Lupe Vélez: Images on and off the Screen." In *Writing the Range: Race, Class, and Culture in the Women's West,* ed. Elizabeth Jameson and Susan Armitage, 475–492. Norman: University of Oklahoma Press, 1997.

Roediger, David R. *The Wages of Whiteness: Race and the Making of the American Working Class.* New York: Verso, 1991.

Rogin, Michael. *Black Face, White Noise: Jewish Immigrants in the Hollywood Melting Pot.* Berkeley: University of California Press, 1996.

Rony, Fatimah Tobing. *The Third Eye: Race, Cinema, and the Ethnographic Spectacle*. Durham, NC: Duke University Press, 1996.

Rosaldo, Renato. "Cultural Citizenship, Inequality, and Multiculturalism." In *Latino Cultural Citizenship: Claiming Identity, Space, and Rights,* ed. William V. Flores and Rina Benmayor, 27–38. Boston: Beacon Press, 1997.

Rose, Phyllis. *Jazz Cleopatra: Josephine Baker in Her Time*. New York: Doubleday, 1989.

Ruiz, Vicki. *From Out of the Shadows: Women in Twentieth-Century America*. New York: Oxford University Press, 1998.

Russell, Catherine. *Archiveology: Walter Benjamin and Archival Film Practice*. Durham, NC: Duke University Press, 2018.

Rydell, Robert. *All the World's a Fair: Visions of Empire at American International Expositions, 1876–1916*. Chicago: University of Chicago Press, 1984.

Said, Edward. *Orientalism*. New York: Random House, 1979.

Sauvage, Marcel, and Josephine Baker. *Les Mémoires de Josephine Baker*. Paris: KRA, 1927.

Scanlon, Jennifer. *Inarticulate Longings: The "Ladies' Home Journal," Gender and the Promise of Consumer Culture*. New York: Routledge, 1995.

Schueller, Malini Johar. *U.S. Orientalisms: Race, Nation, and Gender in Literature, 1790–1890*. Ann Arbor: University of Michigan Press, 1998.

Shapley-Whiting, Tracy Denean. *Black Venus: Sexualized Savages, Primal Fears, and Primitive Narratives in French*. Durham, NC: Duke University Press, 1999.

Shih, Shu-mei. *The Lure of the Modern: Writing Modernism in Semicolonial China 1917–1937*. Berkeley: University of California Press, 2001.

Shimakawa, Karen. *National Abjection: The Asian American Body Onstage*. Durham, NC: Duke University Press, 2002.

Shimizu, Celine Parreñas. *The Hypersexuality of Race: Performing Asian/American Women on Screen and Scene*. Durham, NC: Duke University Press, 2007.

Shirley, Graham, and Brian Adams. *Australian Cinema*. Sydney, Australia: Currency Press, 1983.

Sieg, Katrin. *Ethnic Drag: Performing Race, Nation, Sexuality in West Germany*. Ann Arbor: University of Michigan Press, 2002.

Silva, Noenoe. *Aloha Betrayed: Native Hawaiian Resistance to U.S. Imperialism*. Durham, NC: Duke University Press, 2004.

Simpson, Audra. *Mohawk Interruptus: Political Life across the Borders of Settler States*. Durham, NC: Duke University Press, 2014.

Smith, Andrea, and Audra Simpson. *Theorizing Native Studies*. Durham, NC: Duke University Press, 2014.

Smith, Valerie. *Not Just Race, Not Just Gender: Black Feminist Readings*. New York: Routledge, 1998.

———. *Representing Blackness: Issues in Film and Video*. New Brunswick, NJ: Rutgers University Press, 1997.

Spiegel, Lynn. *Make Room for TV: Television and the Family Ideal in Postwar America*. Chicago: University of Chicago Press, 1992.

Spivak, Gayatri Chakravorty. *Other Asias*. Malden, MA: Blackwell Publishing, 2008.

Stam, Robert, and Louise Spence. "Colonialism, Racism and Representation: An Introduction." *Screen* 24, no. 2 (1983): 2–20.

Stauffer, John. "Frederick Douglass's Self-Fashioning and the Making of a Representative

American Man." In *The Cambridge Companion to the African American Slave Narrative*, ed. Audrey Fisch, 201–217. Cambridge: Cambridge University Press, 2007.

Stearns, Marshall, and Jean Stearns. *Jazz Dance: The Story of American Vernacular Dance*. New York: Macmillan, 1968.

Steen, Shannon. *Racial Geometries of the Black Atlantic, Asian Pacific and American Theatre*. London: Palgrave Macmillan, 2010.

Steichen, Edward Steichen. *A Life in Photography*. New York: Doubleday, 1963.

Stovall, Tyler. *Paris Noir: African Americans in the City of Light*. New York: Mariner Books, 1996.

Streeby, Shelly. *American Sensations: Class, Empire, and the Production of Popular Culture*. Berkeley: University of California Press, 2002.

Sturtevant, Victoria. "Spitfire: Lupe Vélez and the Ambivalent Pleasure of Ethnic Masquerade." *Velvet Light Trap*, no. 22 (Spring 2005): 19–32.

Susman, Warren. *Culture as History: The Transformation of American Society in the Twentieth Century*. New York: Pantheon Books, 1984.

Taylor, Diana. *The Archive and the Repertoire: Performing Cultural Memory in the Americas*. Durham, NC: Duke University Press, 2003.

Tchen, Jack. *Genthe's Photographs of San Francisco's Old Chinatown*. New York: Dover, 1984.

———. *New York before Chinatown: Orientalism and the Shaping of American Culture, 1776–1882*. Baltimore: Johns Hopkins University Press, 1999.

Teng, Emma. "Artifacts of a Lost City: Arnold Genthe's Pictures of Old Chinatown and Its Intertexts." In *Re/collecting Early Asian America: Essays in Cultural History*, ed. Josephine Lee, Imogene L. Lim, and Yuko Matsukawa, 54–77. Philadelphia: Temple University Press, 2002.

Thompson, Robert Farris. *African Art in Motion: Icon and Art in the Collection of Katherine Coryton White*. Berkeley: University of California Press, 1974.

Tomes, Nancy. *Remaking the American Patient: How Madison Avenue and Modern Medicine Turned Patients into Consumers*. Chapel Hill: University of North Carolina Press, 2016.

Torgovnik, Mariana. *Gone Primitive: Savage Intellects, Modern Lives*. Chicago: University of Chicago Press, 1990.

Trachtenberg, Alan. *Reading American Photographs: Images as History, Mathew Brady to Walker Evans*. New York: Hill and Wang, 1990.

Vogel, Michelle. *Lupe Vélez: The Life and Career of Hollywood's "Mexican Spitfire."* Jefferson, NC: McFarland, 2012.

Walk, Cynthia. "Anna May Wong and Weimar Cinema: Orientalism in Postcolonial Germany." In *Beyond Alterity: German Encounters with Modern East Asia,* ed. Qinna Shen and Martin Rosenstock, 137–167. New York: Berghahn Books, 2014.

Walker, David. *Anxious Nation: Australia and the Rise of Asia 1850–1939*. St. Lucia, Australia: University of Queensland Press, 1999.

Wang, Yiman. "The Art of Screen Passing: Anna May Wong's Yellow Yellowface Performance in the Art Deco Era." *Camera Obscura* 60 (2005): 159–191.

———. "Star Talk: Anna May Wong's Scriptural Orientalism and Poly-phonic (Dis-)play." In *The Multilingual Screen: New Reflections on Cinema and Linguistic Difference,* ed. Tijana Mamula and Lisa Patti, 297–315. New York: Bloomsbury, 2016.

———. "Watching Anna May Wong in Republican China." In *American and Chinese-Language Cinemas: Examining Cultural Flows,* ed. Lisa Funnell and Man-Fung Yip, 169–185. New York: Routledge, 2014.

White, Edward. *The Tastemaker: Carl Van Vechten and the Birth of Modern America.* New York: Farrar, Straus and Giroux, 2014.

Wilson, Kathleen. *Island Race: Englishmen, Empire, and Gender in the Eighteenth Century.* New York: Routledge, 2002.

Wong, Eugene M. *On Visual Media Racism: Asians in the American Motion Pictures.* North Stratford, NH: Ayer, 1979.

Wong, Sau-ling. "Denationalization Reconsidered: Asian American Cultural Criticism at a Theoretical Crossroads." In *Postcolonial Theory and the United States: Race, Ethnicity, Literature,* ed. Amritjit Singh and Peter Schmidt, 122–134. Jackson: University of Mississippi Press, 2000.

Woollacott, Angela. "Rose Quong Becomes Chinese: An Australian in London and New York." *Australian Historical Studies* 129 (2007): 16–31.

Wu, Judy Tzu-Chun. *Dr. Mom Chung of the Fair-Haired Bastards: The Life of a Wartime Celebrity.* Berkeley: University of California Press, 2005.

Xing, Jun. "Cinematic Asian Representation in Hollywood." In *Performing Difference: Representations of the "Other" in Film and Theatre,* ed. Jonathan C. Friedman, 113–143. Lanham, MD: Rowman and Littlefield, 2008.

Yoshihara, Mari. *Embracing the East: White Women and American Orientalism.* New York: Oxford University Press, 2003.

Young, Robert. *Colonial Desire: Hybridity in Theory, Culture, and Race.* London: Routledge, 1995.

Yu, Henry. *Thinking Orientals: Migration, Contact, and Exoticism in Modern America.* Oxford: Oxford University Press, 2001.

Yung, Judy. *Unbound Feet: A Social History of Chinese Women in San Francisco.* Berkeley: University of California Press, 1995.

Index

Page numbers in *italics* refer to illustrations.

129, 130, 132–133; and Vélez, 11, 13; and Wong, 11, 12–13, 33, *129,* 130, 132–133
Owen, David, 214

Pabst, G. W., 51–52
Paisley, Fiona, 195
Pandora's Box, 51
Paramount Pictures, 8, 32, 209; B-list films of, 17, 128, 149, 156, 176–179
Paris qui Remue, 80, 96, 97, 101, 107
"Parlez-moi D'Amour," 109, 186
Parnell, Wallace, 184
Parrish, Bob, 185
Pascoe, Peggy, 140–141
passing: in film, 10; in "My China Film," 161, 162; in *Song/Show Life,* 37
Pavement Butterfly, 32, 74, 107n41
Pegler-Gordon, Anna, 119–120
performance: African American, 4, 59–60, 69; and American modernity, 58; and authenticity, 95, 103, 107; of Baker, 4, 88, 95–98, 107, 113; and Chinese immigrant women, 60; colonial, 56, 95, 96; cross-cultural, 4–5, 186–187; of empire, 103; of gender, 164–168; and imperialism, 86; of the modern, 19; oriental, 56; primitive, 56; of race, 59–61, 88, 107, 138, 142, 146; transnational, 18, 86. *See also* cross-racial performance
performance studies, 8, 103, 104, 138, 164
performativity, 8
"Petite Tonkinoise, La," 80, 88, 90, 91, 95, 96–99, 106–107; costuming in, 105
Petro, Patrice, 52
photography: and Chinese women, 119–120; and gender, 115, 118, 120; glamour in, 18, 117, 126; and modernity, 118–119; and race, 115, 117–120, 123, 136, 152, 188. *See also* Steichen, Edward; Van Vechten, Carl
Picasso, Pablo, 63, 79, 89, 123
Piccadilly, 4, 34, 35, 41, 58, 71; costuming in, 39, 88, 104–105; dance performances in, 101, 102–103; and orientalism, 90
Pickford, Mary, 158
Plessy v Ferguson, 61
Poinger, Uta, 51
primitivism, 18; and Baker, 79, 86; and colonialism, 59; and colonization, 71; and

European imperialism, 62; and modernity, 63–64; and orientalism, 59, 107
Princess Tam Tam, 91
production codes, 25–26

Quinn, Anthony, 179
Quong, Rose, 71–72, 187

race: and advertising, 120, *121,* 140, 141–145; and aesthetics, 18; and American modernity, 185; and colonialism, 89; and commodification, 143; and cosmopolitanism, 29, 44; and dance, 106; and essentialism, 136, 187; in Europe, 62; and mass media, 107; and migration, 182; and modernism, 98; and modernity, 4, 25, 29, 42, 88, 102; and nation, 190; and national origin, 71; and orientalism, 88; performance of, 59–61, 88, 107, 138, 142, 146; and photography, 115, 117–120, 123, 136, 152, 188; and self-fashioning, 11; in United States, 59
racial difference, 14; European fascination with, 59; and modernity, 29, 118, 120, 185; and Wong, 108
racial formation, transnational, 182
racialization of Chinese in Australia, 183–184
racism: anti-Chinese, 173, 182–183; in Hollywood, 205
Raeburn, John, 126, 137
Rainier, Luise, 1, 26, 158
Ray, Man, 126
Red Lantern, The, 22
respectability: of Chinese immigrants, 60; performance of, 198
Revue Nègre, La, 80
Reynolds, Henry, 182
Riefenstahl, Leni, 29, 52–53, 152
Rivera, Diego, 134
Robeson, Paul, 185
Rodin, Auguste, 123
Roosevelt, Franklin Delano, 146
Rork, Kate, 74
Rosaldo, Renato, 195
Rose, Phyllis, 62

Said, Edward, 12
Salazar, Antonio de Oliviera, 84

SHIRLEY JENNIFER LIM is Associate Professor of History at SUNY Stony Brook and the author of *A Feeling of Belonging: Asian American Women's Public Culture, 1930–1960*.

Jere Takahashi, *Nisei/Sansei: Shifting Japanese American Identities and Politics*

Velina Hasu Houston, ed., *But Still, Like Air, I'll Rise: New Asian American Plays*

Josephine Lee, *Performing Asian America: Race and Ethnicity on the Contemporary Stage*

Deepika Bahri and Mary Vasudeva, eds., *Between the Lines: South Asians and Postcoloniality*

E. San Juan Jr., *The Philippine Temptation: Dialectics of Philippines–U.S. Literary Relations*

Carlos Bulosan and E. San Juan Jr., eds., *The Cry and the Dedication*

Carlos Bulosan and E. San Juan Jr., eds., *On Becoming Filipino: Selected Writings of Carlos Bulosan*

Vicente L. Rafael, ed., *Discrepant Histories: Translocal Essays on Filipino Cultures*

Yen Le Espiritu, *Filipino American Lives*

Paul Ong, Edna Bonacich, and Lucie Cheng, eds., *The New Asian Immigration in Los Angeles and Global Restructuring*

Chris Friday, *Organizing Asian American Labor: The Pacific Coast Canned-Salmon Industry, 1870–1942*

Sucheng Chan, ed., *Hmong Means Free: Life in Laos and America*

Timothy P. Fong, *The First Suburban Chinatown: The Remaking of Monterey Park, California*

William Wei, *The Asian American Movement*

Yen Le Espiritu, *Asian American Panethnicity*

Velina Hasu Houston, ed., *The Politics of Life*

Renqiu Yu, *To Save China, To Save Ourselves: The Chinese Hand Laundry Alliance of New York*

Shirley Geok-lin Lim and Amy Ling, eds., *Reading the Literatures of Asian America*

Karen Isaksen Leonard, *Making Ethnic Choices: California's Punjabi Mexican Americans*

Gary Y. Okihiro, *Cane Fires: The Anti-Japanese Movement in Hawaii, 1865–1945*

Sucheng Chan, *Entry Denied: Exclusion and the Chinese Community in America, 1882–1943*